PROFIT+
User's Guide

James B. Pettijohn
Southwest Missouri State University

THE DRYDEN PRESS
Chicago New York San Francisco
Philadelphia Montreal Toronto
London Sydney Tokyo

Acquisitions Editor: Ann Heath
Assistant Editor: Betsy Webster
Project Editor: Karen Steib
Design Director: Alan Wendt
Production Manager: Barb Bahnsen
Permissions Editor: Doris Milligan
Director of Editing, Design, and Production: Jane Perkins
Computer Services Coordinator: Kathy Harsch
Copy Editor: Kathy Pruno

Library of Congress CIP Data

Pettijohn, James B., 1947-
PROFIT+ [computer file]

System requirements: IBM PC computers or PC compatibles; 256K RAM; PC or MS DOS 2.0 (or greater); MicroSoft Quick BASIC; 2 dual sided, double density floppy disk drives (or 1 floppy and 1 hard); monochrome monitor (color optional); 80 column printer.
Title from title screen.
Not copy protected.
Audience: College.
Summary: Allows students of financial management classes, especially beginning financial management classes, to make use of the computer as they solve various problems.
1. Business enterprises—Finance—Software.
2. Corporations—Finance—Software. I. Evans, Joe K. II. Title. III. Title: PROFIT plus.
HG4012.5.P47 1988 658.1'02855369 87-30480
ISBN 0-03-013557-5
ISBN 0-03-013558-3 (user's guide)

Printed in the United States of America
90-066-98765432

Address orders:
The Dryden Press
Orlando, Florida 32887

Address editorial correspondence:
The Dryden Press
908 N. Elm St.
Hinsdale, IL 60521

The Dryden Press
Holt, Rinehart and Winston
Saunders College Publishing

Preface

When PROFIT (the predecessor to PROFIT+) was published in early 1985, the preface to the User's Guide began with the following statement:

> The computer has become such a part of everyday business life that it is almost mandatory that more use be made of this time-saving tool in the college classroom.

The many developments that have taken place in the field of microcomputers during the three years since PROFIT was introduced serve to make the preceding statement even more valid than when it was first written. PROFIT was developed to allow instructors and students to use the computer as they solved various types of numerical problems in managerial finance. PROFIT+ was created with the same goal in mind, but as the plus sign in its name implies, many new features have been added to the new version of the software. The following list describes the enhancements found in PROFIT+:

1. The entire program was given a more professional look. Data entry and output screens are presented in an easy-to-read format.

2. The software was given a more professional feel. All special functions—printing, recalculating, clearing the screen, calling up help and review screens, and paging backward and forward from screen to screen—are invoked with the computer's function keys or special purpose keys such as [PG UP] and [PG DN]. Users can move from input to input using the [TAB] key.

3. Context-sensitive review screens that summarize basic concepts have been added and are available within the program at the touch of a single key.

4. Recommendations by reviewers led to the addition of several new programs, including Capital Asset Pricing Model, sources and uses of funds, receivables management, and effective rates on short-term financing routines.

5. Reviewers' suggestions also led to improvements/additions to several existing programs. Whenever possible, dollar entries in time value of money problems are now made on time lines, and an entire cash budgeting spreadsheet is included. A spreadsheet for calculating projected cash inflows for capital spending projects has been added to the capital budgeting routine, while the cost of capital routine has

been expanded to calculate both the costs of capital components and the retained earnings break point.

6. A major strength of PROFIT+ is that the software is not based on a commercially available spreadsheet; it does not require students to learn how to use a spreadsheet before using the routines. Included with the software, however, is a basic spreadsheet program, PROFIT+ Calc, that can be called up from the Main Menu. Chapter Twenty-One of this guide is a tutorial for its use. Thus, PROFIT+ gives instructors the option of introducing students to electronic spreadsheets.

7. A basic text editor, PROFIT+ Write, has been included as an option on the Main Menu. It gives students the ability to include printed discussion along with the output of PROFIT+ routines.

8. PROFIT+ gives students the option of printing output either to the printer or to a floppy disk. Thus, PROFIT+ can be used on computers that are not connected to printers and output can be saved for printing at the student's convenience.

The *PROFIT+ User's Guide* also contains some important changes, additions, and improvements.

1. Two chapters (Chapters Two and Three) have been added to the guide to introduce students first to the computer and then to PROFIT+.

2. A separate chapter in the guide is devoted to each of the selections on the PROFIT+ Main Menu.

3. The number of end-of-chapter problems has been increased substantially to provide a much broader problem set for students.

4. Much of the guide was either newly written or was substantially rewritten to provide concise reviews of the basic concepts on which the PROFIT+ routines are based.

Although PROFIT+ was written in a format similar to that of the Brigham, Weston and Brigham, Campsey and Brigham, and Cooley and Roden textbooks published by The Dryden Press, both this guide and the software package can be used in conjunction with most basic financial management textbooks. Table I, located at the end of the Preface, is intended to help you coordinate PROFIT+ with an assortment of popular financial management textbooks, including those published by The Dryden Press.

A project such as PROFIT+ cannot be completed without the help, advice, and support of many individuals. Both Fred Weston and Eugene Brigham deserve thanks for their many years of writing the financial management textbooks that contributed the basic format for routines included in PROFIT+. Joe K. Evans, my friend, colleague, and programmer, merits much recognition for his work in developing and debugging the actual PROFIT+ programs. Without his dedication to the project, the software itself would not have been a reality. Both the editorial and production staffs at The Dryden Press deserve a great deal of thanks for their work on PROFIT+. In particular, I want to thank Ann Heath, Betsy Webster, Kathy Pruno, Karen Steib, and Kathy Harsch for their editorial guidance. I also want to thank and acknowledge the following individuals for their efforts in reviewing PROFIT+:

Claire Bronson, *Western New England College*
John Earl, *University of Richmond*
John Fletcher, *University of Tennessee–Martin*
Lorraine Gilbertson, *Avila College*
John Lasik, *Central Washington University*
Wold Zemedkun, *Norfolk State University*
Lankford Walker, *Eastern Illinois University*

Finally, I would like to thank my family—Robin, Heidi, and Cory—for the tremendous love and support they have given me as I worked on this project. In particular, I so appreciate the constant reminders from my wife, Robin, that things temporal should not be taken too seriously. It is to my family that I dedicate this work.

James B. Pettijohn
November 1987

TABLE I
KEY FOR USING PROFIT+ WITH VARIOUS TEXTBOOKS

In the left-hand column, you will find a listing of popular financial management textbooks. Other columns are labeled with chapter numbers Three through Twenty from the *PROFIT+ User's Guide*. In the cells of the table are listed the chapter numbers of each textbook that correspond to each *User's Guide* chapter.

	PROFIT+ USER'S GUIDE CHAPTERS									
TEXTBOOK/AUTHOR(S)	**3**	**4**	**5**	**6**	**7**	**8**	**9**	**10**	**11**	**12**
Fundamentals of Financial Management, 4/e Brigham	2	4	5	5	5	6	6	7	7	8
Introduction to Financial Management Campsey and Brigham	2	14	17	17	18	16	16	7	6	8
Business Financial Management Cooley and Roden	1	4	5	5	5	6	6	15	11	16
Essentials of Financial Management, 8/e Weston and Brigham	2	4	5	5	5	6	6	7	7	8
Foundations of Financial Management, 4/e Block and Hirt	2	9	10	10	10	13	13	3	2	4
Basic Managerial Finance Gitman	2	11	12	12	12	12	12	4	3	6
Contemporary Financial Management, 3/e Moyer, McGuigan, and Kretlow	2	3	4	4	4	5	5	6	8	8
Essentials of Financial Management, 2/e Pinches		5	7	7	7	6	6	3	3	4
Essentials of Managerial Finance, 2/e Pringle and Harris	2	3	4	4	4	5	5	6	6	8
Introduction to Financial Management, 4/e Schall and Haley	3	4	5	5	5	6	6	12	12	14

TABLE I (CONTINUED)

TEXTBOOK/AUTHOR(S)	PROFIT+ USER'S GUIDE CHAPTERS 13	14	15	16	17	18	19	20
Fundamentals of Financial Management, 4/e Brigham	19	19	18	17	9	10	15	14
Introduction to Financial Management Campsey and Brigham	12	12	11	13	15	16	9/19	20
Business Financial Management Cooley and Roden	13	13	12	14	8/9	10	7/16	7
Essentials of Financial Management, 8/e Weston and Brigham	13	12	9	14	15	16	9/18	17
Foundations of Financial Management, 4/e Block and Hirt	7	7	4	8	12	13	5	11
Basic Managerial Finance Gitman	9	9	6	10	14	15	5	13
Contemporary Financial Management, 3/c Moyer, McGuigan, and Kretlow	21	20	8	22	9/10	11	7	12
Essentials of Financial Management, 2/e Pinches	18	18	4/17	19	8/9	10	14	13
Essentials of Managerial Finance, 2/e Pringle and Harris	20	20	8	18	9	11	7/13	10
Introduction to Financial Management, 4/e Schall and Haley	15	15	14/15	16	8	9	13	7

The Dryden Press Series in Finance

Brigham
Fundamentals of Financial Management, Fourth Edition

Brigham and Gapenski
Financial Management: Theory and Practice, Fifth Edition

Brigham and Gapenski
Intermediate Financial Management, Second Edition

Campsey and Brigham
Introduction to Financial Management

Clayton and Spivey
The Time Value of Money

Cooley and Roden
Business Financial Management

Cretien, Ball, and Brigham
Financial Management with Lotus 1-2-3

Crum and Brigham
Cases in Managerial Finance, Sixth Edition

Fama and Miller
The Theory of Finance

Gardner and Mills
Managing Financial Institutions: An Asset/Liability Approach

Gitman and Joehnk
Personal Financial Planning, Fourth Edition

Goldstein Software, Inc.
Joe Spreadsheet

Harrington
Case Studies in Financial Decision Making

Johnson
Issues and Readings in Managerial Finance, Third Edition

Johnson and Johnson
Commercial Bank Management

Kidwell and Peterson
Financial Institutions, Markets, and Money, Third Edition

Koch
Bank Management

Martin, Cox, and MacMinn
The Theory of Finance: Evidence and Applications

Mayo
Finance: An Introduction, Second Edition

Mayo
Investments: An Introduction, Second Edition

Myers
Modern Developments in Financial Management

Pettijohn
PROFIT+

Reilly
Investment Analysis and Portfolio Management, Second Edition

Reilly
Investments, Second Edition

Smith and Weston
PC Self-Study Manual for Finance

Tallman and Neal
Financial Analysis and Planning Package

Turnbull
Option Valuation

Weston and Brigham
Essentials of Managerial Finance, Eighth Edition

Weston and Copeland
Managerial Finance, Eighth Edition

Table of Contents

Chapter One
What is PROFIT+

Roger Jones, Bridger Corporation's assistant vice-president of finance for an importer of electronics components, got home from a three-day business trip at 8:30 p.m. Roger's work day was not over, however. After eating a microwave dinner, he went into the extra bedroom and sat down in front of his computer terminal. Roger booted the system, loaded a communications software package, and dialed the home office.

A few seconds and a couple of passwords later, he was going through the electronic mail that had been sent to his "slot" during his absence. A 10:00 a.m. video teleconference with representatives of the company's Seattle bank had been scheduled for tomorrow morning, and his boss wanted to meet with him following the conference. Another message, from Roger's assistant, said that one of the assumptions in the corporate financial model needed to be reevaluated. Roger acted quickly on this message by calling up the model on computer and making the suggested alteration, then left a memo for his assistant thanking her for the suggestion. He left another message for his secretary, asking her to dial up CompuServe Information Services on her computer tomorrow morning and check the flight schedule to Anchorage for his Friday meeting with the president of a Korean manufacturing firm.

Following all of this, Roger "went" to the host computer's electronic data base and reviewed several of the company's short-term credit arrangements. A $250,000 note was coming due in two weeks and would need to be renewed at that time. Using the computer's financial software, Roger quickly calculated the interest that would be due if the note were renewed for 180 days at the prevailing rate of interest. He also took a quick look at how the firm's liquidity would be affected if, rather than renewing the note, the company paid it off in cash.

During Roger's business trip, a district sales manager had given Roger the application of a New York wholesaler who wanted to purchase a substantial number of compact disk players on credit. A few strokes of the keyboard allowed Roger to obtain the latest Dun & Bradstreet Composite Credit Report on the wholesaler. After reviewing the report, Roger became suspicious about some of the data that it contained. Although he ordinarily had very little to do with day-to-day credit operations, Roger had instructed the firm's district sales managers to give him applications such as this one for direct approval. Extracting certain financial data from the credit report and entering it into a special software program designed in-house, Roger calculated a few key financial ratios for the applicant. In addition, he dialed up Dow Jones News/ Retrieval Service to see if any news items on the wholesaler had crossed over the wire in the past 90 days. One article indicated that the applicant's president was under suspicion of racketeering. Given this information, Roger sent a message to the district manager instructing her to reject the application.

Roger's story could go on and on, and similar stories for thousands of managers just like Roger could be told. However, the point should be clear by now that not only have computers become an increasingly important part of our everyday lives, but also that they are used in virtually every area of business activity. As the not-so-old saying goes, "If you have not had at least some exposure to what computers can do for you today, you are going to be left behind tomorrow."

This book and the computer software package that it accompanies have been written with this last point in mind. That is, they have been designed to provide you with practical exposure to some of the ways in which computers can be used to make you a more efficient and effective manager. Furthermore, they have been written in a way that lets the noncomputer major benefit from their use. Roger was neither a computer programmer nor a management information systems major. Roger was a computer user, just as most of the readers of this book will be. So that you might understand more fully what this book and the PROFIT+ software package are all about, the following summarizes both what to expect and what not to expect from PROFIT+.

WHAT PROFIT+ IS

PROFIT+ is an acronym that stands for Provides an Opportunity For Integrating Technology. (The + sign indicates that this is the second edition of PROFIT. The software contains all the features of the first edition plus a variety of additional ones.) In substance, PROFIT+ is a set of user-friendly, interactive computer software programs designed for use in college and university classes dealing with business financial management.

The term *user friendly* simply means that the software is easy to use, easy to understand, and a "friend," rather than a threat. Interactive denotes that the user must enter some input for the program to work. In other words, the user must interact with the computer for it to help him or her solve problems. The computer will do in seconds what might have taken someone minutes, or even hours, to do by hand.

Thus, PROFIT+ is a software package that has been designed to give you, the student, exposure using a computer to help you in everyday business tasks. Even though you may not be a finance major, your experiences with PROFIT+ should help prepare you for the kinds of assistance that computers are going to be giving you once you are out in the real world. PROFIT+ gives you and your professors the opportunity to integrate some of the benefits of computer technology into the traditional business school curriculum, just as the computer has been integrated into many heretofore noncomputerized areas of business.

WHAT PROFIT+ IS *NOT*

PROFIT+ Is Not a Business Financial Software Package

Although PROFIT+ has been designed to provide you with the practical exposure outlined above, to help provide solutions to many of the types of problems encountered in business finance, and to "feel" like a professional software package, it is not an exact duplicate of computer programs actually being used by business. Business financial software packages are generally much more sophisticated than PROFIT+, both in what they can accomplish and in the amount of data that they can handle and manage. At the same time, many of these software packages are much more difficult to learn to use than PROFIT+, since they require adaptation to the firm in which they are being used. Attempting to learn to use these advanced software packages in addition to learning all of the material presented in financial management classes would be a difficult, if not impossible, task. However, if you know how to speak English and understand the types of problems that you want to solve, you can use PROFIT+ without any previous computer experience. Thus, even though PROFIT+ is not identical to the many real-world financial management software packages, its many utilities will still expose you to some of the ways in which computers can help in the business world.

PROFIT+ Is Not a Substitute for Your Reasoning Ability

One of the misconceptions regarding computers is that they can be a substitute for human decision making. Although computers can certainly be programmed to make decisions under some circumstances, their use does not relieve managers from their decision-making responsibilities. For the types of tasks that can be accomplished by PROFIT+, the computer is being used primarily as a timesaver. It allows more numbers to be "crunched" and provides the manager with more alternatives to consider, but it does not make decisions.

Furthermore, to make PROFIT+ work for you, you have to understand the type of problem that you want to solve, and you have to be able to provide PROFIT+ with the proper input. In other words. you have to know what buttons to push, or PROFIT+ is going to give you the wrong answers. The old computer adage, GIGO—garbage in, garbage out—applies to the use of PROFIT+ just as it applies to the use of any computer or computer software.

WHAT PROFIT+ DOES

PROFIT+ Saves You Time

PROFIT+ is primarily a timesaver. Many decisions in business financial management must be based at least in part on numerical calculations. Financial management, by definition, involves the managing of the financial affairs of the business, and the traditional—and only—way of expressing financial information is through the use of numbers. Consider the following facts:

1. What a business owns (its assets) and the various claims against those assets are expressed by numbers on a balance sheet.

2. The ability of a business to produce profits over a given period of time is expressed in numbers on the income statement.

3. Ratio analysis, one of the most widely used methods of evaluating a firm's financial strengths and weaknesses, involves numerical calculations.

4. The monetary rewards to the owners of businesses are measured by numbers (dollars and/or rates of return).

5. When a business borrows money, numbers must be manipulated to determine the cost (interest) of that money.

6. The day-to-day operations of any business involve a constant inflow and outflow of funds, which must be recorded and followed. These flows are measured and evaluated using numbers.

7. The entire economic and financial environments in which businesses operate are constantly being analyzed and interpreted so that current decisions and future plans can be made. Businesses analyze these environments with numbers.

8. Employees' pay, salespersons' commissions, shareholders' dividends, inventory markups, credit management, international operations, a company's growth record, potential investments, and many other financial and business decisions in some way involve numbers.

Although financial management must be carried out by people, these people must have a way of measuring business performance. To a great extent, these performance measures involve numbers. Nothing is inherently wrong with numbers; lots of people (even students) simply get "turned off" when they have to spend hours and hours "number crunching." They get bored when they have to spend their time making calculations they know how to perform, and they get frustrated if, after spending hours on some particular calculation, they find they have made a careless mistake and have to start all over.

Computers to the rescue! A long time ago, business people found out that computers could be used to do all of those time-consuming calculations. This freed up managers' time for more decision making. The educational environment, however, was rather reluctant to develop and use computer programs in the lower-level, number-crunching business classes. PROFIT was designed to bridge this gap, and PROFIT+ carries on its tradition. The programs included in PROFIT+ have been developed to save you, the student, a great deal of time on basic calculations, thus freeing you to spend more time on the more exciting, decision-making aspects of financial management. We hope that after using PROFIT+ in your financial management classes, you will fully appreciate how PROFIT+ saves you time!

Areas in Which PROFIT+ Can Help

Although computer software such as PROFIT+ could be designed for many areas of financial management, PROFIT+ has been developed to include programs that deal with the problems most common to the more basic classes in financial management. The package also includes a basic spreadsheet routine to introduce students to the fundamentals of electronic spreadsheets. In addition, PROFIT+ provides a basic text editor for preparing printouts of verbal comments along with the software's numerical outputs. Finally, PROFIT+ has context-sensitive review screens that you can use to review key concepts as you are making your calculations. The following provides a brief overview of the contents of the PROFIT+ software package:

A. *Corporate Income Tax:* basic taxable income calculations along with federal income tax computation

B. *Financial Calculator:* a complete "time value of money" calculator for computing future and present values, annuity payments (ordinary and due), yield or growth rates, and number of periods (deals with equal, as well as unequal, payment series); dollar values are entered on time lines

C. *Bond Valuation:* calculates the market value of a bond given maturity value, coupon rate, and the market rate of interest

D. *Yield to Maturity:* given a bond's market price, coupon rate, and maturity value, the yield to maturity (i.e., the market rate of interest) is calculated

E. *Common Stock Valuation:* calculates the value of a common stock using either the constant growth or the supernormal growth dividend valuation model

F. *Basic Risk/Return Calculations:* calculates the expected value, variance, standard deviation, and coefficient of variation of a probability distribution of expected returns—also calculates the arithmetic and geometric means, variance, standard deviation, and coefficient of variation of a series of historic returns

G. *Capital Asset Pricing Model:* carries out a three-stage calculation using the result of one stage as a critical input for the next stage: (1) beta calculation/simple regression; (2) required return using the Security Market Line; and (3) common stock valuation as described in E above

H. *Financial Statement Analysis:* based on financial statement data entered by the user, calculates 13 financial ratios and common-size financial statements

I. *Sources and Uses of Funds Analysis:* based on user inputs, calculates sources and uses from comparative balance sheets

J. *Financial Forecasting:* provides two options for financial projections—percentage of sales forecasting and simple linear regression analysis

K. *Inventory Management:* economic order quantity, reorder point, and related calculations

L. *Receivables Management:* analyzes the results changing certain elements of credit policy

M. *Cash Budgeting:* spreadsheet for calculating projected cash inflows and outflows along with estimates of borrowing needs and projections of surplus cash

N. *Effective Rates on Short-Term Financing:* calculates the effective annual interest rate for various types of short-term credit arrangements

O. *Capital Budgeting Basics:* provides two options—net present value and internal rate of return; calculations based on user-entered cash outflows and inflows—and employs a spreadsheet for calculating projected cash inflows that are used along with cash outflows to compute net present value and internal rate of return

P. *Net Present Value (NPV) Sensitivity Analysis:* from a spreadsheet used for cash inflow calculations, PROFIT+ varies each input by plus and minus 10 percent and calculates NPV based on these changes; reports NPVs along with slope of sensitivity line for risk analysis

Q. *Breakeven Analysis and Leverage:* provides two options—calculation of breakeven point based on basic inputs and calculation of degrees of operating, financial, and total leverage from more detailed income statement data

R. *Cost of Capital:* provides three options—marginal cost of capital with component costs given, marginal cost of capital including component cost calculations, and marginal cost of capital with component cost and retained earnings break point calculation

S. *PROFIT+ Calc:* a basic, but quite functional, electronic spreadsheet program

T. *PROFIT+ Write:* a basic text processor for use in including discussion along with PROFIT+ numerical outputs

Calculations performed by each of these programs are explained later in this book.

PROFIT+ Gives You the Ability to Ask "What If?" Questions

One of the main factors that led to the increased use of personal computers by business managers was the availability of so-called electronic spreadsheet programs. These programs give managers who are not computer programmers the ability to develop various models for use in the planning process. For example, budgets, projected financial statements, production schedules, and many other models can all be created on electronic spreadsheets. Once a model has been developed, its user can change, at will, various values or assumptions. When one particular value or assumption is changed, the model automatically will change all other values affected by the initial change. Thus, after developing, for instance, a cash budget for a given period of time based on the most likely estimates of sales, a manager can ask the model, "What if sales in January are 20 percent below the initial estimate?" The model will then adjust the entire budget for this one change.

Spreadsheet software that automatically recalculates the entire budget based on just one or a few changes gives the manager a tremendously powerful planning tool. It allows him or her to evaluate many more possible occurrences in a given period of time and leads to improved decision making.

All PROFIT+ routines give you the ability to ask these "what if?" questions. Performing this analysis is as easy as changing one of your inputs and pressing the [CALC] key, whereupon you see the results of your change instantaneously. Furthermore, PROFIT+ includes a basic electronic spreadsheet program, PROFIT+ Calc (and a tutorial on its use), as one of its routines. Thus, PROFIT+ gives you ample opportunity to use and observe the benefits of electronic spreadsheets.

Without an electronic spreadsheet, or without PROFIT+, finding the answers to "what if?" questions would take a great deal of time. Thus, just as electronic spreadsheets have given business managers the ability to evaluate the consequences of a number of possible occurrences in a relatively short period of time, PROFIT+ gives you the ability to do the same thing. Those users in financial management case courses should find this ability particularly useful, since it allows for a more efficient evaluation of a broader range of possible outcomes. In addition, PROFIT+ is a useful analytical tool to use in classes such as business policy, where quite a bit of manipulation of financial data is generally required.

HOW TO GET THE MOST OUT OF PROFIT+

Some of the most common difficulties experienced by business people when they get their first computer, or when they acquire new computer software, stem from not really knowing what the computer or the software can do for them. The acquisition was made with the feeling or the assurances that the computer or the software would be greatly beneficial to the operations of the business, but no one really took the time to learn about the ways and the means for obtaining these benefits. This problem leads to several others, including a waste of valuable resources, lost time trying to make the computer perform jobs it was not designed to perform, and the frustrations that occur when it takes longer to get the job done on the computer than it did before the computer or the software was purchased. Had a bit more time and thought been devoted to the question of what the computer or the software could do and how it would do it before the acquisition was made, the severity of this problem could have been significantly reduced.

Similar difficulties can be avoided when using PROFIT+ if you will just devote some time to thinking and learning about how PROFIT+ can help you before you actually attempt to use a particular program included in the PROFIT+ software. The following suggests a series of activities that will assist you in getting the most out of your PROFIT+ software.

Learn about Your Hardware

You will be using PROFIT+ on one of several IBM PC-compatible computer systems. Before you attempt to use the software, make sure you understand such basics about your hardware as how to turn the computer on, how to turn your printer on, how to load DOS, how to start PROFIT+ and call up the Main Menu, and how to shut your system down when you have completed a session. Chapter Two of this user's guide deals more fully with this subject.

Learn about the Problem You Will Be Working

Before you attempt to use PROFIT+, make certain you understand the nature of the problem you will be working. This understanding should be gathered from three primary sources.

Your first source of information about the type of problem you are working should be a basic financial management textbook such as *Fundamentals of Financial Management,* 4th ed., by Eugene F. Brigham, *Essentials of Managerial Finance,* 8th ed., by J. Fred Weston and Eugene F. Brigham, or the particular text used at your institution in the beginning financial management class. The routines performed by PROFIT+ have been designed to follow those discussed in most beginning financial management textbooks, thus a complete explanation of why a financial manager would encounter a particular problem and suggestions regarding how he or she might go about solving it are included in these texts.

Your second source of information about the type of problem you will be working is your instructor. Through class lecture, discussion, and outside consultation you will gain an even better understanding of the whys and hows surrounding a particular problem.

The final source of information regarding the type of problem with which you will be dealing is this user's guide. Each chapter of the guide provides a brief review of concepts related to the routine that the chapter presents. Not only will you find these reviews useful as you prepare for a session using PROFIT+, but you will also find that they serve as good summaries as you study for examinations.

Trying to use PROFIT+ without first understanding the problem situation could result in a great deal of wasted time. In other words, learn about the situation and understand the problem from a financial manager's point of view, and then use PROFIT+.

Learn about How PROFIT+ Solves the Problem

Once you understand the problem to be solved, use this guide to make certain you understand how PROFIT+ goes about the arithmetic of finding a solution. Using answers when you do not understand how those answers were obtained is a frivolous practice, both in a business and in the classroom. Double-check to confirm that PROFIT+'s problem-solving methodology is the same as that employed in your text. Where slight differences exist, make certain you understand what they are and their implications. Make a note of any limitations of a particular PROFIT+ routine.

Review a User Session of the Routine You Will Be Using

Once you have followed the preceding steps, turn to the portion of the chapter of this guide that includes a sample user session for the particular program you want to run. Notice the types of input you must provide and the form it must take. Where you have any doubts regarding a particular input required by PROFIT+, review the appropriate materials in your textbook, your class notes, and the user's guide to clear up these doubts. Not only will following this process help you avoid many of the frustrations that could result when using PROFIT+, but adherence to these suggestions should also be valuable in helping you learn what financial management is all about.

ABOUT THIS GUIDE

The second chapter of this guide introduces you to the basics of using a microcomputer. In it you will learn about the basic hardware that you will need to get the most out of PROFIT+ and how to prepare a copy of PROFIT+ for your personal use. In Chapter Three, you will learn the basics of using PROFIT+ itself. To facilitate this instruction, a tutorial based on one of the simpler routines included with PROFIT+ is presented. Subsequent chapters of this guide deal with the remainder of the routines included in the PROFIT+ software. The general outline of these chapters is discussed below.

Each chapter begins with a brief discussion of the type or types of problems with which the chapter deals. It is not the goal of this guide to provide a complete explanation of the nature and setting of each of these problems. Instead, the guide will provide you with a basic discussion of the problem and its setting, and you must supplement this discussion with material from a financial management text and from your financial management classes. After the brief overview of a problem, the methodology used by PROFIT+ in its calculations is described. Where applicable, the most commonly used mathematical notation will be employed to foster consistency between this guide and financial management textbooks. Making certain that you understand these calculations will help assure that you provide the proper input as requested by PROFIT+. In addition, this understanding will contribute to your interpretation of the output once you have completed using a particular PROFIT+ routine.

Once a particular problem has been explained and the calculations it involves outlined, you will be presented with a sample problem. The guide then will include an exact replication of the PROFIT+ screen(s) from which the numerical solution to the problem is obtained. Familiarizing yourself with the "look" of a particular routine will help you avoid any surprises as you work through a particular PROFIT+ program. In addition, this familiarity will acquaint you with the form taken by the final output of a program.

Each chapter ends with a summary followed by end-of-chapter questions and/or problems. The questions are designed to promote your understanding of various terms and concepts covered in the chapter, while the problems will provide exercises for using the PROFIT+ programs.

SUMMARY

PROFIT+ is a set of user-friendly, interactive computer software programs designed for use in college and university classes in financial management. Although PROFIT+ is not a business financial software package per se, it does provide the opportunity to integrate many of the advantages of such packages into the finance curriculum.

PROFIT+ has been devised to be primarily a timesaver. It will perform many of the routine numerical calculations found in basic financial management classes. When using PROFIT+, you must remember that final decisions are left up to you, the user. PROFIT+ provides answers to numerical problems, but in many cases you must evaluate PROFIT+'s output to arrive at a suggested course of action in a particular situation. Thus, PROFIT+ is not a substitute for your ability to think; instead, it is an aid to help you evaluate various problems encountered by financial managers. This guide is your reference book for using PROFIT+. It is designed to be used in conjunction with most popular financial management textbooks.

END-OF-CHAPTER QUESTIONS

1. From a source other than this guide, obtain the definitions of the following terms: computer hardware, computer software, user friendly, interactive, electronic spreadsheet, financial model.

2. Using the Business Periodicals Index, locate a relatively recent article dealing in some way with the use of computer technology by business managers (ideally financial managers). Read the article and prepare a brief report for presentation to your class. (Referring to microcomputers' managerial uses, financial modeling, financial management, electronic spreadsheets, and related key terms should help you in your search.)

Chapter Two
Using a Microcomputer: Basic Concepts

While you will not need much time to learn how to use PROFIT+, you must be familiar with some basic concepts regarding microcomputers before you start to use the program. This chapter introduces you to these fundamentals in a concise manner so that you quickly can begin to benefit from the power of PROFIT+.

SOFTWARE AND HARDWARE

In Chapter One, you learned that PROFIT+ is a microcomputer software package designed for use in the beginning financial management class. In an introductory computer class, you learn that software is simply a set of instructions that tells the computer what to do. In PROFIT+, the software tells the computer how to ask you questions about particular types of finance problems, how to take the answers to those questions and use them to determine the problems' numerical solutions, how to display or store these answers, and how to provide you with on-screen reviews of the topics being covered. The remaining chapters of this guide are devoted to teaching you about the PROFIT+ software package.

To use PROFIT+ you must be familiar with the hardware, or computer components, on which you will be running the package. PROFIT+ has been written to be used on IBM PC computers and a wide range of PC compatibles. Regardless of the brand of computer you will be using, it must have the following components:

1. at least 256K bytes of random access memory (RAM) for the temporary storage of PROFIT+ routines as they are being used

2. two floppy disk drives, or one floppy disk drive and one hard disk drive for permanent storage of the PROFIT+ software, its outputs, if necessary, and any spreadsheets created with PROFIT+ Calc

3. a monitor—color or monochrome

4. a printer—or access to a printer on a similar computer (you can save PROFIT+ outputs for printing at a later time)

Exhibit 2.1 depicts a typical hardware configuration on which each of the preceding components has been identified. The next few paragraphs discuss some of the basic elements of using your system.

Exhibit 2.1

Source: Courtesy of International Business Machines Corporation.

Most students will be using PROFIT+ on a microcomputer with two floppy disk drives. One of these drives is known as the "A-drive," while the other is the "B-drive." Different manufacturers build these drives into their computers in two basic arrangements: side by side, or one on top of the other. When the drives are located side-by-side, the one on the left is typically the A-drive and the one on the right is the B-drive. While most manufacturers of computers with the two drives stacked one on top of the other configure the top drive to be the A-drive and the bottom to be the B-drive, there can be exceptions. The important point here is this: learn which drive is the A-drive and which is the B-drive on your microcomputer. You must know this as you continue with this chapter, since you will be running PROFIT+ from the A-drive and storing personal files (output or spreadsheets) that you have created while using the software on the B-drive.

Hard Disk Drive Layout

Microcomputers that have a hard, or fixed, disk drive ordinarily have at least one floppy drive as well. If your computer has a hard drive, your instructor already will have loaded PROFIT+ into the hard drive for your use. You will use the floppy drive (called the A-drive) for storage of any personal files that you have created while using PROFIT+.

Keyboard Layout

As can be seen from Exhibit 2.2, the layout of a computer keyboard does not look all that different from a typewriter's. The typewriter keys work just as you would expect. There are, however, some additional keys with whose locations and functions you must be familiar if you are going to use PROFIT+. Each of these is described below. (Note: In this discussion, and throughout this guide, whenever a particular computer key is mentioned, it is set off by an extra space on each side and is enclosed in brackets.)

Function Keys Usually located to the far left of the keyboard (but sometimes located above the typewriter number keys), these keys are identified with the letter F followed by a number, [F1], for example. As the name implies, function keys are used for special functions. PROFIT+ makes heavy use of function keys in all of its routines for such tasks as calling up help and review screens, recalculating values, erasing the screen, and printing.

The "Escape" Key PROFIT+ uses the escape key to return the program to menu screens. On most keyboards, the escape key, [ESC], is located just to the left of

Exhibit 2.2

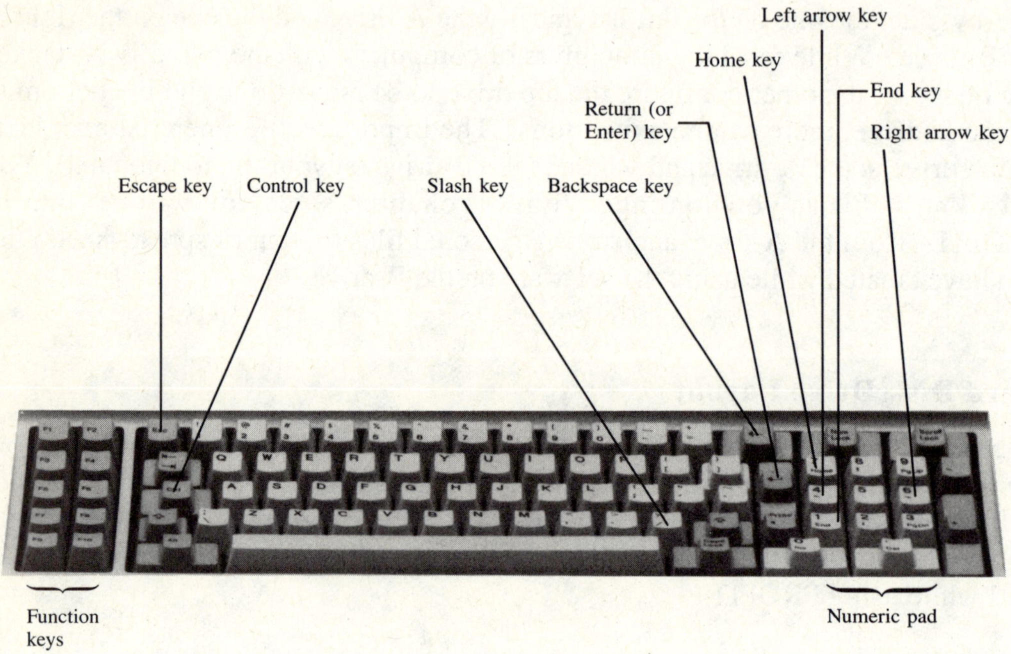

The center portion of the keyboard resembles a typewriter keyboard.

Source: Courtesy of International Business Machines Corporation.

the number 1 key. On some computers you will find it in the upper-right region of the keyboard.

The "Tab" Key Once you have entered your initial set of data into a PROFIT+ screen, you have the ability to change any piece of that data. To move from one data entry field to the next, you must use the tab key, [TAB]. On most computers, it is located just below the [ESC] key on the keyboard's left.

The "Number Pad" Most microcomputers have a number pad located to the keyboard's far right. The pad facilitates rapid entry of numerical data. To use it, you must engage the [NUM LOCK] key. On many keyboards, this key has a red or green light that turns on when the key is engaged. When [NUM LOCK] is on, the number pad keys type in their respective numbers.

The "Cursor Control" Keys On many computers, as can be seen in Exhibit 2.2, the number keys 4, 6, 8, and 2 serve to move the computer's cursor around the screen in the direction of the arrow printed on a key when the [NUM LOCK] key is turned off. (The cursor is the blinking box that identifies where the next character will be typed.) Because several PROFIT+ routines make use of the cursor control keys, you may find it inconvenient to have [NUM LOCK] on while using these routines. Use the regular typewriter number keys instead for entering numerical data. (Note: The trend in newer keyboards is to include a separate set of cursor control keys so that the problem with [NUM LOCK] is not encountered.)

The "Page-up" and "Page-down" Keys When [NUM LOCK] is turned off, the number keys 9 and 3 serve as the page-up, [PG UP], and page-down, [PG DN], keys, respectively. On multiscreen PROFIT+ routines, these keys are used to move back and forth through the screens. Because several PROFIT+ routines make use of the page-up and page-down keys, you may find it inconvenient to have [NUM LOCK] on while using these routines. Use the regular typewriter number keys instead for entering numerical data.

The "Editing" Keys You may edit, or change, anything you have entered while on a PROFIT+ screen by using the editing keys: [INSERT], [DELETE], and [BACKSPACE]. Engaging the insert key allows you to insert keys at the point of the cursor (the cursor expands to indicate that [INSERT] is on). Pressing the [DELETE] key erases the character underneath the cursor, while pressing the [BACKSPACE] key erases the character to the cursor's immediate left.

The "Enter" or "Return" Key The enter or return key is located just to the right of the typewriter keyboard (in the space occupied by the carriage return key on a typewriter). This key must be pressed after each piece of data is typed in on a PROFIT+ screen. In this guide when you are told to "enter" something, that means to type the requested input, and then press the [ENTER] or [RETURN] key.

The "Print Screen" Key While all PROFIT+ routines have their own set of instructions for sending a program's output to a printer, your microcomputer has a special key combination for sending the contents of any one screen to the printer. This key combination consists of holding down the [SHIFT] key (used for making uppercase letters) and pressing the [PR SCRN] key. When this is done, your printer will print a reproduction of the entire contents of the present screen. (Depending on your printer, some graphics characters—lines and boxes—may not print out, but all letters and numbers will.) Ordinarily, you will want to use

PROFIT+'s printing capabilities to send output to the printer, but the print screen capability of your computer is also available.

Power Switch Configurations

The microcomputer, its monitor, and the printer all have their own power switches that must be turned on if the separate components are going to operate. Learn their locations before you continue with the instructions in this chapter. (Note: Some computers and their peripherals have been connected to a power bus that allows the computer, the monitor, and the printer all to be turned on with one switch. Check to see whether or not your system is set up in this manner.)

POWERING UP ON A FLOPPY DRIVE SYSTEM

At this point, you should have identified all the elements of your computer system that are discussed above. Now you are ready to "power up" so that you can begin computing with PROFIT+. If you are going to read these instructions and use them as a tutorial for obtaining your own copy of PROFIT+, you should have the following items available:

1. three double-sided, double-density floppy disks (two for obtaining your own copy of PROFIT+ and one for use as a storage disk)
2. a copy of the two PROFIT+ "Master Disks"
3. a copy of the appropriate "DOS Master" disk (operating system disk) for your computer.

Instructions for obtaining these items will be provided by your instructor. (If your instructor does not have the PROFIT+ master disks, they can be purchased from The Dryden Press at the address indicated in the front of this guide.)

Booting the System

The phrase *booting the system* is computerese for getting your computer going. So that the hardware knows how to perform, it must be booted with an operating system (DOS) disk. Carefully place the DOS master disk in the A-drive, and close the drive's latch. Now you are ready to boot. Turn on the printer's switch, the monitor's switch, and finally the computer's switch. At this point, you may or may not see anything on your screen depending on the brand of computer you are using.

After a few seconds, however, the computer's disk drives will begin to "whir," and a message will appear on the screen requesting that you enter today's date. Enter the date in the format requested by the computer (That is, type in the date, and then press the [ENTER] key). Another message will appear asking you for the current time. Using the format specified on the screen, enter the time (a 24-hour clock is usually used).

You have now successfully booted your computer and are ready to compute. The computer essentially is "asking" you what you want to do next by displaying the "A-prompt":

A>

You must always boot the system with the DOS master disk before you run PROFIT+.

Formatting Your Floppies

Now you must get your three floppy disks ready for use with PROFIT+. As they come from the supplier, the floppies are completely blank. At this point, they could be used by a variety of computers. So that they can be used on IBM PCs and compatibles you must format thc disks (that is, have your computer magnetically divide the disks into segments) so that your system can write information to them and read information from them. Assuming that the A-prompt (A>) is still on the screen, and that your DOS master disk is still in the A-drive, type and enter the following:

format B:

Your A-drive will whir a few seconds, and then instructions will appear on the screen. These instructions will ask you to put a disk (one of your three blank disks) into the B-drive and press any key when ready. Go ahead and do this now. The format program will start working (usually the message "formatting" will appear on the screen) and will take a minute or so to complete its task. When the disk has been formatted, the computer will tell you what it has done with a message similar to the following:

Format complete
362496 bytes total disk space
362496 bytes available on disk
Format another (Y/N)?

(Note: Some format routines will ask you for a disk label at this point. Simply press the [RETURN] key if this request appears.)

Since you still have two more disks that you want to format, type "Y" to tell the computer that you do wish to format another. The format program will now format your second disk. Repeat the procedure for the third disk, also.

Copying PROFIT+

You should now have three formatted disks ready for use by your computer. Using the labels that came with your disk, identify the three disks as follows:

Disk 1: PROFIT+ — Disk 1

Disk 2: PROFIT+ — Disk 2

Disk 3: PROFIT+ — Storage

You are now ready to make your own working copies of the two PROFIT+ disks. With the DOS master disk still in the A-drive, type and enter the following:

diskcopy a: b:

The A-drive will whir, and a message will appear telling you that your system's "diskcopy" routine has been loaded. It will ask you to insert your "source disk" into drive A and your "destination disk" into drive B, and then to press any key when you are ready to copy the disk. Place the PROFIT+ master disk 1 in the A-drive and your formatted disk labelled "PROFIT+ — Disk 1" in the B-drive and press a key. The diskcopy program will copy the programs from the PROFIT+ master disk 1 onto your disk. When the disk has been copied, you will be asked if you want to "Copy another (Y/N)?" Type "Y" and go through the procedure again, this type copying PROFIT+ master disk 2 onto your floppy labeled "PROFIT+ — Disk 2." (Note: Some diskcopy routines return to the A-prompt after they have copied one disk. If yours does this, insert the DOS master disk in drive A and type diskcopy a: b: prior to copying Disk 2.) After disk 2 has been copied, tell the computer that you do not wish to copy another (i.e., type "N"). You will be returned to the A-prompt. Remove your disks from their respective drives, and return the PROFIT+ master disks to their permanent location.

You now are ready to begin using PROFIT+! Before you proceed to the next chapter, however, you should check to make certain that the copies you have just made are not flawed. To do this, place your disk labeled "PROFIT+ — Disk 1" in the A-drive and type and enter the following:

PROFIT

Exhibit 2.3

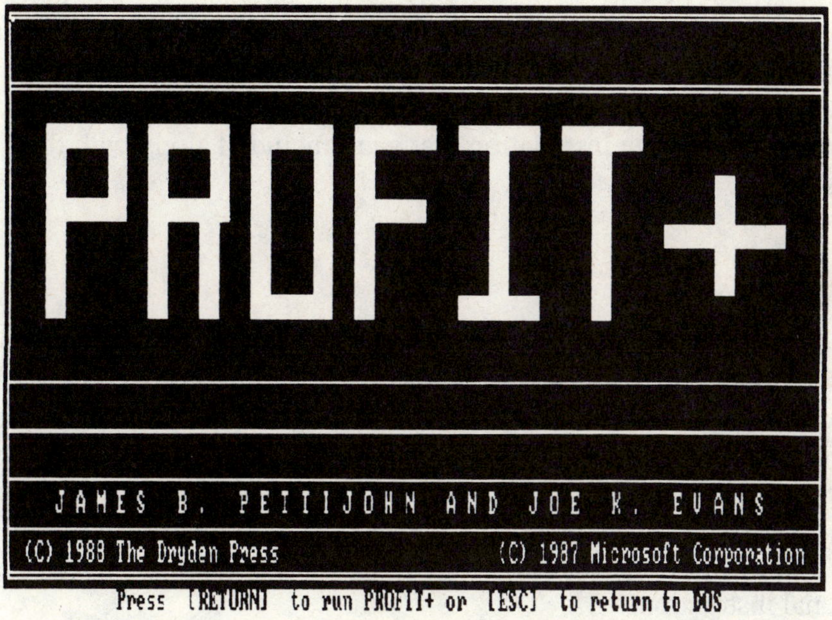

If you have successfully copied the disk, the A-drive should whir for several seconds, a few messages should appear on the screen, and you should be presented with the PROFIT+ Logo screen that appears in Exhibit 2.3. From the Logo screen, press the [ESC] key to return to DOS. If you do not get to the PROFIT+ Logo screen, try reformatting the disks and recopying PROFIT+. If you still cannot obtain a working copy, consult your instructor or lab assistant.

Assuming that you were able to call up the PROFIT+ Logo screen from Disk 1, you are now ready to use PROFIT+ for the first time. Turn to Chapter Three and follow its tutorial for teaching you the basics of using the software. *Remember, however, that you must always boot the system with the DOS master disk before you run PROFIT+ on a floppy disk system.*

POWERING UP ON A HARD DRIVE SYSTEM

In the tutorial that follows, you will need one blank double-sided, double-density floppy disk for formatting as your PROFIT+ storage disk.

Installing PROFIT+ on a Hard Drive

If you are using a computer with a hard drive system, this guide assumes that your instructor has already installed PROFIT+ on the hard drive. If you wish to install PROFIT+ on your own hard drive, ask your instructor for a copy of the instructions for hard drive installation that were included along with the PROFIT+ master disks.

Booting the System

The phrase booting the system is computerese for getting the computer going. With a hard drive system all that you must do to accomplish this is switch on your printer, switch on the monitor, and finally switch on the computer. After a few seconds you may be asked to enter the current date. Do so in the format specified on the screen. Next the computer may request that the correct time be entered (usually on a 24-hour clock basis). Once again, do so in the format specified on the screen. You have now successfully booted the system, and the computer is ready for additional instructions.

Using PROFIT+ on a Hard Drive System

Since there several ways in which computer facilities can set up hard drive management systems, this guide does not provide a specific set of instructions for using PROFIT+ on a hard drive system. Regardless of how a particular hard drive system is managed, however, you will need to obtain from your instructor information on the following:

1. how to format a floppy disk for storage
2. how to access PROFIT+

Once you have obtained this information, you should be able call up PROFIT+ and obtain the Logo screen shown in Exhibit 2.3.

END-OF-CHAPTER QUESTIONS

1. Distinguish between computer software and computer hardware.
2. What four computer components are necessary for using PROFIT+?
3. Will you be using PROFIT+ on a floppy drive system or on a hard drive system?

Chapter Three
Getting Started with PROFIT+: Corporate Income Tax Calculation

In the first chapter of this guide you were introduced to the conceptual aspects of PROFIT+. The second chapter acquainted you with the microcomputer on which you will be using PROFIT+ and led you, by means of tutorials, to the point of being able to boot your system and call up the PROFIT+ Main Menu. This chapter resumes where Chapter Two left off. You will have your first chance to actually use PROFIT+ as you work through a tutorial centering around one of the simpler routines included in the software: the "Corporate Income Tax" program. In addition to providing a tutorial that leads you through most of the features of PROFIT+, the chapter also introduces you to the format used in the remainder of this guide: first, the basic concepts behind a particular PROFIT+ routine are discussed, then a sample problem is worked using PROFIT+.

BASIC CONCEPTS OF FEDERAL CORPORATE INCOME TAXATION

Most firms are in the business of investing in various types of assets to produce a stream of cash flows. These cash flows determine whether a business experiences sustained success and growth. Just as the value of a business depends on the cash flows that it generates, so too do the values of most other investments. In your financial management textbook, you will learn that the cash flows produced by any asset or by any business consist of *usable* income plus depreciation (see *Essentials of Managerial Finance,* 8th ed, by J. Fred Weston and Eugene F. Brigham, p. 31).

Usable income implies income after taxes; thus, investors and financial managers must have a basic understanding of how taxes affect the cash flow streams produced by the assets in which they invest.

Because of the impact of income taxes on cash flows, beginning financial management textbooks discuss some fundamental aspects of federal corporate income tax legislation. These texts and this guide are not attempting to make a tax expert out of you; instead, they are striving to show you some of the most important ways in which our federal tax laws affect business decisions. The following paragraphs summarize the typical tax provisions that are covered in beginning financial management texts. They are based on the tax legislation enacted by the Tax Reform Act of 1986.

Corporate Income Tax Rates

The Tax Reform Act of 1986 established the following rate structure for determining a corporation's federal corporate income tax liability:

Taxable Income	Tax Rate
Up to $50,000	15%
$50,001 to $75,000	25%
Over $75,000	34%
$100,001 to $335,000	5%*

* This 5% surtax eliminates the effect of the lower rates for high income corporations.

For example, if a corporation had $400,000 of taxable income, its tax liability would be:

$$\begin{aligned} \text{Taxes} &= 0.15(\$50{,}000) + 0.25(\$25{,}000) + 0.34(\$325{,}000) + 0.05(\$235{,}000) \\ &= \$7{,}500 + \$6{,}250 + \$110{,}500 + \$11{,}750 \\ &= \$136{,}000. \end{aligned}$$

As indicated in the table, the effect of the 5 percent surtax for income between $100,000 and $335,000 is to eliminate the effect of the 15 and 25 percent tax rates for corporations with higher levels of taxable income. The ultimate result of the surtax is that corporations earning over $335,000 pay a flat 34 percent of their income as taxes. (To verify this fact, refer to the example and calculate the firm's average tax rate as follows: $136,000 / $400,000 = 0.34 = 34 percent.)

While this rate structure is reasonably simple to learn and apply, many factors go into determining the amount of taxable income that a corporation generates. Among these factors is the tax treatment of interest and dividend *income* received by a corporation and interest and dividends *paid* by a corporation.

Interest and Dividend Income Received by a Corporation

Interest income received by a corporation is considered as ordinary income and is taxed as such. However, only 20 percent of dividend income that one corporation receives from another is treated as ordinary income. In other words, 80 percent of the dividend income earned by a corporation is *exempt* from taxation. Thus, if a firm has $300,000 of income before the consideration interest and dividend income of $5,000 and $20,000, respectively, its taxable income would be:

$$\text{Taxable Income} = \$300{,}000 + \$5{,}000 + 0.20(\$20{,}000)$$
$$= \$300{,}000 + \$5{,}000 + \$4{,}000 = \$309{,}000.$$

Interest and Dividends Paid by a Corporation

While interest payments are considered a legitimate expense of doing business, and as such can be deducted from revenues in the determination of taxable income, dividends paid by a corporation are considered as a distribution of profits to owners and are not tax deductible. For example, if a corporation has $200,000 of operating income before the payment of $4,000 of interest expense and $10,000 of dividends, its taxable income would be:

$$\text{Taxable Income} = \$200{,}000 - \$4{,}000 = \$196{,}000.$$

In this calculation, only interest expense was deducted to obtain taxable income. The dividends paid had no effect on the calculation.

THE PROFIT+ CORPORATE INCOME TAX ROUTINE

Choice A on the PROFIT+ Main Menu is the "Corporate Income Tax" routine. It allows you to determine taxable income based on your inputs for operating income, dividend and interest income, and interest expense, and then calculates the federal corporate income tax due on that level of income. The paragraphs that follow present a step-by-step tutorial for using the routine to solve the following sample problem. Since this is your first encounter with PROFIT+, this tutorial is much more detailed than those that you will find in later chapters.

Sample Problem: The Davis Corporation has $250,000 of operating income before the consideration of the following: $20,000 of interest income; $10,000 of dividend income; and, $30,000 of interest expense. What is the firm's federal corporate income tax liability?

Step 1: Booting the System

Follow the instructions included in Chapter Two of this guide for booting your system with DOS. If you have a floppy drive system, remove the DOS master disk from the A-drive after the system is booted.

Step 2: Starting PROFIT+

Follow the instructions included in Chapter Two for starting PROFIT+. On a floppy disk system this means inserting PROFIT+ — Disk 1 in the A-drive and entering PROFIT at the A-prompt. (Remember, when you are instructed in this guide to enter a word or a number, type the word or number and then press the [RETURN] or [ENTER] key. The [RETURN] and [ENTER] symbols will be used interchangeably from this point on in the guide.) On a hard disk system, follow the instructions given to you by your instructor for starting the software.

After PROFIT+ has started and you see the Logo screen, press [RETURN] and the Main Menu shown in Exhibit 3.1 will appear.

Step 3: Calling the "Corporate Income Tax" Routine from the PROFIT+ Main Menu

All the choices on the PROFIT+ Main Menu are preceded by a letter. There are two methods you can use for making your choice from the menu: (1) typing the letter preceding your selection (you do *not* have to press [RETURN] after typing the letter); or, (2) using the arrow keys to move the selection bar to the routine of your choice and then pressing [RETURN]. Ordinarily the first method is the easier, but the final choice of methods is left up to the user. Since you want to run the "Corporate Income Tax" routine, and since the selection bar's "home position" is directly over this choice, you can simply press A or [RETURN] to start the routine.

Exhibit 3.1

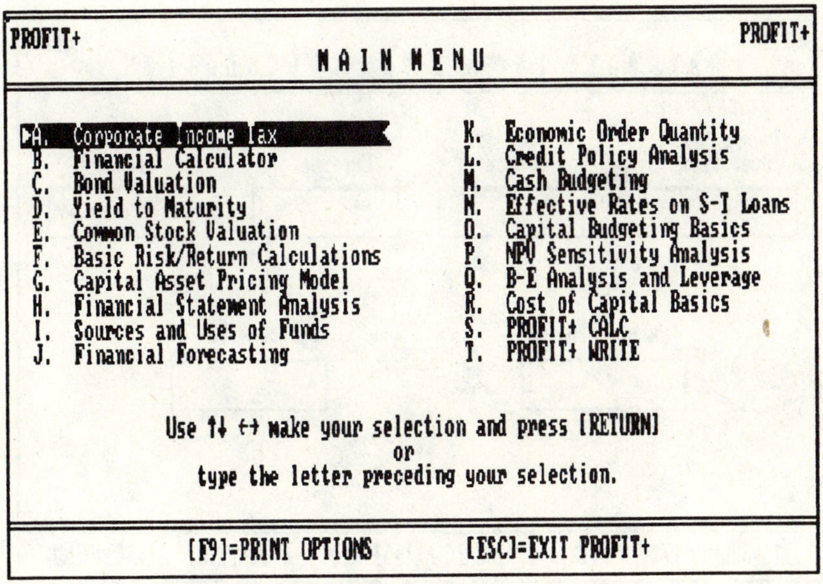

Step 4: A "Tour" of the PROFIT+ Screen

You should now have in front of you on your computer's monitor the "Corporate Income Tax" screen as it appears in Exhibit 3.2. Before you enter any data, become acquainted with the general layout of the screen. You will find this layout to be consistent throughout PROFIT+ (with the exception of the spreadsheet, PROFIT+ Calc). The screen can be divided into four distinct regions:

a. The *title area* located at the top of the screen — This area identifies the routine with which you are working.

b. The *data entry and answer area* that occupies the bulk of the screen — It is in this area that you will enter the information necessary to work your problems, and in which you will receive your problem's answer(s). In the present screen, your inputs will consist of income from operations, interest income, interest expense, and dividend income, while the answers or output calculated by PROFIT+ will be taxable income and income tax. (To assist with this tutorial, a line appears in

Exhibit 3.2

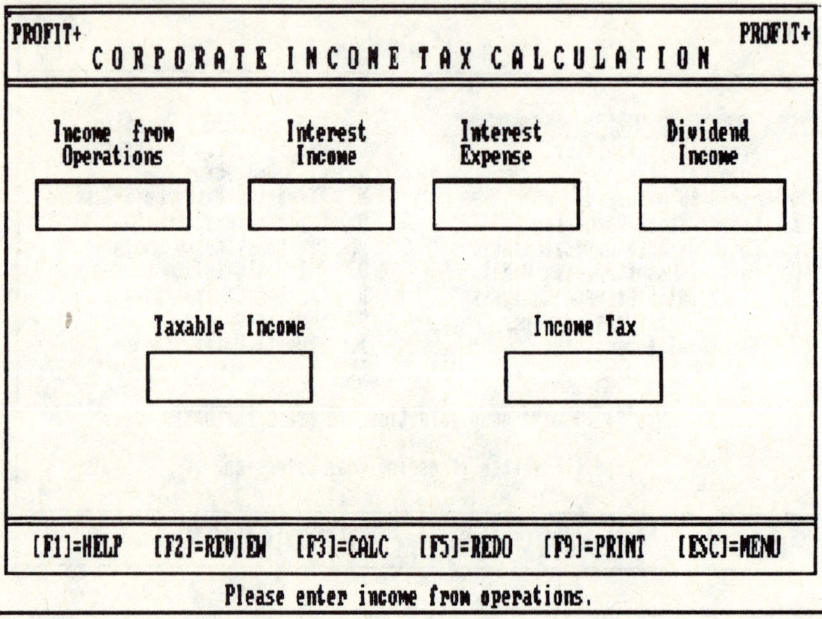

Exhibit 3.2 and subsequent figures in this chapter to identify the answer fields. These lines do not appear on the actual PROFIT+ screens.)

c. The *active function key prompt area* located just above the bottom of the screen (the area that begins with [F1]=HELP) — These prompts identify which function keys are active for this screen and provide a brief description of each key.

d. The *message line* at the very bottom of the screen — This is a very important element of PROFIT+. On this line you will be given instructions for entering data and various types of error messages when you make a mistake while using PROFIT+.

Step 5: Working the Sample Problem

When the Corporate Income Tax screen first appears, the blinking cursor is located at the very left of the income from operations field (the first data entry field), and the message line at the bottom of the screen instructs you to "Please enter income from operations." PROFIT+ is telling you that it is ready for your first input. Type in 250000 (just as it appears here...*no dollar sign* and *no comma* separating the thousands), but do not press [RETURN]. At this point, your screen should look like the one in Exhibit 3.3.

Exhibit 3.3

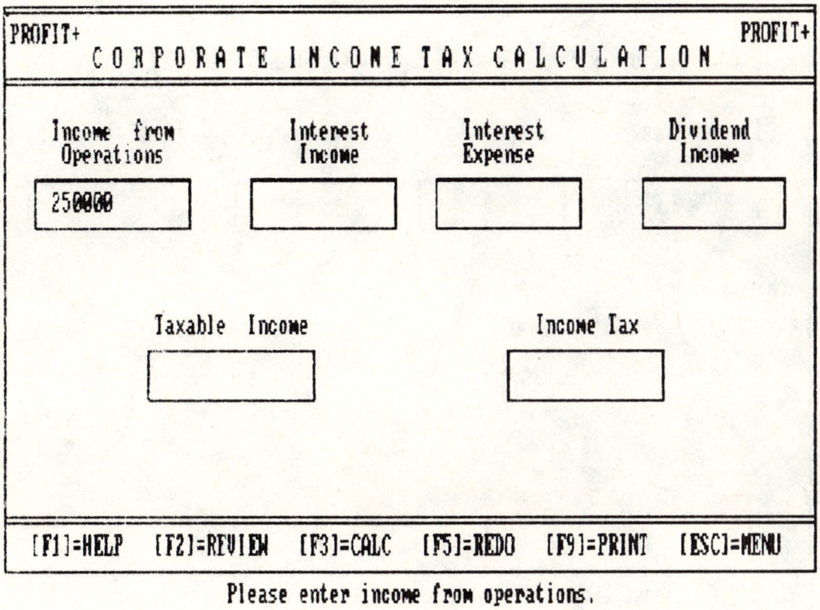

The 250000 that you entered is located on the left side of the entry box just where you typed it. Press [RETURN] and observe the result. Four things happen, as can be seen in Exhibit 3.4. First, a decimal point and two decimal places are added to the 250000 that you entered. Second, the 250000.00 is now right-justified within the entry field (i.e., it is located at the right, rather than the left, side of the field). Third, the cursor has moved to the second data entry field, interest income. Finally, the message line now reads, "Please enter interest income (or 0 if not applicable)." Now PROFIT+ is waiting for you to enter interest income. (If the problem with which you were dealing did not mention any interest income, you could at this point enter a 0 and go on to the next entry. Simply pressing [RETURN] produces the same results as entering a 0.) Interest income in the sample problem is $20,000. Enter 20000 into this field and press [RETURN]. Once you have done this, your screen should look like the one in Exhibit 3.5. The cursor now has moved to the interest expense field, and the message line is instructing you to "Please enter interest expense (or 0 if not applicable)." In our sample problem, interest expense is $30,000. Type and enter 30000. Your screen should now look like the one that is displayed in Exhibit 3.6. The cursor has jumped to the fourth and final entry that you must make to work the sample problem—dividend income. The message line says, "Please enter dividend income

Exhibit 3.4

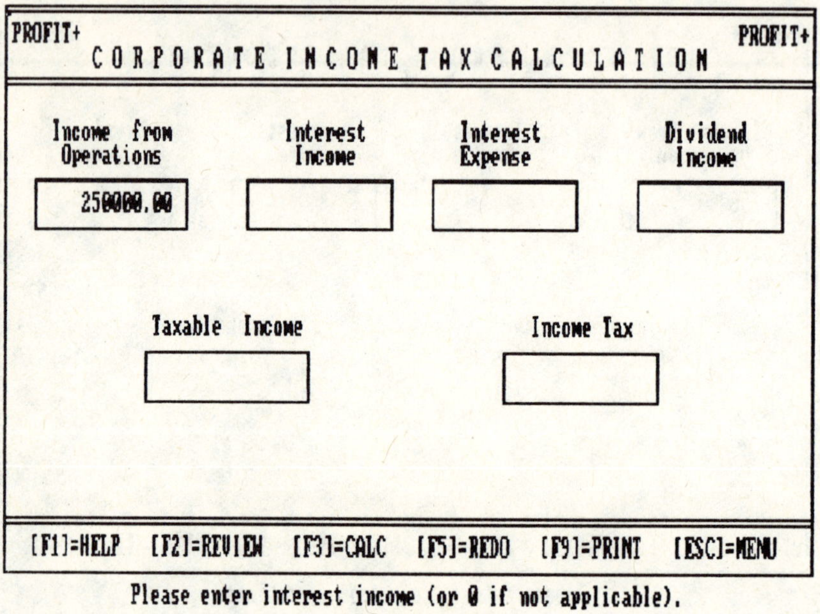

Exhibit 3.5

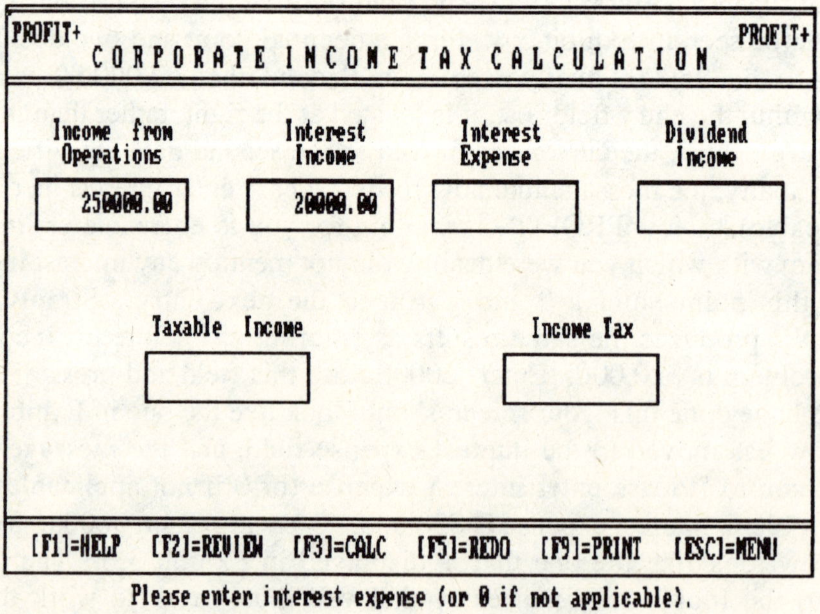

Exhibit 3.6

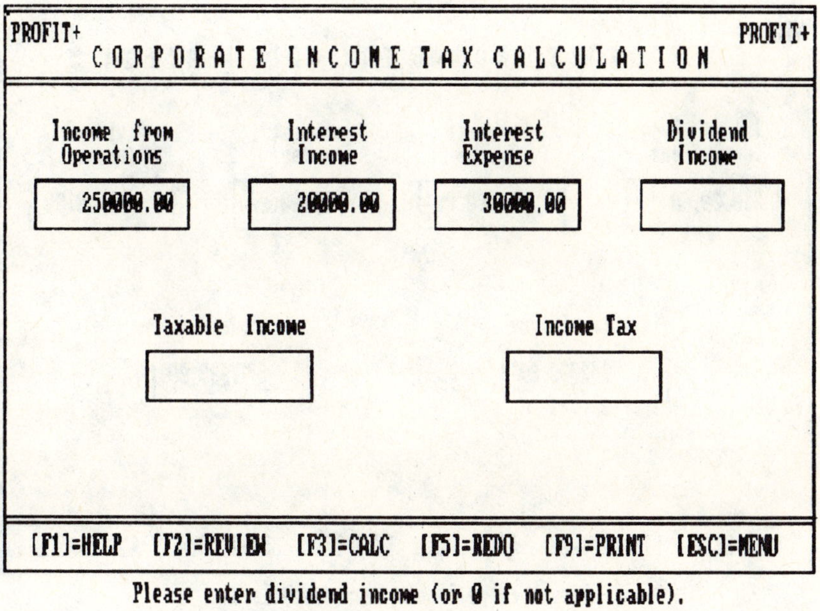

Exhibit 3.7

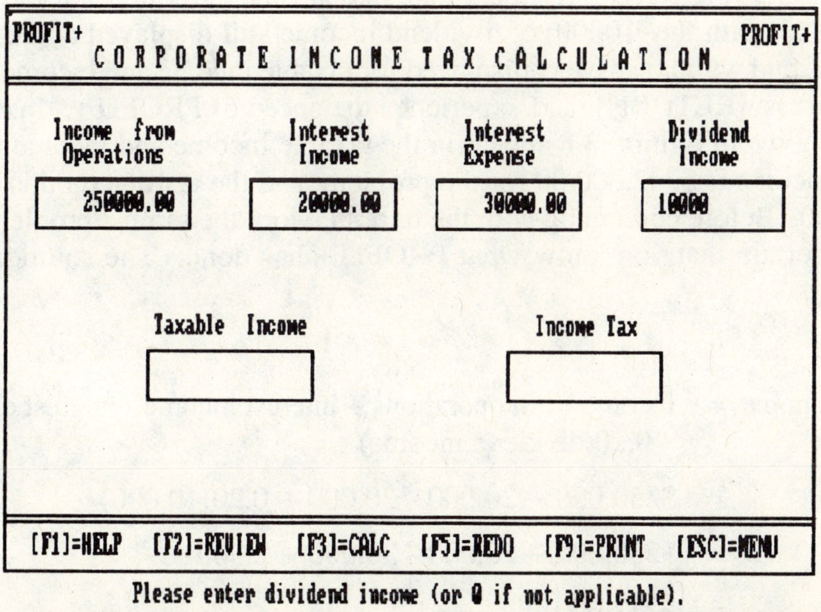

Exhibit 3.8

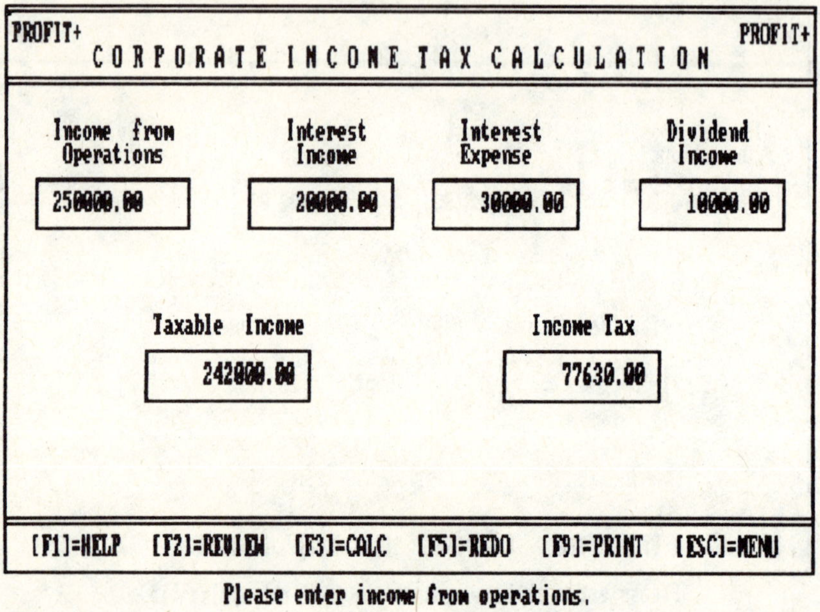

(or 0 if not applicable)." Type in 10000, but do not press [RETURN] yet. Instead, examine your screen. It should look like the one in Exhibit 3.7: all four data entries filled, with the 10000 of dividend income still displayed at the left of its entry field, and with no answers displayed for taxable income and income tax.

Now, press [RETURN] and experience the speed of PROFIT+. Instantly, the answers shown in Exhibit 3.8 appear in the taxable income and income tax fields. Taxable income is \$242,000.00 for the problem, and the tax due on this income is \$77,630.00. Before continuing with the tutorial, work the sample problem by hand to make certain that you know what PROFIT+ has done. The solution appears below:

Taxable Income = Income from operations + interest income - interest expense + 0.20(dividend income)

= \$250,000 + 20,000 - 30,000 + 0.20(10,000)

= \$250,000 + 20,000 - 30,000 + 2,000

= \$242,000.

Exhibit 3.9

```
PROFIT+                                                          PROFIT+
                     M A I N   H E L P   S C R E E N

 Several keys have the same or similar actions, throughout PROFIT+.  At the
 bottom of each screen  is a listing of the  keys that are active for  that
 screen.  The [RETURN] key is always active  and  should  be  pressed after
 each input has been entered.

   [F1]  Displays this Help screen.
   [F2]  Displays a brief review of the concepts behind a particular screen.
   [F3]  Recalculates using current input values.   Must be used when inputs
         have been changed from their initial values.  See [TAB].
   [F5]  Clears all input values, but remains in the same routine.
   [F9]  Prints the current results.
  [TAB]  Moves to the next input field for possible revision.  See [F3].
  [ESC]  Return to previous menu.
 [PGDN]  Changes display to next screen in multiscreen routines.
 [PGUP]  Changes display to previous screen in multiscreen routines.

                           Press [ESC] to return.
```

Income Tax = 0.15($50,000) + 0.25($25,000) + 0.34($167,000) + 0.05($142,000)

= $7,500 + $6,250 + $56,780 + $7,100

– $77,630.

Finally, Exhibit 3.8 shows that the cursor has "jumped back" to the first entry field, income from operations, where it is awaiting your instructions.

Step 6: Using the Active Function Keys

Now that you have worked the problem, you have a variety of alternatives available as to what to do next. These are initiated by pressing one of the active function keys listed at the bottom of the screen. While each of these is described in the following paragraphs, you can also press the [F1] key at any time and the PROFIT+ Main Help Screen will remind you of the action that each invokes. Exhibit 3.9 shows the Main Help Screen.

[F2]=REVIEW Key Pressing the [F2] key will pop in a special review window on top of the screen with which you are working. The review in this window is designed to acquaint you with the basic concepts behind the particular type of

Exhibit 3.10

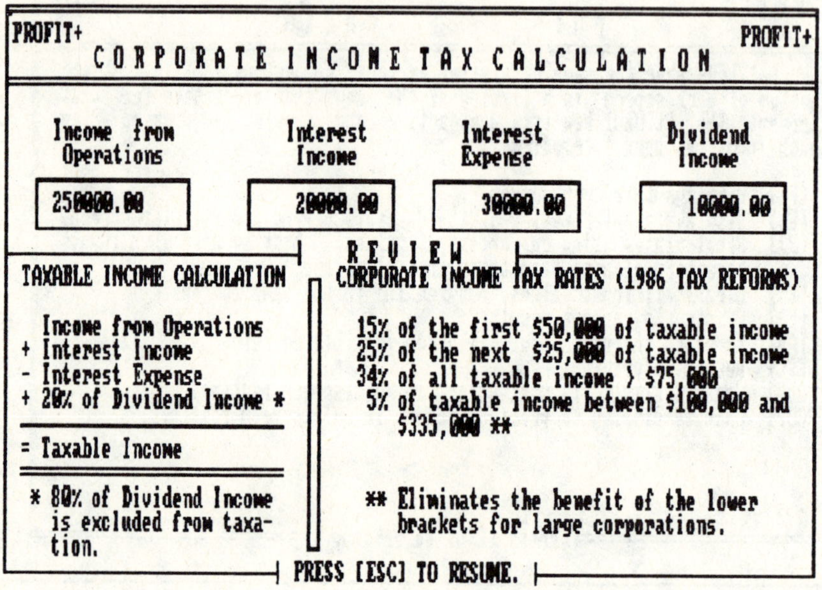

problem that you are solving. It may occupy only a portion of the screen, such as the corporate income tax review shown in Exhibit 3.10, or it may be an entire screen in itself. Regardless of their size, the review windows are designed to help you learn, and remember, the fundamental facts about the routines with which you are dealing. In essence, they provide you with what might be called context-sensitive review, and should be a great deal of help to you as you use PROFIT+ as a tool to help you learn about financial management. A good habit to develop is to always call up and study the review screen(s) associated with each routine you use.

[F3]=CALC Key [F3] is the calculation, or calc, key. When it is pressed, PROFIT+ recalculates a problem's answer using the inputs that appear in the data fields. While this key is of no use if you are simply working a problem one time, it is vital if you elect to correct or revise some of your inputs after the initial calculation. If you change any of your inputs after your first use of a routine, you must press the [F3] key to recalculate. Pressing [RETURN] will not lead to recalculation. (The only exception to this rule is when [RETURN] is pressed after entering the last input requested by a routine—dividend income in the sample problem. If you elect to change this input after your initial calculation, either [F3] or [RETURN] will recalculate. For developing good usage habits, however, it is

recommended that you always employ the [F3] key to recalculate.) You will learn more about changing inputs in the discussion of the [TAB] key.

[F5]=REDO Key Pressing the [F5] key erases all inputs and all outputs from the present screen. While PROFIT+ allows you to change all inputs one at a time, you may find it more convenient to begin working with a clean slate. The [F5] key allows you to do this.

[F9]=PRINT Key When pressed, the [F9] key causes both your inputs and your outputs to be printed—either to your printer or to your storage disk, depending upon the printing instructions that you have given PROFIT+. By default, PROFIT+ assumes that you want printed output to go to the printer, but it is a simple matter to route this output to your storage diskette for printing at a later time.

If it is a hard copy (i.e., on the printer) you want, make certain that your computer is connected to a printer, that the printer is correctly loaded with a sufficient supply of paper, and that it is on-line prior to pressing [F9]; otherwise, you may cause PROFIT+ to return you to the computer's operating system (DOS).

If you wish to save your output on your storage disk so that you can print it out later, you must instruct PROFIT+ to change its default setting before you work any problems. To do this, you must press the [F9] key while the PROFIT+ Main Menu is on the screen. When this is done, the Print Option window "pops" in as shown in Exhibit 3.11 giving you a choice of two print options: print to printer or print to disk. If you select print to disk, another window appears on top of the Print Option window. As can be seen Exhibit 3.12, this window asks for a file name for the output. You may use any combination of letters and numbers up to a total of eight characters for the file name. You must, however, remember the name you have chosen so that you can instruct your computer to route the file to a printer at a later time. If you choose a file name that already exists, PROFIT+ will inform you and give you the opportunity to enter another name. The file name you select will be used by PROFIT+ to save all output from a session. You do not have to go back to the Main Menu and select [F9] again during a session. Once selected, the print to disk option remains in force until you change it, or until you exit PROFIT+.

Once you have told PROFIT+ that you want to print to disk, make certain that your formatted disk labeled PROFIT+ — Storage is in the B-drive (A-drive if your computer has a hard drive). When [F9] is pressed after you have worked a problem, PROFIT+ will automatically print the output to your disk. (Do not become alarmed if the light on your disk drive does not come on each time you press [F9]. If only a small amount of output is being saved, PROFIT+ sometimes waits for

Exhibit 3.11

PROFIT+ PROFIT+

PRINT OPTION MENU

OUTPUT DEVICE:

1. PRINTER
When the [F9] key is pressed, output from a routine will be sent to your printer.

2. DISKETTE
When the [F9] key is pressed, output from a routine will be sent to Drive-B on a floppy disk system, or to Drive-A on a hard disk system.

Use ↑↓ to make your selection and press [RETURN]
or
type the number preceding your choice.

[F1]=HELP [ESC]=MENU

Exhibit 3.12

PROFIT+ PROFIT+

PRINT OPTION MENU

OUTPUT DEVICE:

DISKETTE OUTPUT INSTRUCTIONS

You have chosen to route output to diskette, place your PROFIT+ Data Diskette in Drive-B (Drive-A for hard drive systems), and enter the file name under which you wish to save this session's output.

FILE NAME:

[ESC]=MENU

Please enter a file name that is no more than 8 characters long.

more output before writing it on your disk. Any output that has not been saved when you exit a program will be saved at that point.)

When you are ready to print the contents of a file containing the results of a PROFIT+ session to your printer, you must perform the following steps:

1. Exit PROFIT+ by pressing [ESC] from the Main Menu.

2. Place your storage disk with the file you want printed out in the A-drive of a computer that is connected to a printer and that has been booted with a DOS master disk.

3. Make certain that the printer is switched on.

4. Type and enter the following:

TYPE A:FILENAME.OUT >PRN

where "FILENAME" is the name of the file you want printed. Your computer will respond by printing out the results of your PROFIT+ session.

5. Once you are certain that you have the hard copy you want, it is good practice to erase the file from your storage disk. If you do not do this, you run the risk of completely filling the disk and producing a "Disk Full" error that would cause PROFIT+ to return to DOS during a user session. (This could cause you to lose any output saved prior to the error.) To erase a file, type and enter the following:

ERASE A:FILENAME.*

where "FILENAME" is the name of the file you want erased.

As a safeguard to prevent printing incorrect results, PROFIT+ automatically recalculates when [F9] is pressed. Thus, the [F9] key is also a recalculation key, but is only practical for use as such when you desire a hard copy, or when you want to save a file that shows the results of any changed inputs.

The [TAB] Key If you wish to change any of your inputs, you can use the [TAB] key to move the cursor from one input variable entry field to the next. (PROFIT+ moves the cursor from left to right. When the last input variable on the right of a line is reached, the cursor jumps to the first variable on the left of the next lower input line. When the last input variable requested is reached—dividend income in the sample pro-blem—the cursor returns to the very first input variable—income from operations in the sample problem.) When you use the [TAB] key to move to a given input field, any data in the field becomes left-justified and is ready to be changed or edited. The normal keyboard editing keys—[INSERT], [DELETE], [BACKSPACE], and the right and left arrow keys—can be used to assist in making changes. The revised input can be entered in two ways: by pressing [RETURN] or by pressing the [TAB] key. As was mentioned above, however, no recalculation occurs until you press the [F3] key (or the [F9] key if you want to print your work). Even though the [TAB] key is not listed on the active function key line, it is ordinarily active on all PROFIT+ data entry screens.

The [ESC]=MENU Key A special function key, active on virtually all PROFIT+ screens, is the [ESC] key. On single-screen routines, pressing [ESC] will cause PROFIT+ to return to the last menu that was presented. For example, if [ESC] is pressed while using the "Corporate Income Tax" routine, the program will return to the PROFIT+ Main Menu. Some routines have their own menus ("Financial Calculator," for example). If [ESC] is pressed while one of these sub-menus is displayed, you will return to the PROFIT+ Main Menu. If, however, you press [ESC] while another screen under one of these submenus is active, you will return to the submenu. When either the Main Help Screen or a review window has been requested, [ESC] removes that screen or window and returns you to your original location.

The [PGUP] and [PGDN] Keys In PROFIT+ routines that employ more than one screen, the [PGUP] and [PGDN] keys are used to page back and forth between or among the screens. When these keys can be used, they will be displayed in the active function key area, and their action will be identified. (Since the Corporate Income Tax routine is a single-screen program, there is no need to page between screens, so the [PGUP] and [PGDN] keys are not active.)

Some Practice Using the Special Function Keys

At this point, you should still have the sample problem entries on your screen. If you do not, reenter the inputs so that your screen looks like that displayed in Exhibit 3.8. Now, perform each of the following actions:

1. Press [F1] and examine the Main Help Screen.
2. Press [ESC] to exit the Main Help Screen.
3. Press [F2] to examine the Corporate Income Tax Review Screen.
4. Press [ESC] to exit the review screen.
5. Use the [TAB] key to move the cursor to the dividend income entry field.
6. Use the [DELETE] key to erase your 10000 input.

7. Enter 40000 into the dividend income field.

8. Press [F3] to calculate the results of changing dividend income. Your screen should now appear as that shown in Exhibit 3.13.

9. Making certain that your printer is ready (on line), press the [F9] key. The hard copy produced should look like that presented in Exhibit 3.14.

10. Press [F5] to clear the screen.

11. Press [ESC] to return to the PROFIT+ Main Menu.

12. Press [F9] to bring up the Print Option Menu.

13. Press 2 to tell PROFIT+ that you want to print to disk.

14. Place your PROFIT+ storage disk in the B-drive if you are using a floppy disk machine, or in the A-drive if your computer has a hard drive.

15. Enter TEST1 as the filename for the output that will be saved to disk.

16. Select Option A, Corporate Income Tax, from the PROFIT+ Main Menu.

17. Reenter the inputs for the original sample problem so that your screen appears as the one shown in Exhibit 3.8.

18. Press [F9] to print your results to disk.

19. Press [ESC] to return to the PROFIT+ Main Menu.

20. Press [ESC] to exit PROFIT+. (If necessary, place your DOS master disk in the A-drive.)

21. Place your storage disk with the TEST1 file on it in the A-drive.

22. Make certain that your printer is turned on and is on line with your computer.

23. Type and enter the following:

TYPE A:TEST1.OUT >PRN

24. Examine your printed output to see that it looks like that in Exhibit 3.14.

25. Erase the TEST1 file by typing and entering the following:

ERASE A:TEST1.*

Exhibit 3.13

PROFIT+ PROFIT+

CORPORATE INCOME TAX CALCULATION

Income from Operations	Interest Income	Interest Expense	Dividend Income
250000.00	20000.00	30000.00	40000.00

Taxable Income	Income Tax
248000.00	79970.00

[F1]=HELP [F2]=REVIEW [F3]=CALC [F5]=REDO [F9]=PRINT [ESC]=MENU

Please enter dividend income (or 0 if not applicable).

Exhibit 3.14

```
*****                CORPORATE INCOME TAX                           *****

   INCOME FROM OPERATIONS       $       250,000.00
 + INTEREST INCOME                       20,000.00
 - INTEREST EXPENSE                      30,000.00
 + 20% OF DIVIDEND INCOME                 8,000.00
                                 ------------------
   TAXABLE INCOME               $       248,000.00

FEDERAL CORPORATE TAX RATES UNDER 1986 REFORMS ARE AS FOLLOWS:

     15% OF THE FIRST     $50,000  OF TAXABLE INCOME
     25% OF THE NEXT      $25,000  OF TAXABLE INCOME
     34% OF ALL INCOME > $75,000
      5% OF TAXABLE INCOME BETWEEN $100,000  AND  $335,000

USING THESE RATES, THE FEDERAL TAX DUE ON         $248000.00
                                        IS          $79970.00

------------------------------------------------------------------------------
```

ADDITIONAL INFORMATION, ANSWERS, AND ADVICE

Assuming that you have successfully negotiated all of the steps in the PROFIT+ tutorial included in this chapter, you have learned the operations that are necessary to use the vast majority of the software's routines. A few words of information and advice, plus answers to some typical questions, are appropriate at this junction, however.

PROFIT+ Calc and PROFIT+ Write

The only programs that use some operations that differ from those in this chapter's tutorial are PROFIT+ Calc and PROFIT+ Write. Actually, PROFIT+ Write uses many of these operations so that you must learn only a few additional skills to use it effectively. Since you probably will want to use it to include verbal discussions along with the numerical printouts from most PROFIT+ routines, you should take time to work through the brief PROFIT+ Write tutorial in Chapter Twenty-Two of this guide.

Since PROFIT+ Calc is a spreadsheet program, its use requires that you learn a separate command system. If your instructor wishes you to use PROFIT+ Calc for the class, or if you want to learn how to use it for use in this or another class, a comprehensive tutorial is included in Chapter Twenty-One.

What Do I Do with the PROFIT+—Disk 2?

If you are using PROFIT+ on a floppy disk system, you have two PROFIT+ program disks. While you only used Disk 1 in this chapter's tutorial, some PROFIT+ routines are on Disk 2. You must always start PROFIT+ with Disk 1 and PROFIT+ will tell you to switch disks if you select a routine that is on Disk 2. (Note: If you exit PROFIT+ with Disk 2 in the A-drive, your computer may ask you to insert your DOS or COMMAND.COM disk. If this happens, remove Disk 2, replace it with Disk 1, and press [RETURN].)

Can PROFIT+ "Crash"?

Anyone who has used a computer knows that very few programs are completely "crash proof." That is, there is generally some sequence of events, no matter how unlikely they might be, that can cause the program to stop, freeze up, and/or return to DOS. PROFIT+ is no exception to this rule. While every effort has been taken to trap user errors that can lead to a crash (division by zero, for example), some unlikely key combinations or some illogical inputs might lead to difficulties.

The best way to avoid any problems is to use PROFIT+ in a manner consistent with good business logic. That is, use the software for working problems encountered in your financial management text and in the real world. Do not enter "garbage figures" into the system or just pound away on the computer keyboard. If you avoid the latter practices, you will find that PROFIT+ is, indeed, crash proof for the uses to which you will be putting it. (Fortunately, nothing really disastrous can happen if you do cause a crash. At the worst, you simply must reboot the computer and reenter your inputs for the problem that you were working when the crash occurred.)

Will PROFIT+ Work with Numbers of Any Size?

Any time a program such as PROFIT+ is written, certain assumptions regarding the size of numbers the program will accept must be made. Most routines that require dollar entries allow you to enter values of at least $1 million in size. Many allow values up to $99 million. If you attempt to enter a number larger than that which is allowed into an entry field, PROFIT+ will not let you do so. The field simply will not accommodate the number. In addition, while every attempt has been made to make calculated fields large enough to display the results from all possible inputs in the entry fields, very large entries can lead to outputs that cannot be displayed in the regular output field. When this occurs, PROFIT+ will generate a warning tone, and the message line will display the value of the offending output after the message, "Value out of range." In the unlikely event that this happens, simply press the [RETURN] key to remove the message and continue the operation of the program. When your inputs are obviously going to be larger than those accommodated by PROFIT+, simply divide them by 1,000 or 1,000,000 and then enter them. (If appropriate, remember to multiply your outputs by the divisor that you used.)

Does PROFIT+ Have Color?

PROFIT+ was written to work on either monochrome or color monitors. If you have a color monitor available, you will find that the colors used on PROFIT+ make it a more attractive program to use.

Will PROFIT+ Make All of the Calculations that I Will Encounter in the Beginning Financial Management Class?

While PROFIT+ performs most of the difficult calculations that are found in beginning financial management textbooks, some of the simpler calculations have been omitted from the software. This has been done for an important pedagogical reason. It is vital that you know how to interpret the results that are produced by computers. One of the ways that this guide, and your instructor, can make certain that you understand the output from PROFIT+ is to require you to answer questions and perform simple calculations using the results. Question number 2 at the end of this chapter is an excellent example of this type of question. You will find others like it included in most of the end-of-chapter questions and problems throughout this guide.

Can I Use PROFIT+ beyond the Beginning Financial Management Class?

While PROFIT+ is not a business software package per se, it contains a variety of routines that you will find useful in other classes. If you are a finance major, you probably will discover that PROFIT+ can be used in your subsequent finance classes. (Not only will the program's number- crunching abilities be appreciated, but you will also find the review screens to be an efficient way to recall the basic concepts underlying the calculations.)

If you are not a finance major, you will find PROFIT+ of use in such classes as business policy, where cases requiring financial analysis are discussed. In addition, you will find PROFIT+ Calc to be a basic spreadsheet with many potential uses for handling numbers that lend themselves to a basic spreadsheet format. Finally, the "Financial Calculator" routine included with PROFIT+ gives you a time value of money calculator that you will find useful in your everyday personal finance life. Thus, PROFIT+ is more than a software package for use in the basic financial management class, even though that was the main purpose behind its creation. Keep the disks in the handy envelopes in this guide, and you will have access to a software package with a variety of uses for many years to come.

END-OF-CHAPTER PROBLEMS

1. Determine the federal corporate income tax due on the following amounts of ordinary taxable income (Hint—simply enter these amounts as income from operations, and enter 0 into the other three entry fields. Remember to press the [F3]=CALC key after making each change.):

a. $20,000	**b.** $44,000	**c.** $56,500
d. $77,000	**e.** $102,250	**f.** $207,586
g. $300,000	**h.** $445,000	**i.** $766,222
j. $2,457,500	**k.** $22,744,567	**l.** $111,765,889

2. By hand, calculate the average tax rate (income tax / taxable income) for parts g, h, i, and l in problem 1. For higher income corporations (those with taxable income greater than $335,000) what is their effective (average) tax rate?

3. This year, Betterway Corporation had $275,000 of income from operations. This amount does not include the following items: interest expense of $22,454; interest income of $19,782; dividend income of $76,500; and dividends paid of $25,750. What is the corporation's taxable income and income tax liability for the year?

4. Hollingsworth Incorporated has provided you with the following information regarding its operations for the year:

Operating income..................................	$1,254,350
Interest expense..................................	122,243
Interest income..................................	137,650
Dividend income..................................	202,400
Dividends paid..................................	401,667

a. What is the corporation's taxable income for the year?

b. What is Hollingsworth's income tax liability for the year?

c. What is the company's marginal tax rate? Its average tax rate?

5. The Kemp's Mountain Corporation had $120,000 of taxable income from operations in 1988.

a. What is the company's federal income tax liability?

b. Assume that Kemp's Mountain receives an additional $12,000 of interest income from some marketable securities that it owns. What is the firm's tax liability after the inclusion of this income? By how much did the interest income increase the firm's tax liability?

c. Now assume that the company does not receive the interest income, but does receive an additional $12,000 as dividends on some stock it owns. What is its tax liability after the inclusion of this income? By how much did the dividend income increase the firm's tax liability?

6. The Forefront Corporation had 1988 income from operations of $300,000 after all costs of operation, but before (1) interest charges of $21,000, (2) dividends received of $15,000, and income taxes. What is Forefront's income tax liability and its after-tax income?

7. Holdington Corporation lists the following information regarding its operations for the year:

Operating income..................................	$4,678,350
Interest expense..................................	232,650
Interest income..................................	230,010
Dividend income..................................	56,000

a. What is the corporation's taxable income for the year?

b. What is Holdington's income tax liability for the year?

c. How would the firm's tax liability change if its operating income were $3,500,000 rather than the amount listed? (Hold the other items constant.)

8. Hedgehog Sofa, Inc., had income from operations of $20,400 for 1988. This amount is exclusive of $1,500 of interest expense, and $1,225 of interest income. What is the firm's tax liability and *after-tax* income?

9. (Note: This question is designed to get you to make heavy use of PROFIT+'s "what if" capabilities. It is a "for fun" question, but it does give you the opportunity to experience the computer's recalculation power.) During 1988, APM Corporation produced $250,000 of taxable income, exclusive of dividend income and income taxes. If the firm's tax liability was $82,505, what was its dividend income for the year? (Hint: Enter $250,000 as income from operations, and then use PROFIT+'s, "what if", capabilities to zero in on the dividend income necessary to produce the indicated tax liability.)

Chapter Four
The PROFIT+ Financial Calculator

MONEY AND TIME

In business, and in your personal financial dealings, many situations require that the time value of money be taken into consideration. That is, these situations demand that you consider that money is worth different amounts depending on the points in time that you receive, or have to pay, that money. Money has time value because it can be put to work to earn more money. Ordinarily, these earnings are referred to as interest.

For an example of how the time value of money enters into financial decisions, assume that someone has just offered you the choice of being given $100 immediately or receiving that same $100 one year from today. Which alternative would you choose? Assuming that there are no tax considerations that would affect your decision, you would most likely choose to receive the $100 today because you could take the $100, invest it, and end up with more than $100 one year from today. Your choice demonstrates that you know money has time value. You realize that $100 today is worth more than $100 received in one year.

The time value of money concept is constantly being put to use in many areas of business financial management. The concept determines the interest earned and the interest paid on loans and is used to calculate the payments on an amortized loan. It is used to express the rates at which various series, for example, sales or earnings, have been increasing. Time value considerations must enter into decisions to acquire fixed assets, since such investments generate returns that will be received in the future.

Various other situations in financial management also require that money's time value be considered. This chapter explains the types of time value problems that PROFIT+ can help you solve.

Simple Interest

Just as the concept of time value is based on the idea that money can be put to work to earn interest, all time value calculations are based on the computation of simple interest. Simple interest assumes that interest is paid only once on the original amount borrowed (or lent) and is paid at the maturity of the loan. For an example of simple interest, assume that a friend loaned you $1000, for six months, at 12 percent simple interest. When the loan comes due at the end of six months, you will owe your friend $1000, plus interest at a 12 percent annual rate. To compute the interest due, you must solve the simple interest equation

$$I = Prt \tag{4.1}$$

where I = simple interest
P = the loan principal
r = annual rate of interest
t = time (expressed as a fraction of one year).

In this example, you would owe your friend $60 ($1000 x .12 x 6/12) interest.

Time Lines

A useful way to visualize any time value problem is with a time line. A time line is simply a horizontal line that reflects a period of time. Expressed as a time line, the simple interest problem just worked appears as follows:

	6 months	
PV	————————————	FV
$1000		$1060

The time line shows that a present amount, or present value (PV), of $1000 was borrowed, and six months later a future value (FV) of $1060 was due. Time lines are used throughout this chapter and in the PROFIT+ software to help you better understand the various types of time value problems that are being presented or solved.

Compound Interest

While simple interest is relatively easy to understand, many real-world situations requiring the use of time value concepts require that interest be figured on a compound basis. Compound interest differs from simple interest in the number of times that interest is calculated while money is on deposit or is being borrowed. Whereas simple interest assumes that interest is figured only once during the time under consideration, compound interest allows for interest to be computed more than once. For deposits that are earning compound interest (such as bank savings accounts), each time interest is determined it is calculated on the original principal plus all interest earned up to that point in time. This latter point explains why compound interest is frequently called "interest on interest."

The following calculations explain how compound interest works by showing you how much interest would be earned on \$1000, deposited for one year in an account that pays 12 percent interest compounded quarterly. In these calculations, compound interest is based on the simple interest equation (Eq. 4.1). Since interest in the example is compounded quarterly, it will be calculated four times, or every three months. For the first three-month period, the original \$1000 principal will earn \$30 interest (\$1000 x .12 x 3/12). When interest is calculated for the second three-month period, the principal used in the computation is \$1030 (the original \$1000 plus the \$30 interest earned during the first compounding period). Thus, the interest earned for the second period would be \$30.90 (\$1030 x .12 x 3/12). For the third interest calculation, the principal would become \$1060.90 (\$1000 + \$30 + \$30.90) and the interest earned would be \$31.83 (\$1060.90 x .12 x 3/12). Interest for the final quarter of the year will equal \$32.78 (\$1092.73 x .12 x 3/12). The balance in the account at the end of the year will be \$1125.51, composed of the original \$1000 principal plus \$125.51 (\$30 + \$30.90 + \$31.83 + \$32.78) compound interest.

Drawn as a time line, the \$1000 would increase to \$1125.51 as follows:

	3 months	6 months	9 months	1 year
/	/	/	/	/
\$1000	\$1030	\$1060.90	\$1092.73	\$1125.51

Although every problem in this chapter could be worked using some variation of the sample solution that was just discussed, much more appropriate methods exist for solving problems that involve compounding. These methods are based on the compound interest equation

$$FV = PV(1 + i)^n \tag{4.2}$$

where FV = the future value (ending value)
PV = the present value (beginning principal)
i = interest rate per compounding period (nominal interest rate divided by the number of times interest is calculated each year)
n = total number of times interest is figured during the time period involved in the problem.

(Note: Although the symbols used in this guide may not be the same as those that appear in your financial management textbook, they have been chosen for their clarity and practicality. The symbols are clear, because they are taken directly from the words they represent. They are practical, because they are the ones used on financial calculators and in most time value software.) Equation 4.2 can be used to solve the previous sample problem. In that problem, PV = \$1000, i = 12%/4 = 3%, and n = 4. By entering these values in Equation 4.2, you obtain the following results:

$$FV = \$1000(1 + .03)4$$
$$FV = \$1000(1.03)4$$
$$FV = \$1000(1.2550)$$
$$FV = \$1125.51$$

THE PROFIT+ "FINANCIAL CALCULATOR"

All of the problems in this chapter could be solved using some modification of Equations 4.1 and 4.2. In addition, any introductory financial management textbook (for example, *Fundamentals of Financial Management*, 4th ed., by Eugene F. Brigham) will show you how to use tables of compound interest factors to shorten the amount of time it takes to work time value problems.

PROFIT+ includes a routine that allows for even speedier solutions of time value problems: the Financial Calculator. To run Financial Calculator, simply select choice B the Main Menu. Once you have done this, PROFIT+ will load the Financial Calculator routine and then will present you with the Financial Calculator Menu depicted in Exhibit 4.1.

Options A through O on the Financial Calculator Menu allow you to work various types of time value problems. The following paragraphs discuss the basic types of time value problems that can be worked using PROFIT+. More complex problems can be solved using two or more of the options. So that you can be more certain you have chosen the appropriate option, the majority of the routines include a time line representation of the type of problem that it solves. You actually enter

Exhibit 4.1

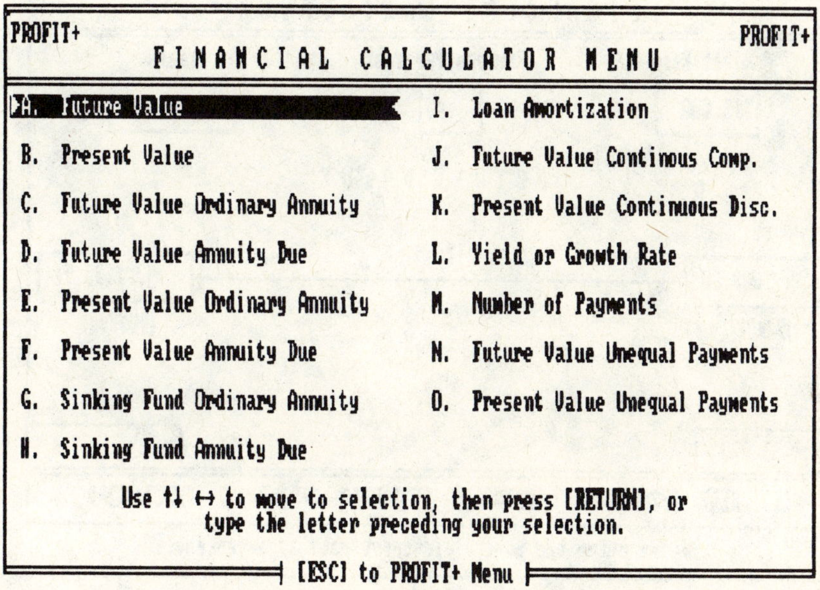

your "known" dollar amounts on these time lines, and the "unknown" amounts are displayed on the lines. You should find that thinking each problem out as a time line, in advance of working it, will help you decide on the correct option to choose from the Financial Calculator Menu.

Option A: Future Value

This option solves problems similar to the sample compound interest problem given earlier in this chapter. As a time line, future value problems take the following form:

PV————————————————FV
Known   Unknown

PROFIT+ uses Equation 4.2 to solve future value problems. The compound interest problem worked earlier asked for the future value of $1000 deposited for one year, at 12 percent interest compounded quarterly. Exhibit 4.2 shows the completed Future Value Screen once it has been used to solve this problem.

PROFIT+ provides not only the answer to the problem, but also the "i" and "n" used in the compound interest equation to solve the problem.

Exhibit 4.2

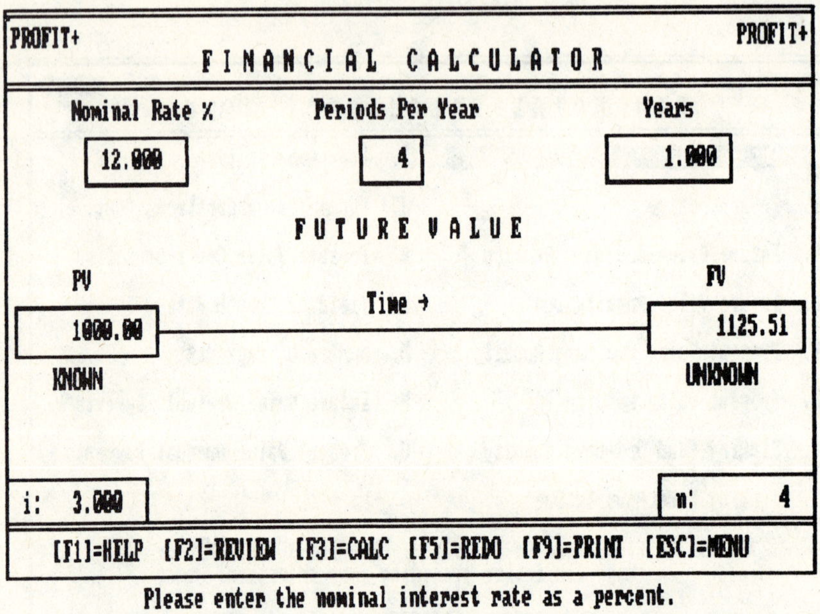

Option B: Present Value

Present value problems take a form that is just opposite of that taken by future value problems. That is, you know a future value and want to determine the present value that would grow to that future amount at a given rate of interest (often called the discount rate in present value problems) over a given period of time. Thought of as a time line, present value problems appear as follows:

PV——————————————————FV
Unknown Known

PROFIT+ uses the following equation to solve present value problems:

$$PV = \frac{FV}{(1 + i)^n} \tag{4.3}$$

Exhibit 4.3 shows you how Financial Calculator Option B can be used to solve the following problem:

Exhibit 4.3

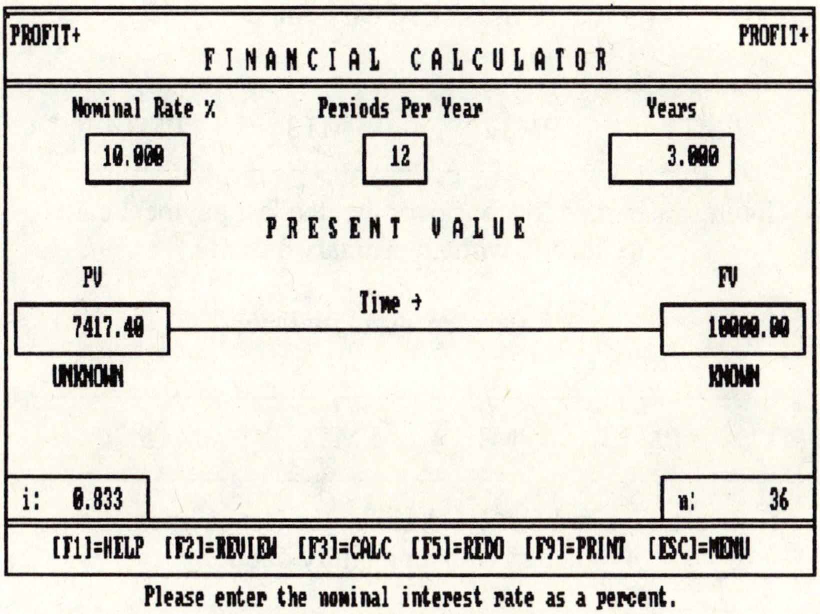

Sample Problem: How much must you invest today in an account that pays 10 percent interest compounded monthly so that you will have accumulated $10,000 by the end of three years?

Annuities

An annuity is a series of equal payments made at equal time intervals for a given period of time. In ordinary annuities, the payments are made at the end of each time period. When the payments come at the beginning of each time period, the annuity is called an annuity due. With both types of annuities, the perodic payments are assumed to coincide with dates on which interest is compounded. Exhibit 4.4 depicts the difference between an ordinary annuity and an annuity due with time lines. With the annuity due, the payments have one more time period in which to earn interest. Because of this, the formulas for working with annuities due always have a factor included to account for the additional interest period. This additional factor takes the form (1 + i). You will see it in this chapter any time you encounter an annuity due problem.

Exhibit 4.4

A 5-Payment Ordinary Annuity

```
——————/——————/——————/——————/——————/
     PMT1       PMT2       PMT3       PMT4       PMT5
     ———1———>———2———>———3———>———4———>
```

(Interest is earned for four periods; the last payment earns no interest with an ordinary annuity.)

A 5-Payment Annuity Due

```
/——————/——————/——————/——————/——————
PMT1     PMT2     PMT3     PMT4     PMT5
———1———>———2———>———3———>———4———>———5———>
```

(Interest is earned for five periods; the last payment earns interest with an annuity due.)

Options C and D: Future Value of an Annuity

The future value of an annuity can be thought of as the amount to which a series of annuity payments will accumulate over a given period of time. This amount includes both the payments themselves and the interest earned on those payments. The formula for calculating the future value of an ordinary annuity is

$$FV = PMT\left(\frac{(1+i)^n - 1}{i}\right) \tag{4.4}$$

where PMT = the size of each of the annuity payments.

Expressed as a time line, a future value of an ordinary annuity problem appears as follows:

FV of an Ordinary Annuity

```
——————/——————/——————/——...——/ FV (Unknown)
     PMT       PMT       PMT        PMT
     Known     Known     Known      Known
```

Option C on the Financial Calculator Menu uses Equation 4.4 to determine the future value of an ordinary annuity.

When calculating the future value of an annuity due, the following formula is used:

$$FV = PMT\left(\frac{(1+i)^n - 1}{i}\right)(1+i) \tag{4.5}$$

A future value of an annuity due problem takes the following form when expressed as a time line:

FV of an Annuity Due

/————/————/———...———/—————/ FV (Unknown)

PMT	PMT	PMT	PMT
Known	Known	Known	Known

Option D on the Financial Calculator Menu uses Equation 4.5 to determine the future value of an annuity due.

Exhibit 4.5 shows how PROFIT+ Financial Calculator Option C uses Equation 4.5 to solve the following problem:

Sample Problem: If you were to deposit $125 at the end of every year into an account that pays 9.25 percent interest compounded monthly, how much would you have in that account at the end of five years? (Note: Since payments are being made at the end of each year, the problem is dealing with an ordinary annuity; therefore, Exhibit 4.5 is a depiction of the Future Value of an Ordinary Annuity Screen.)

In Exhibit 4.5, three annuity payments are shown on a "broken" time line. The time line is broken to show that several (i.e., "n") payments are involved. When you enter the actual payment, you will do so only in the first payment field. PROFIT+ automatically will fill in the remaining payment fields with the value entered in the first one.

Exhibit 4.5

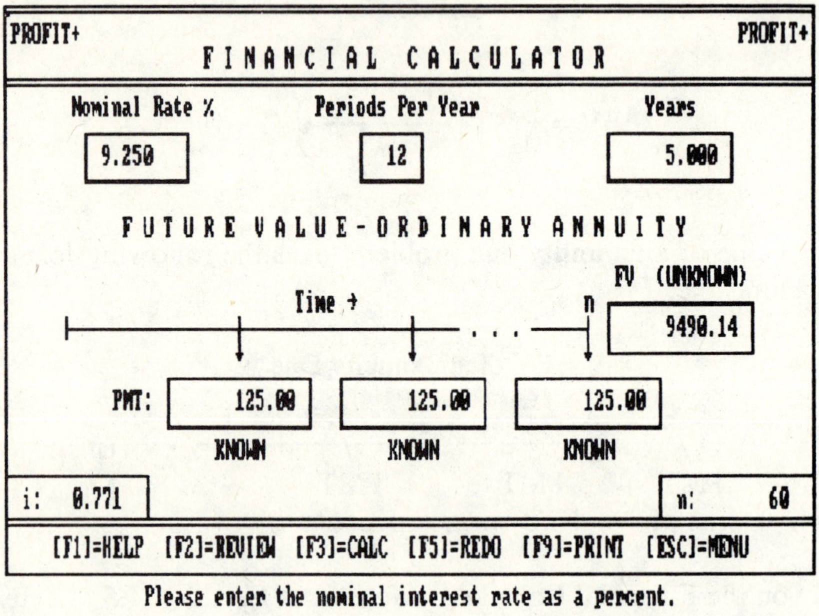

If the payments in the preceding problem were made at the beginning of each time period, you would request Option D from the Financial Calculator Menu and use the Future Value of an Annuity Due routine to solve the problem, as shown in Exhibit 4.6.

In the discussions of the remaining annuity options on PROFIT+'s Financial Calculator Menu, you will be told if a routine gives you the choice of selecting either an ordinary or an annuity due, but a sample printout will be provided for only one of the two types of annuities.

Options E and F: Present Value of an Annuity

An annuity's present value is the amount of money that you would have to put aside today at a given rate of interest to receive a series of equal payments over a given period of time. The formula for calculating the present value of an ordinary annuity is

$$PV = PMT\left(\frac{1}{i} - \frac{1}{i\,(1+i)^n}\right) \tag{4.6}$$

Exhibit 4.6

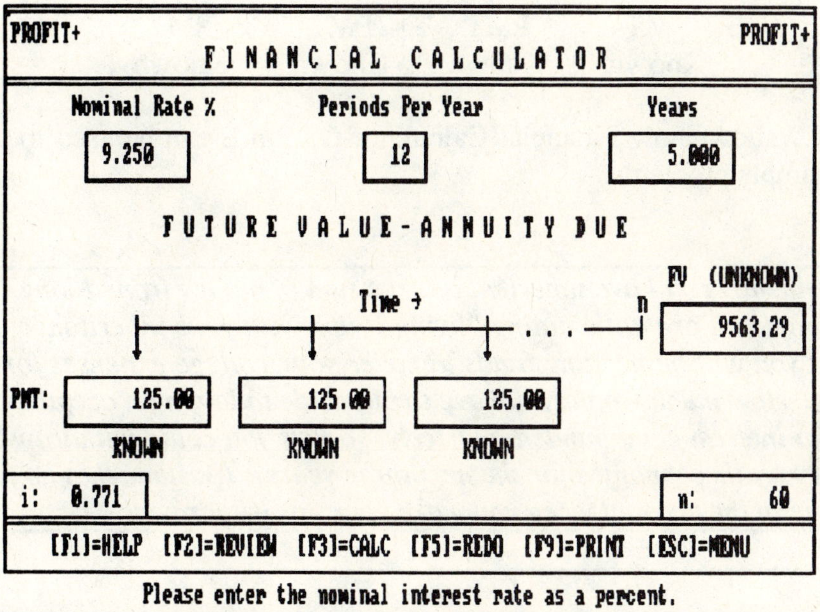

Expressed as a time line, a present value of an ordinary annuity problem appears as follows:

PV of an Ordinary Annuity

(Unknown) PV/————/————/ ... /————/

PMT	PMT	PMT	PMT
Known	Known	Known	Known

The present value of an annuity due is calculated using the following formula:

$$PV = PMT \left(\frac{1}{i} - \frac{1}{i\,(1 + i)^n} \right) (1 + i) \quad \textbf{(4.7)}$$

Expressed as a time line, the present value of an annuity due takes the following form:

PV of an Annuity Due

(Unknown) PV/——————/——————/——————/——...———

PMT Known | PMT Known | PMT Known | PMT Known

Exhibit 4.7 shows how Financial Calculator Option E can be used to solve the following sample problem:

Sample Problem: You have inherited a large sum of money from a long-lost relative. Although you are anticipating "living it up" with your inheritance, you also realize that you will be needing funds to cover your college expenses for the next three years. How much would you have to put aside today in an account that pays 10.5 percent interest compounded quarterly, so that you could withdraw $1200 at the end of every three months for the next three years? (Assume that no funds will be remaining in the account when you make your last withdrawal.)

Exhibit 4.7

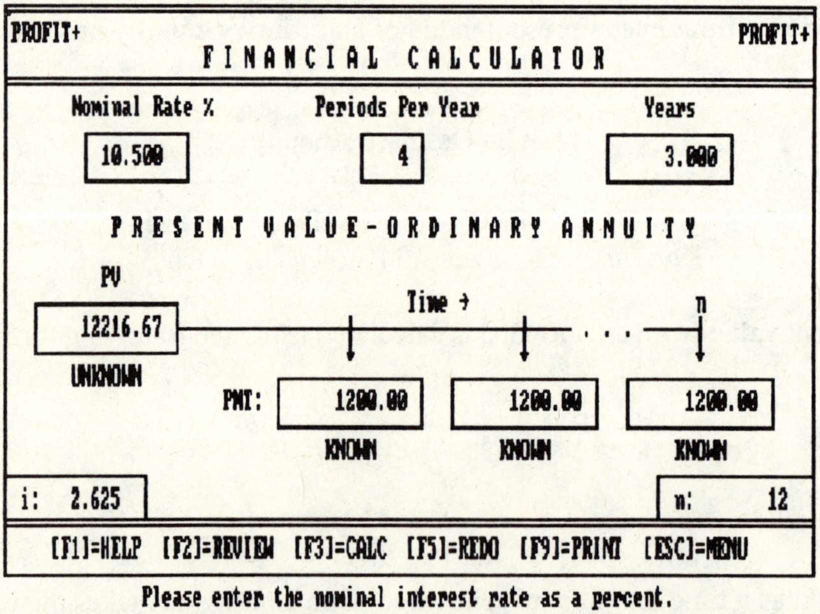

Options G and H: Sinking Fund Payment

In a general sense, sinking funds can be thought of as savings plans. They allow you to accumulate a given future amount by making a series of equal payments into some interest-bearing investment. In most cases, sinking funds are established with the idea of making payments at the end of each of the time periods involved. That is, the sinking fund, or savings plan, user is determining today how much to deposit at the end of every month, for example, to accumulate a desired future amount at the end of a given period of time. PROFIT+ does, however, give you the option of assuming payments at either the ending (ordinary annuity) or the beginning (annuity due) of the time periods involved.

Expressed as a time line, the sinking fund with ordinary annuity payments problem appears as follows:

Sinking Fund - Ordinary Annuity

```
———————/———————/———————/———...———/FV (Known)
     PMT      PMT      PMT        PMT
    Known    Known   Unknown    Unknown
```

The formula used to calculate sinking fund ordinary annuity payments is

$$PMT = FV\left(\frac{i}{(1 + i)^{n} - 1}\right) \tag{4.8}$$

The sinking fund with annuity due payments appears as follows when depicted as a time line:

Sinking Fund - Annuity Due

```
/———————/———————/———...———/———————/FV (Known)
PMT      PMT      PMT      PMT
Unknown  Unknown  Unknown  Unknown
```

When calculating sinking fund annuity due payments, the following formula is used:

$$PMT = FV\left(\frac{i}{(1 + i)^{n} - 1}\right)\frac{1}{(1 + i)} \tag{4.9}$$

The PROFIT+ solution to the following sample problem appears in Exhibit 4.8. The problems deals with sinking fund ordinary annuity payments, and thus uses Financial Calculator Option G.

Exhibit 4.8

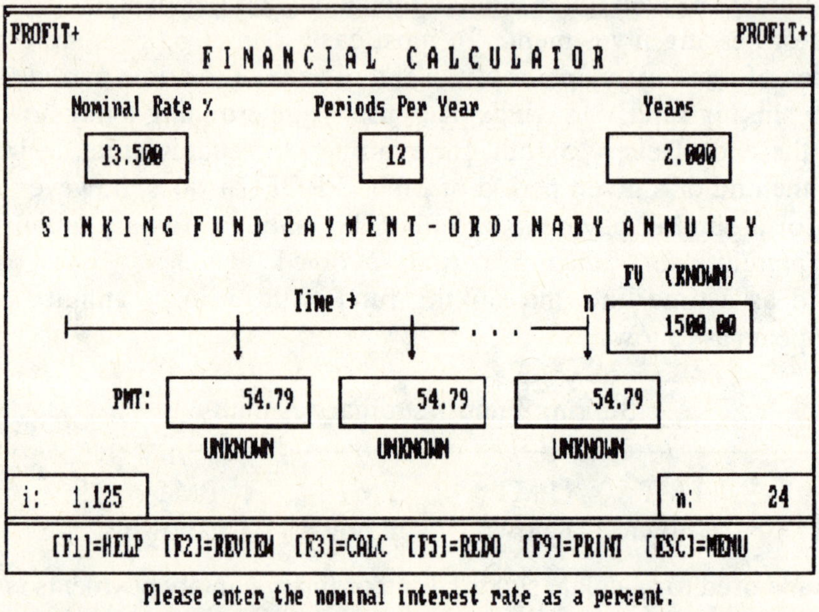

Sample Problem: Frederic Biswell, owner of Fred's Hardware Store, estimates that he will need $1500 at the end of two years to replace the sign in front of his building. How much will Fred have to deposit at the end of every month into an account that pays 13.5 percent interest compounded monthly, so that he will have accumulated the $1500 two years from now?

Option I: Loan Amortization

One of the most frequent uses of the time value concept involves the calculation of the size of a series of equal payments necessary to repay a loan. When a loan is paid off with a series of equal periodic payments, it is said to be amortized. Each of the amortization payments covers the interest due for the period and also includes some funds for the repayment of the outstanding principal balance of the loan. Thus, as time passes, the amount owed declines, interest due on the loan declines, and a greater portion of each of the equal payments goes to further reduce the balance of the loan. A table showing how much of each payment is interest, how much is used to reduce the principal, and the size of the remaining loan balance is called amortization schedule. In addition to calculating the size of a series of equal payments necessary to retire a loan, PROFIT+'s loan amortization routine also can prepare a loan amortization schedule for the problem with which you are dealing.

The following formula is used to determine the size of each of the payments necessary to amortize a loan:

$$PMT = PV\left(\frac{1}{1 - \frac{1}{(1 + i)^n}}\right) \tag{4.10}$$

Expressed as a time line, a loan amortization problem appears as follows:

Loan Amortization

(Known) PV ——————/——————/——————/——...——/

PMT	PMT	PMT		PMT
Unknown	Unknown	Unknown		Unknown

Exhibits 4.9 and 4.10 depict how the Financial Calculator Option I can be used to solve the following sample problem:

Sample Problem: Litvan's Laundry borrows $30,000 from its bank, promising to repay the loan in a series of four equal annual payments. What would be the size of each of these equal payments if the bank is charging 12 percent interest on the outstanding loan balance? Prepare an amortization schedule for this loan.

The second part of the sample problem requires that a loan amortization schedule be prepared. This table shows each loan payment, how much interest each payment must cover, how much of each payment can be used to repay the loan, and the loan balance after each payment has been applied. The loan amortization schedule for the sample problem is shown in Exhibit 4.10. This schedule can be obtained by pressing the [PGDN] key after the loan payment has been calculated.

PROFIT+ uses Equation 4.10 to calculate the loan amortization payment. However, you must also understand how the loan amortization schedule was prepared. The first step in gaining this knowledge is to realize that the interest due from each payment is determined by multiplying the outstanding loan balance for the period times i (the interest rate per payment period). Thus, for the sample problem, the interest due from the first payment is $3,600 ($30,000 x .12). All that must be done to determine how much of a payment can be used to reduce the principal of the loan is to subtract the interest due from the loan payment. When this is done for the sample problem, you obtain $6,277.03 ($9,877.03 - $3,600.00). The loan balance is simply the remaining principal after the principal

Exhibit 4.9

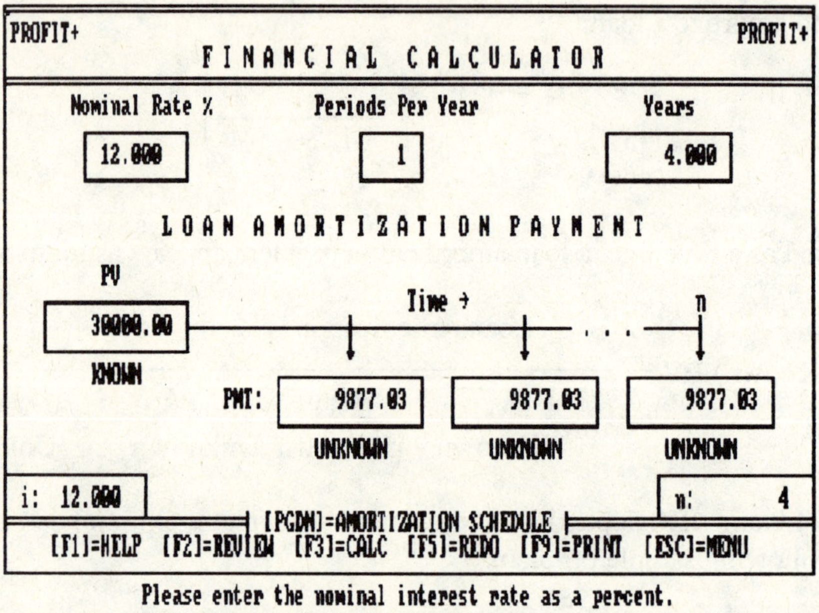

Exhibit 4.10

PROFIT+ PROFIT+

FINANCIAL CALCULATOR

LOAN AMORTIZATION SCHEDULE

n	PMT	TO INTEREST	TO PRINCIPAL	LOAN BALANCE
				30000.00
1	9877.03	3600.00	6277.03	23722.97
2	9877.03	2846.76	7030.28	16692.69
3	9877.03	2003.12	7873.91	8818.78
4	9877.03	1058.25	8818.78	0.00

[F1]=HELP [F2]=REVIEW [F5]=REDO [F9]=PRINT [ESC]=MENU [PGDN]=MORE

[PGUP]=PAYMENT CALCULATION

reduction for a payment has been applied; therefore, the balance after the first payment was made in the sample problem was $23,722.97 ($30,000.00 - $6,277.03). This same procedure is followed for subsequent payments:

Interest due—2nd pmt	= $23,722.97 x .12 = $2,846.76
To principal—2nd pmt	= $9,877.03 - $2,846.76 = $7,030.28*
Loan balance after 2nd pmt	= $23,722.97 - $7,030.28 = $16,692.69
Interest due—3rd pmt	= $16,692.69 x .12 = $2,003.12
To principal—3rd pmt	= $9,877.03 - $2,003.12 = $7,873.91
Loan balance after 3rd pmt	= $16,692.69 - $7,873.91 = $8,818.78
Interest due—4th pmt	= $8,818.78 x .12 = $1,058.25
To principal—4th pmt	= $9,877.03 - $1,058.25 = $8,818.78
Loan balance after 4th pmt	= $8,818.78 - $8,818.78 = 0

* slight discrepancy due to rounding on screen

When many payments are involved, the rounding of the payment to the nearest cent will lead to a slight negative or positive balance at the end of the term of the loan. To account for this, PROFIT+ will adjust the final payment by the amount necessary to "zero out" the loan. Lending institutions follow the same practice.

Option J: Future Value Continuous Compounding

Option A assumes that compounding occurs at discrete time intervals (daily, monthly, quarterly, etc.). Occasionally, however, it is more appropriate to assume that compounding is continuously taking place. This option computes the future value of a present amount, compounded continuously for a given period of time. The formula used to compute future value with continuous compounding is

$$FV = PV(e^{in}) \tag{4.11}$$

where e = the value 2.7183... .

You can read about how this formula is derived in most time value of money chapters in leading financial management textbooks (for example, in Appendix 4A of *Essentials of Managerial Finance,* 8th ed., by J. Fred Weston and Eugene F. Brigham). Depicted as a time line, continuous compounding appears as follows:

FV with Continuous Compounding

PV———————————————FV
Known   Unknown

Exhibit 4.11 shows how Option J can be used to solve the following sample problem:

Sample Problem: What is the future value of $100, deposited for five years in an account that pays 10 percent interest compounded continuously?

Option K: Present Value Continuous Discounting

This option computes the present value of a future amount, assuming that continuous discounting is taking place. Expressed as a time line, the problem appears as follows:

PV, Continuous Discounting

PV———————————————FV
Unknown   Known

The following formula is used to compute present value under the condition of continuous compounding:

$$PV = FV(e^{-in}) \tag{4.12}$$

Exhibit 4.12 demonstrates how Financial Calculator Option K can be used to solve the following sample problem:

Sample Problem: What is the present value of $1649 to be received at the end of five years if the appropriate continuous discount rate is 5 percent?

Exhibit 4.11

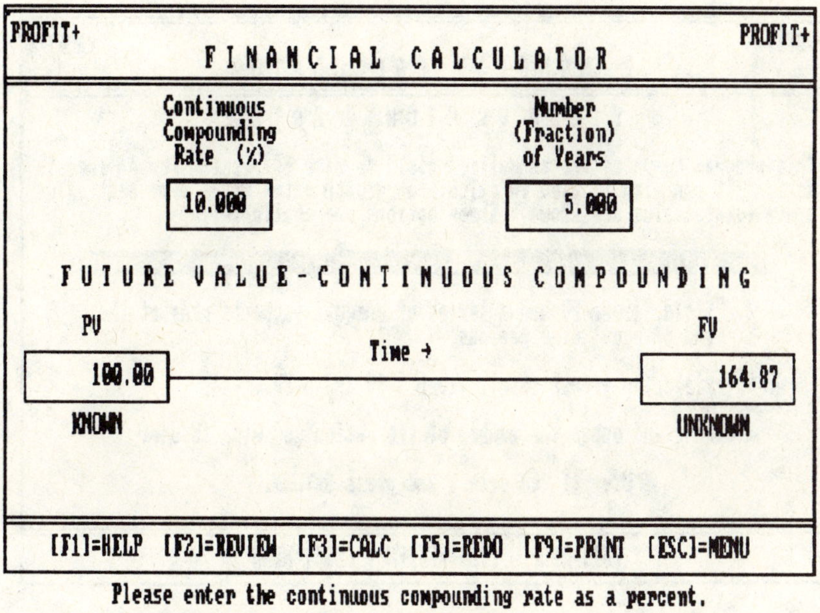

Exhibit 4.12

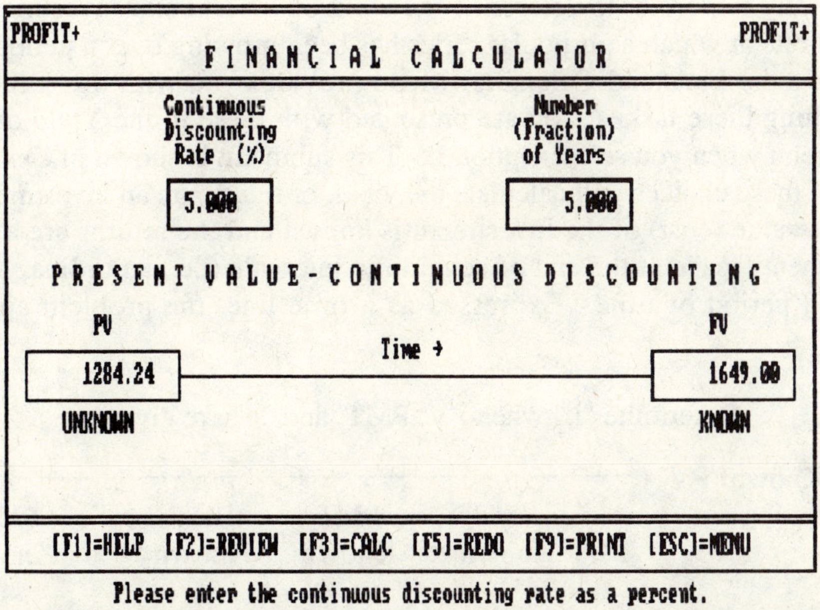

Exhibit 4.13

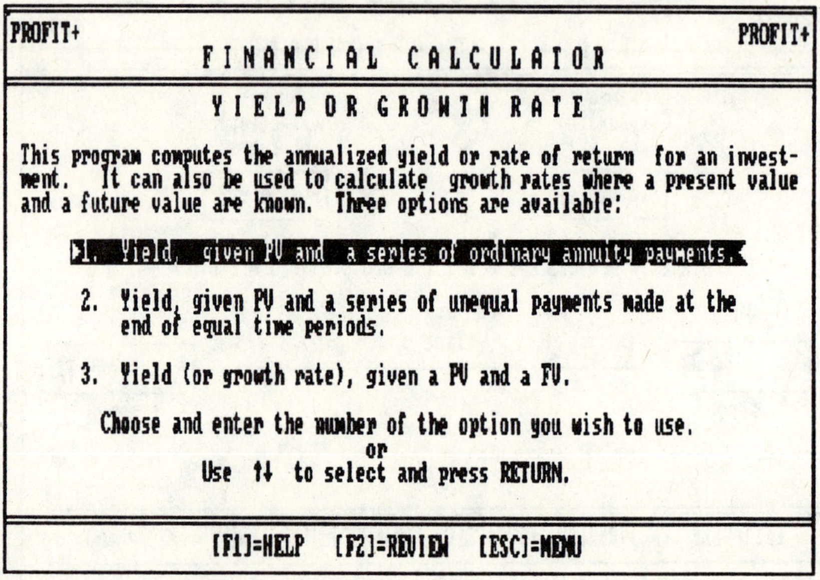

Option L: Yield or Growth Rate

It is frequently important to determine the yield on a particular investment, or the compound rate at which a particular series has been growing over a period of time. Option L on the Financial Calculator Menu provides you with three choices for accomplishing these tasks. You are presented with these in the Yield or Growth Rate submenu when you select Option L. This submenu is shown in Exhibit 4.13. The first of these choices will calculate the yield, or return, on an investment where the present value (cost) of the investment is known and the returns are a series of equal payments made at the end of equal time intervals (i.e., an ordinary annuity) for a given period of time. Expressed as a time line, the problem appears as follows:

Determine "i," when PV, PMT, and "n" are given

```
(Known) PV ————/————/————/——...——/
              PMT    PMT    PMT      PMT
             Known  Known  Known    Known
```

To obtain the yield on the investment, PROFIT+ solves for "i" in the formula used for calculating the present value of an annuity, Equation 4.6:

$$PV = PMT\left(\frac{1}{i} - \frac{1}{i(1 + i)^n}\right) \tag{4.6}$$

Where compounding occurs more frequently than one time per year, PROFIT+ annualizes the yield using the following formula:

$$\text{Effective annual yield} = (1 + i)^m - 1 \tag{4.13}$$

where m = number of compounding periods per year.

Exhibit 4.14 shows how option 1 from the Yield or Growth Rate submenu can be used to solve the following sample problem:

Sample Problem: Your broker is offering you the opportunity to purchase a note for $1,000. In return for your investment you will receive $300 per year for the next five years. What rate of return would you be earning on your investment?

Exhibit 4.14

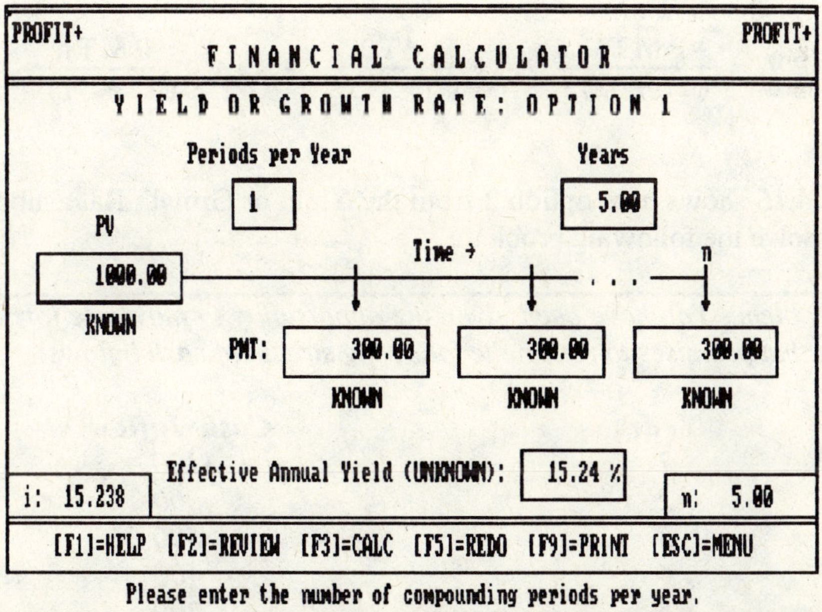

In the solution to the preceding sample problem, the effective annual rate of interest and "i" are identical values, because that compounding is taking place only one time per year. If interest were being compounded more than once per year, these two values would have differed, because PROFIT+ would have used Equation 4.13 to convert "i" to an effective annual rate.

The second choice that you are given on the Yield or Growth Rate submenu is that of calculating yield given a present value (cost) and a series of *unequal* payments being made at the end of equal time periods. Expressed as a time line, the problem appears as follows:

Determine "i," when PV, PMTs(1 - n), and "n" are given

```
(Known) PV ----------/----------/----------/----...----/
                   PMT1       PMT2       PMT3        PMTn
                   Known      Known      Known       Known
```

where PMTs 1 through n are not necessarily equal.

PROFIT+ solves the following formula for "i" to determine the yield for this problem and uses Equation 4.13 to convert "i" to an effective annual yield where compounding takes place more than once per year:

$$PV = \frac{PMT1}{(1 + i)^1} + \frac{PMT2}{(1 + i)^2} + \ldots + \frac{PMTn}{(1 + i)^n} \tag{4.14}$$

Exhibit 4.15 shows how option 2 from the Yield or Growth Rate submenu can be used to solve the following problem:

Sample Problem: You have been given the opportunity to purchase for $1,000 an investment that promises to return the following stream of cash inflows:

Year	***Cash Inflow***
1	*$100*
2	*300*
3	*500*
4	*400*
5	*200*

If these cash inflows are realized, what is the investment's effective annual yield?

Exhibit 4.15

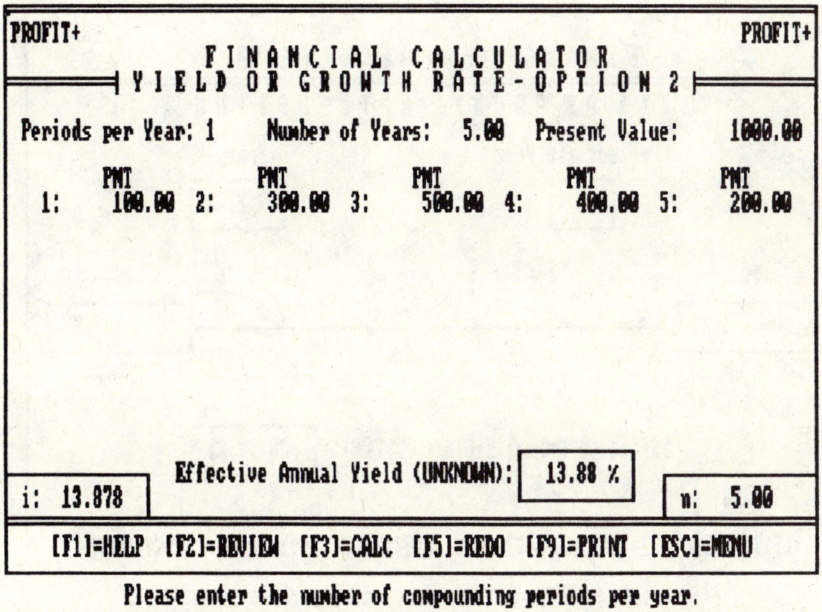

This is the first Financial Calculator routine that does not request that you enter dollar amounts on time lines. The reason for this is that the routine allows for the entry of as many as 50 cash inflows. Screen space simply will not allow the construction of a time line large enough to accommodate that number of flows.

The third and final option available on the Yield or Growth Rate submenu is that of calculating the yield, return, or growth rate when given a present and a future value. This type of computation is frequently used by firms to calculate the average annual compound rate at which some series (i.e., sales, earnings, or dividends) have been growing. Depicted as a time line, the problem appears as follows:

Determine "i" when PV, FV, and "n" are given

(Known) PV————————————————FV (Known)

To obtain the annual growth rate, or yield, PROFIT+ solves for "i" in the basic future value equation

$$FV = PV(1 + i)^n. \tag{4.2}$$

Exhibit 4.16

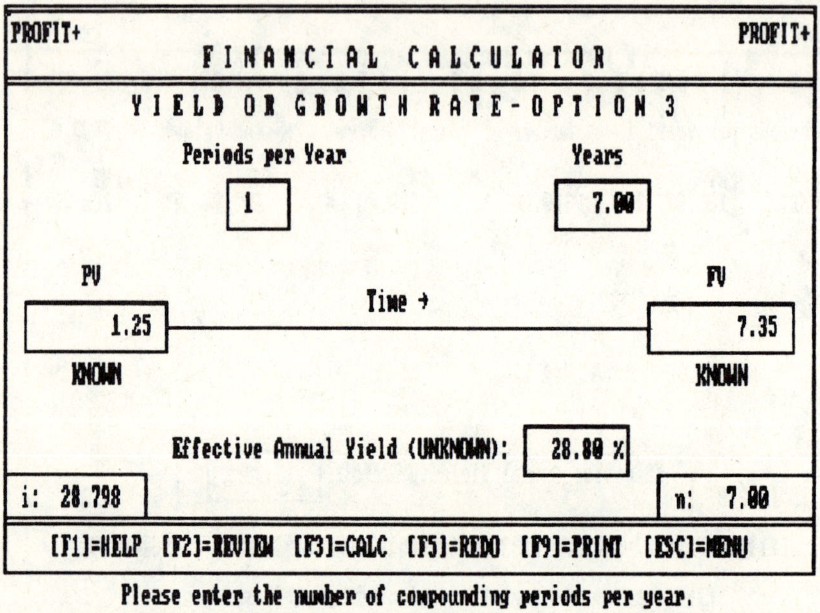

Exhibit 4.16 shows how PROFIT+ uses option 3 from the Yield or Growth Rate submenu to solve the following sample problem:

Sample Problem: The sales for Tom's Corp. have increased from $1.25 million to $7.35 million over the past seven years. At what average annual rate did Tom's sales grow?

In the preceding example, since compounding is annual, i = effective annual rate. The slight difference that appears on the screen is simply due to rounding that takes place in the effective annual yield formula.

Option M: Number of Payments

This option calculates the number of years, or number of payments, needed to achieve a given savings or investment objective under the assumption of a given rate of compound interest. Since there are different circumstances under which you might want to determine the number of payments to attain an objective, Financial Calculator Option M gives you three choices from which to select, depending on the

Exhibit 4.17

```
PROFIT+                                                              PROFIT+
                      F I N A N C I A L   C A L C U L A T O R

                          N U M B E R   O F   P A Y M E N T S

This program computes the number of years of number of payments it takes to
accomplish a certain objective.  Three options are available depending upon
the information that is known:

     ▶1.  Number of PMIs, given PV, FV, and an interest rate.

      2.  Number of PMTs, given PV, ordinary annuity PMT, and an
          interest rate.

      3.  Number of PMTs, given FV, ordinary annuity PMT, and an
          interest rate.

        Choose and enter the number of the option you wish to use,
                                   or
             use ↑↓ to select option and press RETURN.

                  [F1]=HELP   [F2]=REVIEW   [ESC]=MENU
```

information that is given in your problem. These choices are presented in the Number of Payments submenu shown in Exhibit 4.17.

The first choice is that of calculating the number of payments when a present value, a future value, and an interest rate are known. Drawn as a time line, this type of problem appears as follows:

Determine "n," given PV, FV, and "i"

(Known) PV————————————————FV (Known)

The answer to this type of problem is determined by solving for "n" in the basic future value equation

$$FV = PV(1 + i)^n . \qquad \textbf{(4.2)}$$

Where compounding takes place more than one time per year, PROFIT+ divides "n" by the number of compounding periods per year to obtain the "number of years" answer to the problem.

Exhibit 4.18

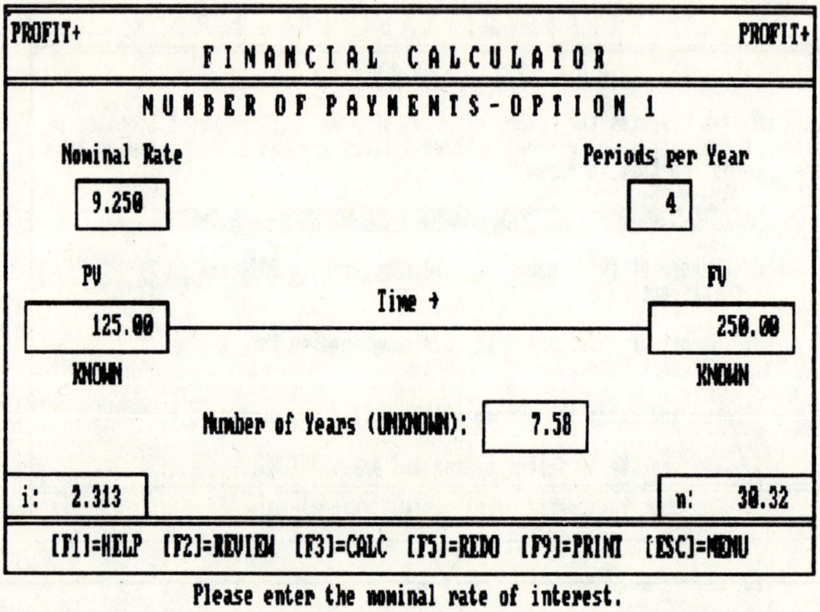

Exhibit 4.18 shows how option 1 from the Number of Payments submenu can be used to solve the following problem:

Sample Problem: John Bowdidge has $125 to place in a savings account that pays 9.25 percent interest compounded quarterly. At this rate of interest, how long will it take John to double his money?

The second choice on the Number of Payments submenu allows you to determine the number of payments, given PV, PMT, and "i." When entering the data for this type of problem, you must make certain that the size of each of the equal payments is more than large enough to cover the interest due at the time the first payment is made. Otherwise, the present value will never be paid off or used up. When depicted as a time line, the problem appears as follows:

Determine "n," given PV, PMT, and "i"

(Known) PV ——————/——————/——————/——...——/

PMT	PMT	PMT	PMT
Known	Known	Known	Known

Exhibit 4.19

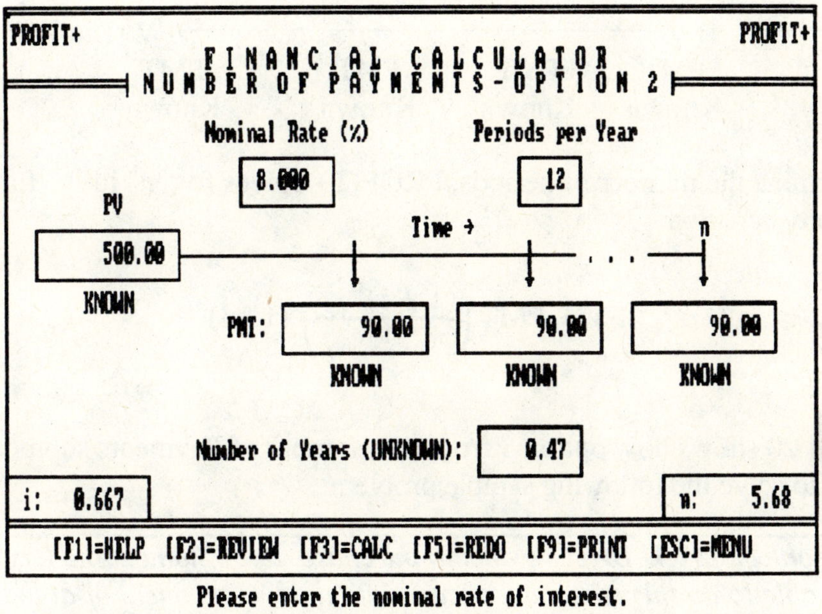

When using this routine, PROFIT+ assumes that payments are made at the end of the time intervals defined by the problem. To determine the number of payments, PROFIT+ solves for "n" in the present value of an annuity formula

$$PV = PMT\left(\frac{1}{i} - \frac{1}{i\,(1 + i)^n}\right) \tag{4.6}$$

Exhibit 4.19 shows how Number of Payments option 2 can be used to solve the following sample problem:

Sample Problem: Kathy Brady has just borrowed $500 from a friend. If her friend is charging Kathy 8 percent interest compounded monthly, and if Kathy can afford to pay her friend $90 per month, how long will it take Kathy to repay the loan?

Your third choice on the Number of Payments submenu computes the number of equal periodic payments, made at the end of each payment period, needed to accumulate a given future amount when the funds are earning a given rate of compound interest. Depicted as a time line, this problem appears as follows:

Determine "n," given FV, PMT, and "i"

```
————————/——————————/————————————/————...—————/FV (Known)
      PMT        PMT         PMT             PMT
     Known      Known       Known           Known
```

To determine the number of periods, PROFIT+ solves for "n" in the future value of an annuity equation

$$FV = PMT\left(\frac{(1 + i)^n - 1}{i}\right)(1 + i) \tag{4.5}$$

Exhibit 4.20 shows how option 3 from the Number of Payments submenu can be employed to solve the following sample problem:

Sample Problem: Vicki Briggs wants to purchase a new home. She has been told that to be able to do this, she must accumulate a down payment of at least $8000. Vicki believes that she can save approximately $250 at the end of every month. If she does this, and if the funds she saves are earning 10 percent interest compounded monthly, how long will it take Vicki to accumulate $8000?

Option N: Future Value of a Series of Unequal Payments

In some instances, for example when a savings program is being established, the future value of a series of unequal payments must be calculated. Since these payments are not of equal size, the annuity techniques covered in the previous sections of this chapter do not apply. To calculate the future value of an unequal payment series, you must compute the future value of each payment separately, and then find the sum of these future values. As a time line, this type of problem appears as follows:

```
————————/——————————/————————————/————...—————/FV (Unknown)
      PMT1       PMT2        PMT3            PMTn
     Known      Known       Known           Known
```

where PMTs 1 through n are not necessarily equal.

Exhibit 4.20

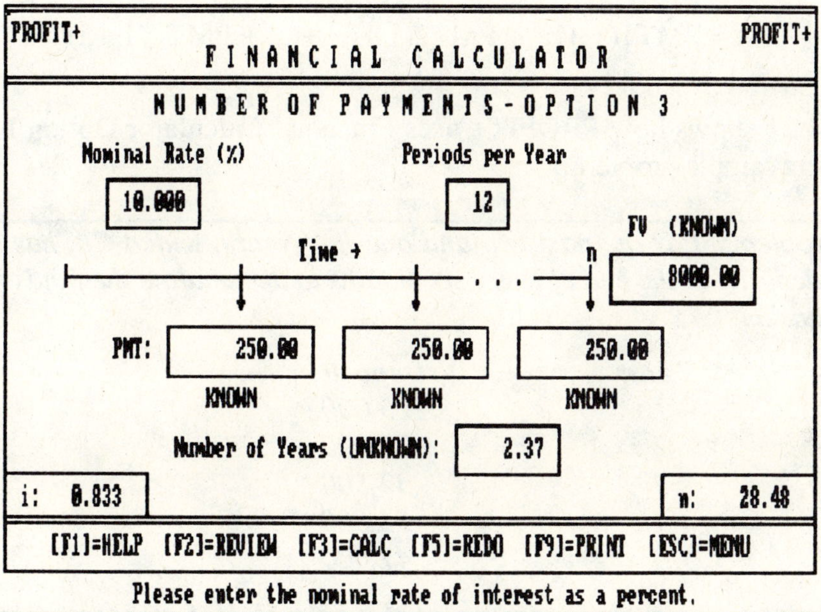

Exhibit 4.21

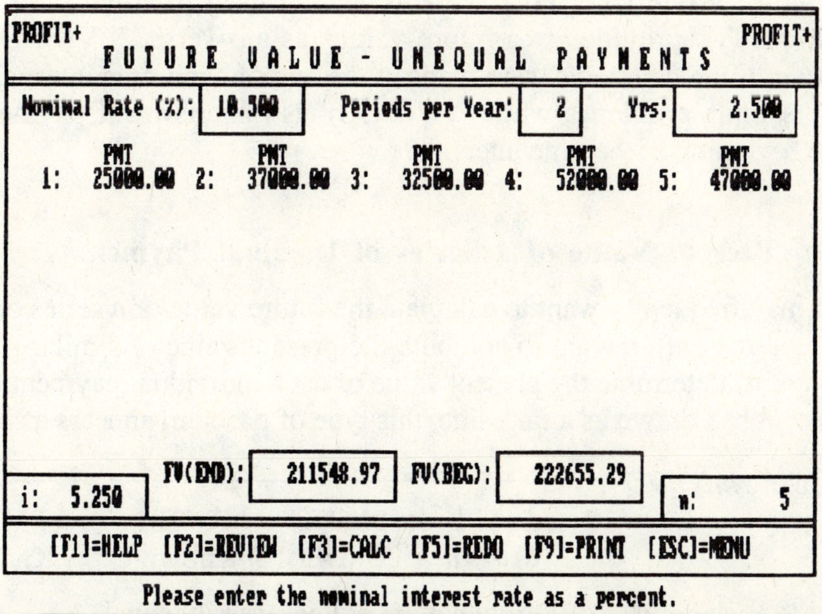

PROFIT+ uses the following formula to calculate the future value of a series of unequal payments:

$$FV = PMT1(1 + i)^1 + PMT2(1 + i)^2 + \ldots + PMTn(1 + i)^n \quad \textbf{(4.15)}$$

Exhibit 4.21 shows how PROFIT+ uses Financial Calculator Option N to solve the following sample problem:

Sample Problem: For the past two and one-half years, Kidco Co. has made the following deposits at the end of every six months to accumulate the funds necessary for an expansion:

Year	***Deposit***
1	*$25,000*
2	*37,000*
3	*32,500*
4	*52,000*
5	*47,000*

If the deposits have been earning at the rate of 10.5 percent compounded semiannually, how much is in the account today?

On the Future Value-Unequal Payments Screen used to solve the preceding problem, PROFIT+ provides two future values as answers. "FV(END)" is the correct answer if the payments were made at the end of each time interval (as they were in the sample problem), while "FV(BEG)" is the answer if payments were made at the beginning of the time intervals.

Option O: Present Value of a Series of Unequal Payments

Just as you may frequently want to calculate the future value of a series of unequal payments, you may often want to compute the present value of similar series. To do this, you must determine the present value of each individual payment, then add your results. When drawn as a time line, this type of problem appears as follows:

(Unknown) PV————	/————	/————	/——...——	/
	PMT1	PMT2	PMT3	PMTn
	Known	Known	Known	Known

where PMTs 1 through n are not necessarily equal.

PROFIT+ uses the following formula to determine the present value of a series of unequal payments:

Exhibit 4.22

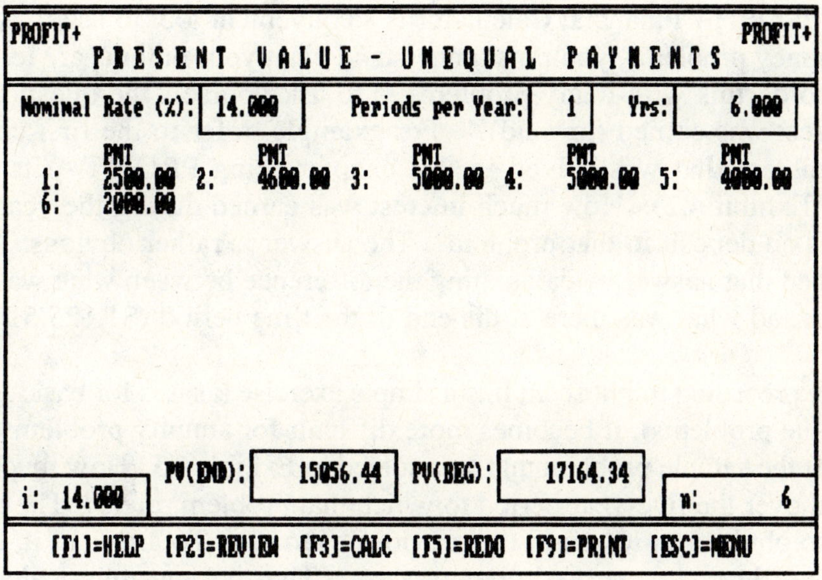
PROFIT+ PROFIT+
PRESENT VALUE - UNEQUAL PAYMENTS
Nominal Rate (%): 14.000 Periods per Year: 1 Yrs: 6.000
1: PMT 2500.00 2: PMT 4600.00 3: PMT 5000.00 4: PMT 5000.00 5: PMT 4000.00
6: 2000.00
i: 14.000 PV(END): 15056.44 PV(BEG): 17164.34 n: 6
[F1]=HELP [F2]=REVIEW [F3]=CALC [F5]=REDO [F9]=PRINT [ESC]=MENU
Please enter the nominal interest rate as a percent.

$$PV = \frac{PMT1}{(1 + i)^1} + \frac{PMT2}{(1 + i)^2} + \ldots + \frac{PMTn}{(1 + i)^n} \tag{4.14}$$

Exhibit 4.22 shows how you can use Financial Calculator Option O to solve the following sample problem:

Sample Problem: Faarco Incorporated is considering investing funds in a project that has the following estimated annual returns:

Year	*Return*
1	*$2,500*
2	*4,600*
3	*5,000*
4	*5,000*
5	*4,000*
6	*2,000*

What is the present value of the estimated returns from this project if the appropriate interest (discount) rate is 14 percent?

HOW MUCH INTEREST WAS EARNED (PAID)?

While the PROFIT+ Financial Calculator is a convenient tool to use to work time value of money problems, you must understand what your outputs are telling you. One way to do this with many problems is to ask yourself the question, "How much interest was earned (or paid)?" For example, refer to the first compound interest problem that was solved in this chapter using PROFIT+ (its solution appears in Exhibit 4.2). How much interest was earned during the year that the $1,000 was on deposit in that problem? The answer is rather obvious: $125.51. You obtained that answer by calculating the difference between what was put into the account and what was there at the end of the time period ($1,125.51 - 1000 = $125.51).

While the preceding might seem like a simple exercise (as it is for basic future and present value problems), it becomes more difficult for annuity problems. Take a look now at the sample problem that was solved in Exhibit 4.5. How much interest was earned over the five-year period to which that problem refers? The answer is not quite so obvious as it was in the previous example. To arrive at it, however, you must go through a very similar process. That is, you must calculate the difference between what was put into the account and what was there at the end of the time period. In the the problem in Exhibit 4.5, 60 payments of $125 each were put into the account; therefore, a total of $7,500 (60 x $125) was deposited. Since $9,563.29 will be in the account at the end of the five-year period, $2,063.29 of interest will be earned on the deposits ($9,563.29 - $7,500.00). Similar calculations can be made for most of the time value problems that are discussed in this chapter. Being able to answer the question of how much interest was earned (paid) will help you understand the compounding process that is taking place in your problems. Several of the problems at the end of this chapter give you an opportunity to work with these calculations.

(Note: Some readers might ask why PROFIT+ does not have the ability to determine the answer to the "How much interest?" question. While this would have been a relatively simple addition to the Financial Calculator routines, it is the author's philosophy as an educator that additional learning takes place if you, the user, are required to exercise some thought and judgment regarding the computer's output. This is just one example of how this philosophy manifests itself in PROFIT+.)

SUMMARY

Some people have said that the concept of time value of money is at the heart of financial management. Because of this, you must understand the types of problems discussed in this chapter and how you can solve them. The PROFIT+ Financial Calculator is a powerful tool to assist with these solutions. In addition, if you will take the time to study the review screens that are associated with the PROFIT+ Financial Calculator routines, and if you begin to think of time value problems in time lines, such as those the software employs, you will discover that PROFIT+ is an excellent tool for developing an understanding of time value concepts.

END-OF-CHAPTER PROBLEMS

1. What is the future value of $4,567 deposited for five years in an account that pays the following?

a. 9 percent compounded annually

b. 9 percent compounded semiannually

c. 9 percent compounded quarterly

d. 9 percent compounded monthly

e. 9 percent compounded daily (use a 365-day year)

f. 9 percent compounded continuously

2. What is the future value of $10,000 deposited for five years at the following rates of interest?

a. 5-1/4 percent compounded monthly

b. 7 percent compounded monthly

c. 10 percent compounded monthly

d. 12 percent compounded monthly

e. 18 percent compounded monthly

3. What is the present value of $15,000 to be received three and one-half years from now if each of the following discount rates is used?

a. 10 percent compounded annually

b. 10 percent compounded semiannually

c. 10 percent compounded quarterly

d. 10 percent compounded monthly

e. 10 percent compounded daily (use a 365-day year)

f. 10 percent compounded continuously

4. What is the present value of $22,000 to be received at the end of five years at each of the following discount rates?

a. 5-1/4 percent compounded monthly

b. 7 percent compounded monthly

c. 10 percent compounded monthly

d. 12 percent compounded monthly

e. 18 percent compounded monthly

5. Five years ago you deposited $124,000 in an account that promised to pay 7.5 percent interest compounded quarterly. How much is in that account today assuming you have made no withdrawals? How much interest did you earn over the five-year period?

6. Control Disks Amalgamated's sales this year were $8,000,822. The company expects sales to grow at an average annual rate of 22 percent over the next four years. If this growth rate is realized, what will be Control Disks' sales two years hence? Four years hence?

7. Five years ago you deposited $1,000 into an account that paid 7 percent interest compounded monthly. You have now removed your money from that account and have transferred it to an account that pays 12 percent interest compounded semiannually. Assuming you left all interest in the first account to accumulate and will do so in the second account too, how much will be in the second account two years from now?

8. Three years from now your company will need $150,450 to satisfy the terms of a contract. How much must you deposit into an account that pays 9 percent interest compounded monthly in order to accumulate the $150,450 by the end of three years? How much interest will you earn during the three years?

9. Your broker has offered to sell you a note that matures in five years and will be worth $10,000 at the end of that time. What is the most you would be willing to pay for the note, assuming you wish to earn 9 percent interest compounded annually on your investment?

10. U.S. Treasury Bills have a maturity value of $10,000 and are sold at a discount from that amount. The discount is the investor's return. How much would you be willing to pay for a nine-month U.S. T-Bill if the prevailing yield on such bills is 6.07 percent compounded annually? What is the size of the discount?

11. How long would it take to double your money at each of the following rates?

a. 5-1/4 percent compounded daily

b. 7.5 percent compounded monthly

c. 10 percent compounded quarterly

12. You have $1,000 to invest and have determined that the best rate you can get on your money is 8.05 percent compounded annually. At this rate, how long will it take for your investment to grow to $2,500?

13. You have been given the opportunity to purchase a five-year note for $1,000. The maturity value of the note at the end of five years is $1,456. What annual compound rate of interest will you be earning on your investment?

14. Ten years ago Golfco's earnings per share (eps) were $1.55. Now the company's eps are $8.10. At what average annual rate have Gulfco's earnings been growing?

15. An advertisement in a local newspaper begins with the following headline: "Give us $1,000 today and we will promise to repay $1,250 at the end of two years!" What annual compound rate of interest is implied by this advertisement?

16. What is the future value of the following annuities at 6 percent compounded annually?

a. A $350, 5-year ordinary annuity

b. A $350, 5-year annuity due

c. A $350, 10-year ordinary annuity

d. A $350, 10-year annuity due

17. At the end of every month for the past three years, your company has been placing $1500 into an account that pays 8 percent compounded monthly. How much is in this account today? How much interest has been earned over this three-year period?

18. Mines-America needs to accumulate $800,000 by the end of five years to meet the provisions of one of its loan contracts. If the company can deposit the money into a trust account that promises to pay 8.5 percent compounded semiannually, what must be the size of each of a series of equal semiannual payments designed to accumulate the $800,000? The payments are to be made at the end of each six months.

19. What is the present value of the following annuities at 7.75 percent compounded annually?

a. A $350, five-year ordinary annuity

b. A $350, five-year annuity due

c. A $350, ten-year ordinary annuity

d. A $350, ten-year annuity due

20. Double Circle, Inc., just signed a five-year loan agreement to purchase a piece of property. If the property's cost was $156,800, and Double Circle made a 20 percent down payment, what would be the size of each of a series of equal quarterly payments to amortize the loan at an interest rate of 10.45 percent? How much interest will the company be paying over the five-year period?

21. Set up a loan amortization table for Double Circle's loan in problem 20. How much of the firm's first loan payment will go toward reducing the principal balance of the loan? How much of the last payment will go toward principal reduction?

22. You are considering the purchase of a note that promises to return you $100 per month for the next four years. If the note's purchase price is $2,750, what rate of return will you be earning? (Note: Your answer should take the form of ... percent compounded monthly.)

23. A friend tells you that her bank will loan her $5,000 to be paid back over two and one-half years in a series of equal monthly payments of $193.74. What rate of interest is the bank charging your friend?

24. The chief engineer of the Williams-Bixler Company was recently killed in an automobile accident. The company had taken out key executive insurance on the engineer and now has to decide from among the following three alternatives for receiving the proceeds of the policy:

a. A single lump-sum payment of $500,000

b. A series of five $130,000 payments, the first to be received today and the remaining four at the beginning of each of the next four years

c. A series of ten $78,000 payments, the first to be received today and the remaining nine at the beginning of each of the next nine years

If the company's opportunity cost is 12 percent, which of these three options should it choose?

25. At the end of each six months for the past four years you have been depositing $1,000 into an account that pays 8.25 percent interest compounded semiannually. Beginning six months from today, you wish to make a series of equal semiannual withdrawals from this same account so that when the last withdrawal is made, no funds will remain in the account. What will be the size of each of these withdrawals?

26. What is the future value of the following stream of payments at 10.5 percent compounded annually? (Payments are made at the end of each year.)

Year	Payment
1	$12,000
2	$12,500
3	$14,750
4	$16,000
5	$18,500
6	$10,600

27. What is the present value of the following stream of payments at 10.5 percent compounded annually? (Payments are made at the end of each year.)

Year	Payment
1	$12,000
2	$12,500
3	$14,750

Year	Payment
4	$16,000
5	$18,500
6	$10,600

28. Reference Incorporated is considering purchasing a machine that costs $8,200. It is anticipated that the machine will last five years and will increase cash flows by the following amounts in each of these years: Yr. 1— $1,000; Yr. 2—$2,200; Yr. 3—$4,500; Yr. 4—$5,000; and Yr. 5—$3,250. If the company desires this project to return 12.5 percent, should it be undertaken?

29. Bill Cress, proprietor of a small camping supply firm, needs to purchase a new delivery truck. The truck Bill has located costs $13,790, and he plans to put $1,790 down and borrow the remaining $12,000. His bank will loan him the money at a rate of 11.5 percent compounded monthly, and Bill believes that he can afford payments of $400 each month. If the bank agrees on the $400 payments, how long will it take Bill to pay off his loan?

30. Tom Bergmann, a recent graduate of a nationally recognized MBA program, has a dream. He wants to sail around the world in a 24-foot vessel of his own design. Tom does not have the money to fulfill his dream at this time, but he would like to make an attempt at it in ten years. If he currently has $9,500 to invest and estimates that he can earn 9 percent compounded annually on his investments, how much must Tom put aside at the end of each of the next ten years in order to accumulate the $75,000 he anticipates will be needed to fulfill his dream?

Chapter Five
Basic Bond Valuation

The goal of financial management is to maximize the value of the firm. Although there are various ways in which this value might be estimated and subsequently monitored, the best measure of value for a publicly held corporation is the market price of its common stock. Thus, if a financial manager is going to achieve his or her goal, he or she must make decisions that have a positive effect on the price of the firm's stock.

An understanding of common stock valuation requires that financial managers be aware of factors that determine the value of any investment. This chapter begins a series of five chapters that deal with topics related to the valuation of assets. It presents a brief overview of the factors affecting investment value, and then discusses the basics of bond pricing and the related PROFIT+ Bond Valuation routine. Chapter Six shows how PROFIT+ can be used to calculate the yield to maturity for a bond, a fundamental determinant of its value. The topic of Chapter Seven is common stock valuation. In it, the basic dividend valuation models used by PROFIT+ will be reviewed, and then you will learn how to use the software's Common Stock Valuation routine. Chapter Eight discusses the basics of investment risk and how they relate to the returns that investors require. The PROFIT+ routines associated with Chapter Eight provide you with a tool for calculating the expected value and risk measures related to a probability distribution of projected returns and for determining the arithmetic and geometric means of a historic series of returns along with the series' variance, standard deviation, and coefficient of variation. The final chapter in this five-chapter valuation sequence, Chapter Nine, provides a description of the theoretical framework for relating investment risk and return to valuation. Then it introduces you to the PROFIT+ Capital Asset Pricing Model routine. This routine is a three-stage program that allows you to calculate the appropriate risk measure for a stock (i.e., the stock's "beta"), use that beta in what is known as the "Security Market Line" equation to estimate the stock's required return, and finally insert the calculated return into the dividend valuation model to arrive at the appropriate price (value) for the stock.

DETERMINANTS OF VALUE

With very few exceptions, the value of any investment depends on three factors:

1. the earnings stream projected for the investment
2. the timing of the earnings stream
3. the risk associated with the earnings stream (which is reflected in the investment's required return)

For an example of the impact of the first of these three factors, assume you are considering the purchase of two virtually identical apartment buildings. The only difference between the two structures is that one is located in a relatively low-rent area, and the other is in an area where rents are higher. Other things being equal, for which would you be willing to pay more? If you answered the one in the high-rent area, you are right, and the reason you gave that answer was because that building has a higher expected earnings stream. (Most property in the high-rent area would cost more, because of the greater earnings streams that could be associated with that property.)

The second factor, timing of the projected earnings stream, also has a significant impact on the value of investments. For an example of this impact, assume once again you are deciding which of two identical apartment buildings to purchase. These two buildings are located side by side in a respectable area of town. The only difference between the two buildings is that one is complete and fully rented, whereas the other will not be ready for occupancy for at least a month and only one-quarter of its units have been leased. You are, however, relatively certain that all the apartments in the second unit will be rented within the next two years. Other things being equal, for which building would you be willing to pay more? In this case, the answer would be the first building because it is fully rented and has an earnings stream that you would immediately realize. To attain the same earnings stream from the second building, you would have to wait at least two years.

For an example of the third factor, risk, assume that you are considering the purchase of one of yet another pair of identical apartment buildings. The two buildings are located in working-class neighborhoods of two midwestern cities. Living costs in both cities have been similar over the past several years and both apartment buildings are fully rented at the present time. The city in which the first building is located has a diversified employment base that has never been very sensitive to slumps in the individual industries of which it is composed. The second building is located in a city that depends on one industry, and rumor has it that foreign competition is going to cause employment in this industry to decline by 75 percent over the next few years. Other things being equal, which of these two buildings should be of greater value? Your answer here should be the first building, because there is less risk associated with the earnings stream that you expect from that investment. With the second building, significant unemployment may be experienced in the city in which it is located, and this could lead to difficulty in collecting rent and/or a decline in tenants. (Another way of looking at your reaction to the higher risk of the second building is to say that you are demanding a greater return from that building. One way of helping to realize a higher return on this risky investment is to pay less for the building. Thus, risk and required return are directly related.)

From these examples, then, you should see that when other things are equal, the value of an investment will be greater if:

1. the expected earnings stream is greater
2. the earnings will be received sooner, and/or
3. the risk associated with the earnings stream is relatively low (the required return is relatively low)

The previous discussion should help you understand why any investment has value. You will find it a useful foundation as you study bond valuation in this chapter, common stock valuation in Chapter Seven, and the capital budgeting process that is discussed later in this guide.

BOND VALUATION

The value of a bond depends on the same three factors as the value of any investment. With a bond, the expected earnings flow takes two forms: the annual or semiannual interest payments (determined by the bond's coupon interest rate), and the repayment of principal when the bond matures. The timing factor enters into bond valuation in the number of interest payments that are left until maturity. This affects not only the number of cash flows that the investor will receive, but also when the principal will be repaid. In general, the closer a bond is to maturity, the nearer its price, or value, will be to its face, or principal, value. Finally, the risk factor is one of the main determinants of the rate of return investors demand from a given bond. The higher the risk factor, the greater the required rate of return and the lower a bond's price. Keeping these three points in mind, we will now take a look at the mathematics of bond valuation.

One very useful way in which to view bond valuation is with a time line. A bond promises to pay its holder a series of equal annual or semiannual interest payments (often called coupon payments) over a period of time, and then at maturity to return the face value. These promised cash flows appear as follows when expressed on time lines:

Interest (Coupon) Payments

———/———/———/———/———/

C C C C C_n

Principal Repayment

————————————————M

When viewed in this manner, you can easily see that the cash flows from bonds are composed of an annuity, or the interest payments (C), and the receipt of a single sum at maturity (M). Since pricing a bond involves determining the value of a bond today, you must find the sum of the present values of these two types of flows to determine a bond's price. Thus, the process of determining the value of a bond can be expressed as follows:

$$\text{Value} = V_b = \text{PV of Interest Payments} + \text{PV of Maturity Value}$$

When calculating present values, you must use an interest, or discount, rate. When valuing bonds, the appropriate discount rate is the required rate of return (also called the market, or going, rate of interest or the yield to maturity) on bonds similar to the one with which you are dealing. This rate reflects the riskiness of the bond.

The model, or formula, for calculating the value of a bond that pays annual interest is

$$V_b = \sum_{t=1}^{n} C \left(\frac{1}{1 + k_b}\right)^t + M\left(\frac{1}{1 + k_b}\right)^n \tag{5.1}$$

where V_b = value (or price) of the bond

C = annual interest payment
= coupon interest rate x maturity value

M = maturity value (usually $1,000)

k_b = required rate of return on the bond

n = number of years remaining until maturity.

When interest payments occur on a semiannual basis, Equation 5.1 must be modified by dividing the annual interest payment and the required rate of return by two, then multiplying the number of years by two so as to reflect the increased number of interest payment periods. The results of this procedure produce Equation 5.2.

$$V_b = \sum_{t=1}^{n} \frac{C}{2} \left(\frac{1}{1 + k_b/2}\right)^t + M\left(\frac{1}{1 + k_b/2}\right)^{2n} \tag{5.2}$$

(Note: In the real world of bond trading, most transactions take place on dates other than those on which interest is paid. That is, most transactions occur in between interest payment dates. Because of this, the price of the bond needs to be adjusted to account for interest that has been earned between these interest payments. Since the methodology of doing this generally is not discussed in beginning financial management textbooks, PROFIT+ does not include a routine for making the necessary calculations.)

The PROFIT+ Bond Valuation Routine

Your PROFIT+ software includes a routine for determining bond value. To use that routine, simply select the Option C, Bond Valuation, from the PROFIT+ Main Menu. As part of the information you must provide PROFIT+ with, you will be asked if the bond being valued pays annual or semiannual interest. Depending on your response to this query, PROFIT+ uses either Equation 5.1 or 5.2 to determine the value of the bond. Exhibit 5.1 shows how this routine can be used to answer the following sample problem:

Sample Problem: A $1,000 Kateco Company bond bears a coupon interest rate of 13.75 percent, pays interest semiannually, and has seven years remaining until maturity. What should be the market price of this bond if bonds of similar risk and maturity are currently yielding 15 percent?

Exhibit 5.1

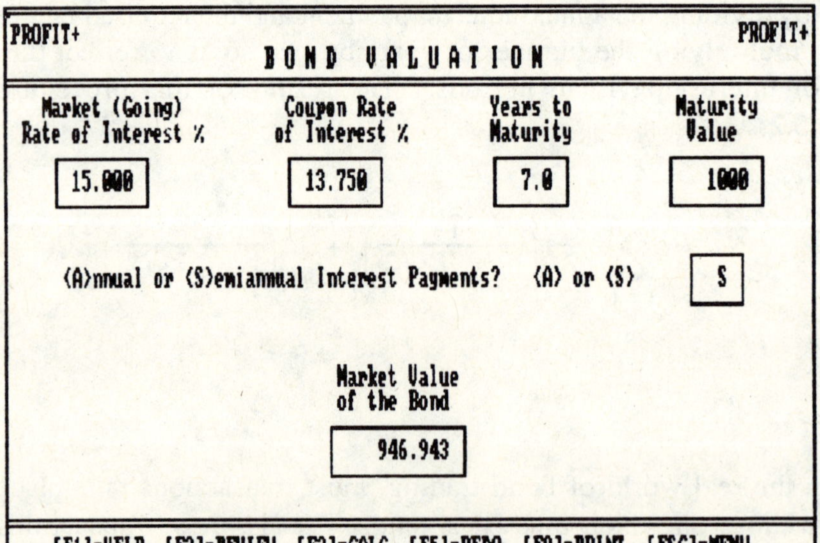

END-OF-CHAPTER PROBLEMS

1. What are the three basic determinants of value for any investment?

2. You are considering the purchase of an Amerweb Corporation bond. The bond has eight years remaining until maturity, carries a 9.5 percent coupon rate of interest paid annually, and has a face value of $1,000.

a. If investors require a 12 percent rate of return on bonds of similar quality and maturity, what is the most that you would be willing to pay for this bond?

b. How would your answer to part a change if investors required a 6 percent rate of return?

3. A $1000 Bowdidge Russian Fur Corporation bond will mature in five years and carries a 15 percent coupon rate of interest paid semiannually. Bonds of this type are currently selling to yield 14 percent.

a. What should be the current market price of this bond?

b. What would be the bond's price if it had eight rather than five years remaining until maturity?

4. Suppose that the Barrton-Cheek Corporation sold an issue of bonds with a 15-year maturity, a $1,000 face value, a 10 percent coupon rate, and semiannual interest payments.

a. Five years after the bonds were issued, the market rate of interest on bonds such as these rose to 12.5 percent. At what price would the bonds sell?

b. Now assume that five years after the date of issue the market rate of interest had declined to 9.15 percent. At what price would the bonds sell?

5. Ten years ago, the Stanson Corporation sold an issue of bonds with a 15-year maturity, a $5,000 face value, a 12 percent coupon rate, and semiannual interest payments.

a. If the going rate of interest on bonds such as these is presently 10 percent, at what price will the bonds sell? (Assume five years remain until maturity.)

b. Suppose that the condition described in part a existed--that is, the going rate of interest is 10 percent and five years remain until maturity. Suppose further that the interest rate remained at 10 percent over the next five years. What would happen to the price of the Stanson bonds over time? (Note: Use the "what if?" capability of PROFIT+ to confirm your answer.)

6. Antistat Company bonds, which pay interest annually, have seven years remaining until maturity. The bonds have a $1,000 face value and bear a coupon rate of interest of 9.25 percent. If the going rate of interest for similar bonds is 11 percent, would you be willing to pay $937.50 for one of these bonds? Explain your answer.

7. Assuming that the following bonds pay interest semiannually, calculate the value of each:

Bond	Face Value	Coupon Rate %	Years to Maturity	Required Return %
ABC	$1000	8.0	7.5	9.5
DEF	$1000	9.5	7.5	8.0
GHI	$5000	12.6	4.0	10.0
JKL	$5000	12.6	6.0	10.5
MNO	$ 500	10.0	7.0	10.0
PQR	$ 500	10.0	10.0	10.0

8. Assuming that the following bonds pay interest semiannually, calculate the value of each:

Bond	Face Value	Coupon Rate %	Years to Maturity	Required Return %
CBA	$1000	8.0	10.0	10.0
FED	$1000	8.0	9.0	10.0
IHG	$1000	8.0	8.0	10.0
LKJ	$1000	8.0	6.0	10.0
ONM	$1000	8.0	4.0	10.0
RQP	$1000	8.0	2.0	10.0
UTS	$1000	8.0	.5	10.0

9. Assuming that the following bonds pay interest semiannually, calculate the value of each:

Bond	Face Value	Coupon Rate %	Years to Maturity	Required Return %
CB	$1000	14.0	10.0	10.0
FE	$1000	13.0	10.0	10.0
IH	$1000	12.0	10.0	10.0
LK	$1000	11.0	10.0	10.0
ON	$1000	10.0	10.0	10.0
RQ	$1000	9.0	10.0	10.0
UT	$1000	8.0	10.0	10.0

10. Assuming that the following bonds pay interest semiannually, calculate the value of each:

Bond	Face Value	Coupon Rate %	Years to Maturity	Required Return %
BA	$1000	14.0	10.0	16.0
EF	$1000	14.0	10.0	15.0
HI	$1000	14.0	10.0	14.0
KL	$1000	14.0	10.0	13.0
NO	$1000	14.0	10.0	12.0

Chapter Six
Yield to Maturity

From the discussion of bond valuation in Chapter Five, you learned that one of the main determinants of the price of a bond is the market, or going, rate of interest. Another common name for the market rate of interest on a bond is "yield to maturity." Thus, it is the yield to maturity that reflects the return that investors require of a bond.

Although being able to calculate the value of bonds is quite important, you frequently will already know the market price of a bond (you can obtain it from price quotations in *The Wall Street Journal* and other publications) and will be interested in the yield to maturity, or rate of return, that this bond will provide. To assist you in determining this rate, PROFIT+ includes a routine for calculating yield to maturity.

CALCULATING YIELD TO MATURITY

The mathematics associated with calculating yield to maturity are identical to those used in Chapter Four to determine yields and growth rates. That is, you know a present value (the market price of the bond), the size of the cash flows (the coupon payments and maturity value), and the number of years until maturity, and you want to determine the rate of return that makes the present value of the cash flows equal to the bond's price.

When a bond pays interest annually, Equation 6.1 can be solved for k_b to calculate the bond's yield to maturity.

$$V_b = \sum_{t=1}^{n} C\left(\frac{1}{1 + k_b}\right)^t + M\left(\frac{1}{1 + k_b}\right)^n$$

(6.1)

where V_b = value (or price) of the bond
C = annual interest payment
= coupon interest rate x maturity value
M = maturity value (usually $1,000)
k_b = required rate of return on the bond
n = number of years remaining until maturity.

When interest payments occur on a semiannual basis, Equation 6.1 must be modified by dividing the annual interest payment and the required rate of return by two, then multiplying the number of years by two so as to reflect the increased number of interest payment periods. The yield to maturity, however, is still determined by solving the equation for k_b.

$$V_b = \sum_{t=1}^{n} \frac{C}{2}\left(\frac{1}{1 + k_b/2}\right)^t + M\left(\frac{1}{1 + k_b/2}\right)^{2n}$$

(6.2)

Exhibit 6.1 shows how PROFIT+ Option D, Yield to Maturity, can by used to solve the following sample problem:

Sample Problem: What is the yield to maturity on a $1,000 RSP Corporation bond that has 12 years remaining until maturity and is currently selling for $675? The bond, which pays interest semiannually, carries a 10 percent coupon interest rate.

Exhibit 6.1

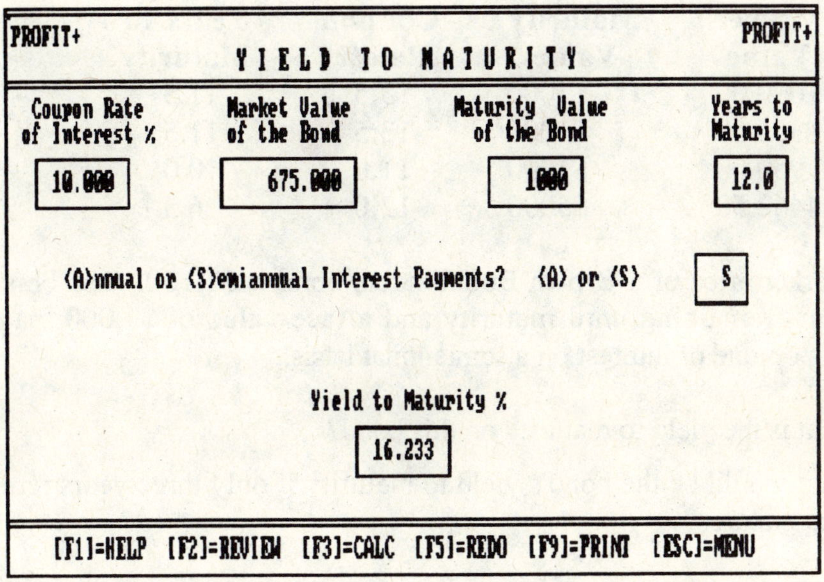

END-OF-CHAPTER PROBLEMS

1. Determine the yield to maturity for each of the following bonds. Assume that each bond pays annual interest.

	Market Value	Maturity Value	Coupon Rate %	Years to Maturity
a.	$1000.00	$1000	12.0	10
b.	$1365.50	$1000	12.0	10
c.	$ 950.00	$1000	12.0	10
d.	$4462.50	$5000	12.0	10

2. Determine the yield to maturity for each of the following bonds. Assume that each bond pays semiannual interest.

	Market Value	Maturity Value	Coupon Rate%	Years to Maturity
a.	$1000.00	$1000	13.5	11.5
b.	$1365.50	$1000	13.5	11.5
c.	$ 950.00	$1000	11.0	10.0
d.	$4462.50	$5000	12.0	6.5

3. The market price of a Brown Bookbinders bond is $1,160. The bond, which has 8.5 years remaining until maturity and a face value of $1,000, pays its 12 percent coupon rate of interest on a semiannual basis.

a. What is the yield to maturity on this bond?

b. What would be the bond's yield to maturity if only three years remain until the bond matures?

4. Using a recent edition of *The Wall Street Journal* and your PROFIT+ software, determine the yield to maturity for three bonds listed on the New York Stock Exchange. Unless your instructor tells you otherwise, assume semiannual interest payment on each bond that you choose.

5. Planer Corporation bonds have a maturity value of $1,000, a coupon rate of 9 percent, annual interest payments, six years until maturity, and presently have a market price of $637.50.

a. What is the yield to maturity on one of these bonds?

b. How would the yield to maturity of the bond change if the coupon rate were 10 percent?

c. How would the yield to maturity of the bond change if the coupon rate were 8 percent?

d. How would the yield to maturity of the bond change if there were 10 years remaining until maturity?

6. Five years ago, Volks, Inc., sold an issue of $1,000, 15-year, 11 percent bonds for $1,000 each. What would the yield to maturity for these bonds be today if their market price were each of the following (assume semiannual interest)?

a. $1537.50
b. $1287.50
c. $1000.00
d. $ 950.00
e. $ 575.00

7. Interco bonds have six and one-half years remaining until maturity, pay semiannual interest, have a maturity value of $5,000, and a current market price of $5,775. What would the yield to maturity of these bonds be if their coupon rate were each of the following?

a. 8.50 percent
b. 10.10 percent
c. 12.75 percent
d. 13.90 percent
e. 14.20 percent

8. Precision Corporation sold an issue of 11.5 percent bonds seven years ago for $1,000 each. The bonds pay interest semiannually. Now the bonds have eight years remaining until maturity and are selling for $1,000.

a. What is the yield to maturity for these bonds?

b. What would the bonds' yield to maturity be if they bore a 13 percent coupon rate, rather than an 11.5 percent rate?

9. A Dataman bond has a face value of $1,000, a coupon interest rate of 12.75 percent paid semiannually, and a current market price of $922.50. What would the yield to maturity be for this bond if it had each of the following numbers of years remaining until maturity?

a. 15 years
b. 10 years
c. 5 years
d. 3 years
e. 1 year
f. 0.5 year

Chapter Seven
Common Stock Valuation

You will remember from Chapter Five that the value of any investment depends on the following three factors:

1. the earnings stream projected for the investment
2. the timing of the earnings stream
3. the risk associated with the earnings stream

The value of a share of common stock also depends on these same three factors.

In this chapter, the process of valuing common stocks will be reviewed, and you will be introduced to PROFIT+'s Common Stock Valuation routine. As a preliminary introduction to common stock valuation, we will review the process involved with valuing preferred stocks.

PREFERRED STOCK VALUATION

An important intermediary step between understanding how bonds are valued and learning about common stock valuation is a discussion of the valuation of preferred stock. Preferred stocks promise to pay their owners regular, fixed dividend payments. Conceptually, these payments can be thought of as being similar to the coupon interest payments on bonds. However, valuation of preferred stocks differs from bonds in at least one important respect. Whereas bonds have a maturity date on which the issuer must return the principal of the bonds to the bondholders, most preferred stocks never mature. That is, most preferred stocks can be thought of as perpetuities, in which the dividend payments will continue for an infinite period of time.

The value of preferred stocks is based on the same three factors that determine the value of any investment: earnings stream, the timing of the earnings, and risk. A preferred stock's dividends form the earnings stream. Since this stream is infinite, it incorporates timing, and the required rate of return on a preferred stock reflects the risk associated with the investment. The value of a preferred stock is calculated by determining the present value of the infinite stream of equal dividends. Expressed as a time line, the process for calculating the value of a preferred stock appears as follows:

Value of a Preferred Stock

(Unknown)PV———/———/———/———/—...—>infinity
Div_1 Div_2 Div_3 Div_4 Div_{inf}

Although determining the present value of an infinite stream of equal dividends might sound imposing at first, the mathematics involved are rather simple. So simple, in fact, that you do not need anything so sophisticated as a PROFIT+ program to determine the value of a share of preferred stock. The present value of a perpetuity, in particular the stream of dividend payments from a preferred stock, can be found using the equation

$$V_{ps} = \frac{D_{ps}}{k_{ps}} \tag{7.1}$$

where V_{ps} = value or price of the preferred stock
D_{ps} = the preferred stock dividend
k_{ps} = the required rate of return for preferred stocks of similar risk.

COMMON STOCK VALUATION

The value of a share of common stock depends on the expected flow of earnings, the timing of those earnings, and risk, just as the value of any investment. The technique for valuing common stocks is essentially the same as that used to value bonds and preferred stock with two important exceptions. First, since the interest and maturity payments for bonds are fixed contractual obligations, and the dividends for most preferred stocks are fixed, earnings forecasts for these securities can be made with a relatively high degree of certainty. With common stocks, however, forecasting future earnings, dividends, and stock prices can be quite difficult. Second, the calculations associated with valuing a share of common stock can be more involved than those associated with bond and preferred stock valuation. This is because the earnings of most common stocks are expected to grow, thus limiting the use of standard annuity and perpetuity techniques for calculating the present values of the expected earnings.

Although models have been developed that use earnings per share as the basis for common stock valuation, the more common dividend valuation, or Gordon, model is used here. This model assumes that the earnings stream associated with a share of common stock is composed of the future dividends expected to be paid on that stock. (Models based on earnings per share should produce a similar estimate of value as those based on dividends, if they are properly used.)

Viewed as a time line, the problem of valuing a share of common stock appears as follows:

Valuing Common Stock

(Unknown)PV———/———/———/———/———>infinity

Div_1 Div_2 Div_3 Div_4 Div_{inf}

On this time line, Div_1 through Div_{inf} represent an infinite stream of common stock dividends, where each individual dividend is not necessarily equal to any other dividend. Given this time line view of the earnings flow associated with common stock, a series of present value calculations based on the projected value of each dividend must be made to determine the value of a share of stock. This process can be expressed as follows:

$$P_0 = \frac{D_1}{(1 + k_s)^1} + \frac{D_2}{(1 + k_s)^2} + \ldots + \frac{D_{inf}}{(1 + k_s)^{inf}} = \sum_{t=1}^{inf} \frac{D_t}{(1 + k_s)^t} \tag{7.2}$$

where P_0 = value of the stock (PV of future dividends)
D_t = value of each dividend out to infinity
k_s = required rate of return on common stocks of similar risk.

Normal or Constant Growth Model

Where no assumptions are made about the rate at which the dividend stream is growing, the process of first estimating future dividends and then finding the present value of each becomes quite lengthy. To make the basic determinants of common stock value conceptually easier to understand, some assumptions are made about the rate at which dividends will be growing. The most common of these is to assume that dividends will be growing at some constant rate into the foreseeable future. Especially when dealing with well-established firms, the assumption of constant growth (usually estimated to be equal to the "normal" growth rate of the economy) is common. When this is done, Equation 7.2 can be reduced to the constant growth dividend model (also called the Gordon model) for common stock valuation given in Equation 7.3.

$$P_0 = \frac{D_1}{(k_s - g)} \tag{7.3}$$

where D_1 = next expected dividend = $D_0(1 + g)$
g = constant rate of dividend growth.

The derivation of Equation 7.3 is beyond the scope of this guide, but can be found in most advanced financial management texts, for example, Appendix 3A of *Intermediate Financial Management,* 2d ed., by Eugene F. Brigham and Louis C. Gapenski. Expressed in words, Equation 7.3 finds the present value of a stream of dividends, growing at a constant rate, for an infinite period of time. The constant growth model can provide useful estimates of value as long as the assumed growth rate (g) is less than the required rate of return on the stock in question (k_s). (Note: A special case of constant growth exists when it is assumed that a company will experience no growth in dividends in the foreseeable future. Equation 7.3 can also be used to value such a "zero growth" stock simply by entering "0" as the expected growth rate. When this is done, the equation becomes similar to that used to value preferred stocks. That is, the resulting answer is the present value of a perpetual stream of equal dividends.)

Nonconstant or Supernormal Growth Model

Although one may presume that the dividends of well-established firms are growing at a constant rate, in many cases the firm being analyzed is not mature and established. Most industries, and the companies of which they are composed, go through life cycles. During the early stage of a typical life cycle, a firm may grow at a rate that is far in excess of that for a normal business in the economy. After this initial period of what is frequently called supernormal growth, a firm's growth rate typically will level off to a rate equal to that of the economy.

Valuation models have been developed that allow their users to assume that a company is experiencing supernormal growth that will be followed by an infinite period of constant growth. The simplest of these models allows for one supernormal growth period, although other models exist that give their users the ability to assume multiple supernormal growth periods, each at a different rate. The simplest model is sufficient for the level of this guide. You will be able to better understand the mathematics of this model if you realize that it is performing the following three tasks:

1. Determining the present value of the dividends during the period of supernormal growth.

2. Determining the price of the stock at the end of the supernormal growth period (using the constant growth model), and then discounting this price back to the present.

3. Adding the results from steps 1 and 2 to find the present value (price) of the stock.

The model for determining the value of a common stock expected to experience a period of supernormal growth is given in the equation

$$P_0 = \sum_{t=1}^{n} \frac{D_0(1 + g_s)^t}{(1 + k_s)^t} + \left(\frac{D_{n+1}}{(k_s - g)}\right)\left(\frac{1}{(1 + k_s)}\right) \tag{7.4}$$

where g_s = supernormal growth rate
g = normal growth rate
n = period of supernormal growth.

Exhibit 7.1

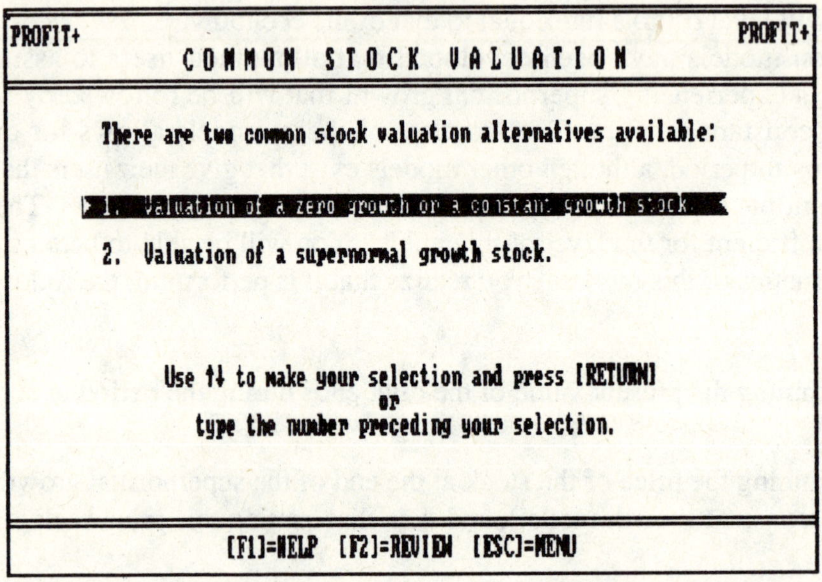

The PROFIT+ Common Stock Valuation Routine

Selecting the Common Stock Valuation (Option E) alternative from the PROFIT+ Main Menu will allow you to run PROFIT+'s routine for valuing common stocks. As you can see from Exhibit 7.1, the routine has two options. The first calculates the value of a zero or a constant growth stock using Equation 7.3. The second option uses Equation 7.4 to determine the value of a supernormal growth stock.

Exhibit 7.2 shows how the PROFIT+ Common Stock Valuation Routine can be used to solve the following constant growth problem:

Sample Problem: Double Ewe Corporation paid a $1.26 dividend this year. If investors require a 16 percent rate of return on stocks of similar risk and anticipate a constant growth rate of 10 percent for the company, what is the value of a share of Double Ewe's common stock?

Exhibit 7.3 shows how the PROFIT+ Common Stock Valuation routine can be used to find the solution to the following supernormal growth dividend valuation problem:

Exhibit 7.2

PROFIT+ PROFIT+

COMMON STOCK VALUATION

ZERO GROWTH OR CONSTANT GROWTH STOCK

Most Recent Dividend	Required Rate of Return %	Expected Growth Rate %
1.260	16.000	10.000

Estimated Value of the Stock

23.100

[F1]=HELP [F2]=REVIEW [F3]=CALC [F5]=REDO [F9]=PRINT [ESC]=MENU

Exhibit 7.3

PROFIT+ PROFIT+

COMMON STOCK VALUATION

SUPERNORMAL GROWTH STOCK

Most Recent Dividend	Required Rate of Return %	Expected Supernormal Growth Rate %	Number of Years of Supernormal Growth
1.820	16.000	30.000	3

Constant Growth Rate (%) Following Supernormal Growth Years: 10.000

Estimated Value of the Stock

53.852

[F1]=HELP [F2]=REVIEW [F3]=CALC [F5]=REDO [F9]=PRINT [ESC]=MENU

Sample Problem: You are examining the stock of a supernormal growth firm. Your analysis leads you to believe that the dividends of the firm will grow at a 30 percent rate for three years, after which the growth rate is expected to fall to 10 percent. If stockholders require a 16 percent rate of return on stocks of similar risk, and if the last dividend (D_0 paid by the firm was $1.82, what is the value of the stock? (Note: A detailed, by-hand solution of this problem is contained on pages 151 and 152 in Essentials of Managerial Finance, *8th ed., by J. Fred Weston and Eugene F. Brigham.)*

SUMMARY

The valuation of common stocks is much more difficult than that of bonds or preferred stocks. Although it may appear to be a rather routine matter to enter the necessary information into the PROFIT+ programs to determine common stock values, remember that this information is the result of forecasts. Not only can a company's growth rate be difficult to forecast, but also a great deal of uncertainty can be associated with determining the rate of return that should be required of a particular company.

However, you should not become discouraged by the discovery that common stocks cannot be valued with 100 percent certainty. This real-world fact is what makes the art and science of stock analysis both challenging and confusing, both exciting and frustrating. Futhermore, you should realize that the basic models of common stock valuation have given you a tool that can be used to help you evaluate the potential consequences of your actions. By examining, for example, the constant growth dividend model

$$P_0 = \frac{D_1}{(k_s - g)} \tag{7.3}$$

you can see that the market price of a share of your firm's common stock is primarily determined by three factors: the expected dividends (earnings stream), the return investors require of your company's stock, and the expected growth rate in dividends. Thinking through the potential impact that each financial decision might have on these three factors can help you see the potential effects a decision will have on your firm's stock. In turn, this process will help keep you focused on the goal of financial management: maximization of owners' wealth as reflected in the market price of the firm's common stock.

END-OF-CHAPTER PROBLEMS

1. What are the three basic determinants of the value of a share of common stock?

2. Other things being equal, what is the most likely effect that each of the following would have on the market price of a firm's common stock?

a. The expected dividend growth rate increases.

b. Investors demand a higher rate of return on all investments.

c. The firm finances a project with debt. Investors believe this decision makes the company's stock a more risky investment.

3. Using the constant growth dividend valuation model, determine the appropriate price for each of the following stocks:

	Last Dividend	Required Return %	Constant Growth Rate %
a.	$2.10	16	6
b.	$2.10	14	6
c.	$2.10	12	6
d.	$2.10	14	10
e.	$2.10	14	7
f.	$2.10	14	5
g.	$1.10	14	6
h.	$2.10	14	6
i.	$3.10	14	6

4. Madd Hattery, Incorporated's last dividend was $2.20 and dividends are expected to grow at a constant rate of 9 percent in the foreseeable future.

a. If investors require a 17 percent rate of return on similar investments, what should be the market price of the company's common stock?

b. How would your answer to part a change if investors require a 15 percent rate of return, rather than the 17 percent rate?

c. How would your answer to part a change if the constant rate of dividend growth is assumed to be 7 percent? (The required return is still 17 percent.)

d. How would your answer to part a change if the last dividend was $1.20, rather than $2.20? (Growth rate is 9 percent, and required return is 17 percent.)

5. Basic Aviation's latest common stock dividend was $4.10. According to a recent security analyst's report, stockholders should require a 17 percent return on the stock and should expect dividends to grow at a constant annual rate of 7 percent.

a. What should be the market price of Basic Aviation's common stock given the above information?

b. After reading a recent article on Basic in the financial section of your local newspaper, you decide that the stock is riskier than was implied in the security analyst's report. Because of this, you believe that investors should require a 20 percent return on the stock. How does this additional information affect the stock's value?

c. How would your answer to part b change if, instead of finding out the stock was more risky, you discovered that it was less risky and decided on a required return of 15 percent?

d. How would your answers to parts a, b, and c change if the projected constant growth rate were 5 percent, rather than 7 percent?

6. Keyboard Company common stock is presently selling for $17.50 per share. If its last dividend was $1.70, and if investors require a 17 percent rate of return on stocks of similar risk, is the $17.50 stock price justifiable? Why or why not? (Assume that dividends are projected to grow at a 5 percent annual rate in the foreseeable future.)

7. Computers For The Masses, Inc., (CFTM) is experiencing above-average, or supernormal, growth. Over the next six years, the company's dividends are expected to grow at an annual rate of 30 percent. After that time, however, it is projected that the dividend growth rate will decline and level off to a normal 7 percent rate. If the firm's last dividend was $1.44, and investors require a 20 percent return on similar investments, what should be the market price of a share of CFTM common stock?

8. How would your answer to question 7 be affected if the supernormal growth rate expected for CFTM were 25 percent, rather than 30 percent?

Chapter Eight
Basic Risk/Return Calculations

In the previous chapters, we saw that one of the main determinants of the value of any investment is the risk associated with the expected flow of returns from that investment. This risk was taken into consideration in the development of bond, preferred stock, and common stock valuation models by incorporating it in the required return for the security in question. In this chapter, we will take a closer look at what investment risk is, how it can be measured, and how these measurements can be incorporated into a model for determining the return required of a particular investment.

INVESTMENT RISK

Investment risk can be defined as the uncertainty inherent in estimating the expected returns from an investment. More specifically, it is the chance that an investment might produce low, or even negative, returns.

Expected Rate of Return

When discussing the risk associated with an investment, it is helpful to be able to express that risk in some quantifiable form. The first step in this process involves the realization that most estimates of investment returns involve forecasts, and any time forecasts are made, some degree of uncertainty exists. If, for example, we say that we expect a 20 percent return next year from an investment in the common stock of Larimer Computers Corporation, what we are really saying is that, given our assumptions about the future, our best estimate of the return on that investment is 20 percent. If some, or all, of our assumptions are inaccurate, our actual return might be different. In other words, we believe there is a good *chance* that we will earn 20 percent on our investment in Larimer, but there also is a *chance* that our actual return will vary.

One way to express that the returns on an investment might vary from predicted levels is to state those returns in terms of a probability distribution. A probability distribution of investment returns lists the possible outcomes from an investment and your estimates of the likelihood, or chance, that each of those events will occur. Returning to the Larimer Computers Corporation (LCC) example, we might construct the following probability distribution of returns we would expect next year on an investment in the company's common stock:

State of the Economy	Probability of the State Occurring (%)	Rate of Return for LCC for this State(%)
Boom	20	50
Normal	60	20
Recession	20	-10

This distribution shows that we think there is a 20 percent chance that the economy will experience a boom, and if it does, we would expect the return on an investment in LCC to be 50 percent next year.Furthermore, we estimate a 60 percent chance of a normal economy accompanied by a 20 percent return and a 20 percent chance of a recession, which would cause us to realize a negative 10 percent return on our investment in LCC.

By multiplying the probability of each outcome by the outcome itself and then adding the results, we can calculate a weighted average outcome. Another name for this weighted average is the "expected value" of the probability distribution, or, in this case, the "expected return" for our investment. From the following calculations, you can see that the expected return for our investment in LCC is 20 percent:

State of the Economy	Probability of this State	Rate of Return for this State (%)	Probability x Return (%)
Boom	20	50	10
Normal	60	20	12
Recession	20	-10	-2
	100	E(Rate of Return) =	20

The following formula can be used to calculate the expected rate of return for an investment:

$$\hat{k} = \sum_{i=1}^{n} P_i k_i \tag{8.1}$$

where $\hat{k}$ = expected rate of return
k_i = the ith possible outcome
P_i = the probability of the ith outcome
n = the number of possible outcomes.

Variance and Standard Deviation of a Probability Distribution

Once we have a probability distribution of the returns expected from an investment, we can begin to think about the risk associated with these returns. Although numerous arguments exist for dealing with what is the right way to measure this risk, one common, and useful, method is to measure the standard deviation of the probability distribution. Standard deviation measures how spread out the possible outcomes in a probability distribution are. Other things being equal (for example, the expected return), the greater a probability distribution's standard deviation, the more spread out the possible returns, and the riskier the investment. (For a more detailed explanation of this measure, see Chapter 6 of *Fundamentals of Financial Management,* 4th ed., by Eugene F. Brigham, or Chapter 6 of *Essentials of Managerial Finance*, 8th ed., by J. Fred Weston and Eugene F. Brigham.)

The standard deviation of a probability distribution can be calculated as follows:

1. Compute the expected value of the probability distribution.

2. Calculate the deviation of each possible outcome from the expected return by subtracting the expected return from each outcome.

3. Square each of the deviations obtained in step 2.

4. Multiply each of the squared deviations from step 3 by the probability of the event related to each deviation.

5. Add the results from step 4. This sum is called the "variance" of the probability distribution.

Exhibit 8.1

$k_i - \hat{k}$					$(k_i - \hat{k})^2$	$(k_i - \hat{k})^2 P_i$		
0.50	-	0.20	=	0.30	0.09	0.09(0.20)	=	0.018
0.20	-	0.20	=	0.00	0.00	0.00(0.60)	=	0.000
-0.10	-	0.20	=	-0.30	0.09	0.09(0.20)	=	0.018
						Variance	=	0.036
							=	3.6 %

Standard Deviation = $\sqrt{\text{Variance}} = \sqrt{0.036} = 0.1897 = 18.97\ \%$

6. Calculate the square root of the variance. The result is the standard deviation of the probability distribution with which you are dealing.

(Note: All percents should be converted to decimals prior to making the calculations given above. If you change the probabilities to decimals, but do not change the outcome for that probability, you will still obtain a correct value for the standard deviation, but the variance will be in error.)

Equation 8.2 shows the formula for determining the variance of a probability distribution, while Equation 8.3 is used for calculating a probability distribution's standard deviation.

$$\text{Variance} = \sigma^2 = \sum_{i=1}^{n}(k_i - \hat{k})^2 P_i \tag{8.2}$$

$$\text{Standard Deviation} = \sigma = \sqrt{\sum_{i=1}^{n}(k_i - \hat{k})^2\ P_i)} \tag{8.3}$$

Exhibit 8.1 shows the calculations for determining the variance and standard deviation of the probability distribution of returns for Larimer Computers Corporation.

Assuming a normal distribution of returns, we would expect 68.26 percent of returns to be within plus or minus 1 standard deviation of the mean, 95.46 percent of returns to be within plus or minus 2 standard deviations of the mean, and 99.74 percent of returns to be within plus or minus 3 standard deviations of the mean return. In the Larimer Computers example where the mean return was 20 percent, a standard deviation of 18.97 percent implies that there is a 68.26 percent probability that the stock will return 1.03 percent to 38.97 percent (20 percent plus or minus 18.97 percent), a 95.46 percent chance the stock will return -17.94 percent to 57.94 percent (20 percent plus or minus 2 x 18.97 percent), and a 99.74 percent chance the stock will return -36.91 percent to 76.91 percent (20 percent plus or minus 3 x 18.97 percent).

Coefficient of Variation

Other things being equal, when you compare two probability distributions of returns, the one with the higher standard deviation is the one with the greater risk. Frequently, however, "other things" may not be equal. Specifically, the expected return for each of the two distributions may not be the same. What is needed when this is the case is a standardized measure of risk that eliminates the effects of different expected values. The coefficient of variation (CV), which is the standard deviation divided by the expected value, is such a measure. It shows the risk per unit of return, and yields a more meaningful comparison when the expected returns of two investments are not identical.

The following equation is used to calculate the coefficient of variation:

$$\text{Coefficient of Variation} = CV = \frac{\sigma}{\hat{k}} \tag{8.4}$$

The PROFIT+ Risk/Return Software

Your PROFIT+ software includes a routine for determining the expected value, variance, standard deviation, and coefficient of variation of a probability distribution of investment returns using Equations 8.1, 8.2, 8.3, and 8.4, respectively. This routine is included under Option F, Basic Risk/Return Calculations, on the Main Menu. When you select Option F, you are presented with the submenu shown in Exhibit 8.2. Option 1 on this submenu brings up the routine for making the calculations that we have been discussing.

Exhibit 8.3 presents a printout of the PROFIT+ screen used to solve the following sample problem:

Exhibit 8.2

PROFIT+ PROFIT+

B A S I C R I S K / R E T U R N C A L C U L A T I O N S

This routine offers two options:

▶ 1. Expected value and descriptive statistics for a probability distribution.

2. Arithmetic mean, geometric mean, and descriptive statistics for a historical series.

Use ↑↓ to make your selection and press [RETURN]
or
type the number of your selection.

[F1]=HELP [F2]=REVIEW [ESC]=MENU

Exhibit 8.3

PROFIT+ PROFIT+

P R O B A B I L I T Y D I S T R I B U T I O N S T A T I S T I C S

Number of probable occurances in the distribution (maximum of 8): 5

	Return %	Probability %		Return %	Probability %
1:	100.00	10.000	2:	50.00	20.000
3:	15.00	40.000	4:	5.00	20.000
5:	-20.00	10.000			

Expected Value %	Variance %	Standard Deviation %	Coefficient of Variation
25.000	10.1000	31.780	1.271

[F1]=HELP [F2]=REVIEW [F3]=CALC [F5]=REDO [F9]=PRINT [ESC]=MENU

Sample Problem: You are considering an investment in the common stock of Novice Corporation. After considerable research, you have constructed the following probability distribution of returns you might earn next year based on your expectations of the level of economic activity:

State of Economy	***Probability (%)***	***Rate of Return (%)***
Boom	*10*	*100*
Above Average Growth	*20*	*50*
Average Growth	*40*	*15*
Below Average Growth	*20*	*5*
Recession	*10*	*-20*

What are the expected value, the variance, the standard deviation, and the coefficient of variation of the returns you expect next year for an investment in Novice?

EXAMINING HISTORIC RETURNS

Examining the pattern and variability of the historic rates of return on investments is often helpful. Not only does such an examination provide insight into what returns would have been had you made a particular investment, but it also gives you a way to compare the relative volatility (i.e., riskiness) of the returns on various investments.

Your PROFIT+ software contains a routine for examining and describing the level and variability of historic returns. This routine includes the following information as its output: arithmetic mean return, geometric mean return, variance, and standard deviation of returns.

Arithmetic and Geometric Mean Returns

Means, or averages, are sometimes called *measures of central tendency*. They attempt to provide one number that can be used to describe the general nature of a group of observations, such as the mean grade on an examination or the mean annual return on an investment in a particular stock. You were probably taught how to calculate the arithmetic mean several years ago. It is obtained by adding all observations and dividing by the number of observations. If, for example, the returns on XYZ common stock over the past three years had been 10, 20, and 30 percent respectively, the arithmetic mean return for these three years would have been 20 percent (10 + 20 + 30 / 3). Equation 8.5 expresses the formula used for computing the arithmetic mean.

$$\text{Arithmetic Mean} = \bar{X}. = \frac{\sum_{i=1}^{n} k_i}{n} \tag{8.5}$$

The geometric mean, on the other hand, is a measure of central tendency with which you may not be so familiar. It is, however, a measure that can be of much use, especially when describing the historical returns for an investment. The arithmetic mean can yield some misleading results when it comes to providing a descriptive measure of investment returns. You can best understand this point by studying the following example. Suppose you bought the common stock of Airline Corporation for $10 a share. At the end of the first year, the market price of the stock was $20; however, two years following your purchase, the stock's market price had declined to $10 once more. If no dividends were paid during this period, what was the arithmetic mean return on your investment? To answer this question, you need only to add the two annual returns and divide by two. The return for year one was 100 percent [(20 - 10) / 10], and the return for year two was -50 percent [(10 - 20) / 20]. Therefore, your arithmetic mean return was 25 percent [100 + (-50) / 2]. However, have you really earned 25 percent per year on your investment? You purchased your stock for $10 per share and now, two years later, it is still worth $10. You have actually experienced a zero return on your investment, not the 25 percent return that the arithmetic mean reported. Therein lies a fault of the arithmetic mean: where negative returns are experienced, the arithmetic mean yields a measure of central tendency that is higher than the actual return. The geometric mean overcomes the upward bias of the arithmetic mean. To calculate the geometric mean return, follow these steps:

1. Change each annual percentage return to a decimal and add it to 1.0.
2. Multiply together the numbers resulting from step 1.
3. Take the nth root of the product obtained in step 2, where "n" is the number of observations.
4. Subtract 1.0 from the result obtained in step 3. This is the geometric mean return for your series of observations.

In our example for an investment in Airline Corporation, the geometric mean would be calculated as follows:

1. Yr. 1 return: 100 percent = 1.00 + 1.00 = 2.00
   Yr. 2 return: -50 percent = -0.50 + 1.00 = 0.50
2. 2.00 x 0.50 = 1.00
3. $1.00^{.5} = 1.00$
4. 1.00 - 1.00 = 0.00 percent return

Thus, the 0.00 percent geometric mean return provides a more representative measure of your actual results. You invested $10, two years later you still have $10, so you have experienced a 0.00 percent return on your investment. Equation 8.6 gives the formula for calculating the geometric mean return for a series of investment returns.

$$\text{Geometric Mean} = \prod_{i=1}^{n}(1 + k_i)^{1/n} - 1.00 \tag{8.6}$$

Variance and Standard Deviation of Historical Returns

The variance and standard deviation of a series are commonly used to describe the variability, or riskiness, of an historic series of returns. As with probability distributions, when other things are equal, a series with a larger variance and standard deviation has greater volatility, and therefore a higher level of risk. Equations 8.7 and 8.8 respectively give the formulas for calculating the variance and standard deviation of a series of returns.

$$\text{Variance} = \sigma^2 = \frac{\sum_{i=1}^{n}(k_i - \bar{X}.)^2}{(n - 1)} \tag{8.7}$$

$$\text{Standard Deviation} = \sigma = \sqrt{\frac{\sum_{i=1}^{n}(k_i - \underline{X}.)^2}{(n - 1)}} \tag{8.8}$$

Exhibit 8.4

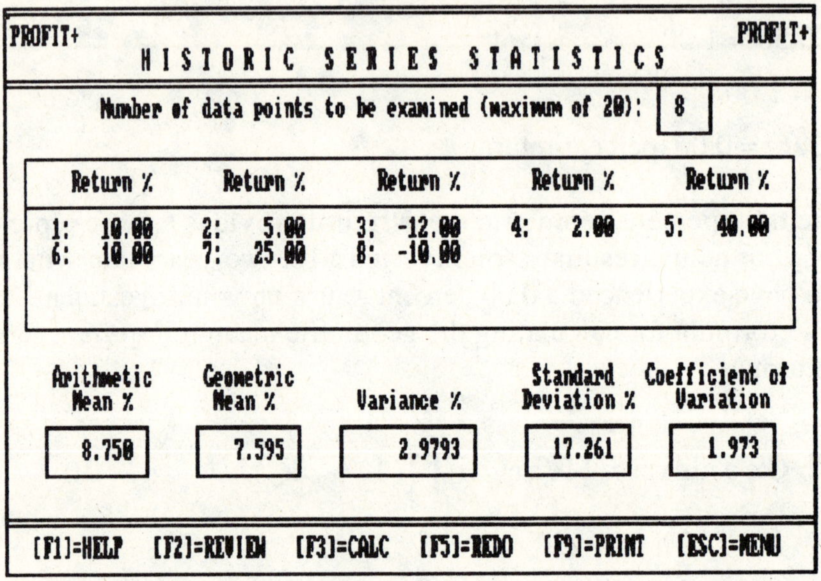

Coefficient of Variation

Just as it is frequently important to determine the coefficient of variation of a probability distribution of expected returns so that the relative riskiness of potential investments can be evaluated, so too is it important to calculate the coefficient of variation of historical series of returns so that their relative volatility can be examined. For historical series, the coefficient of variation is obtained by dividing the standard deviation by the arithmetic mean return. This procedure is shown in Equation 8.9.

$$\text{Coefficient of Variation} = CV = \frac{\sigma}{X} . \qquad \textbf{(8.9)}$$

Option 2 on the PROFIT+ Basic Risk/Return Calculations submenu is a routine for calculating the arithmetic mean, geometric mean, variance, standard deviation, and coefficient of variation of a series of historic returns. PROFIT+ uses Equations 8.5, 8.6, 8.7, 8.8, and 8.9, respectively, to make these calculations.

Exhibit 8.4 shows how this PROFIT+ routine can be used to provide answers to the following sample problem:

Sample Problem: What is the arithmetic mean, geometric mean, variance, and standard deviation of the following series of return data for Standard Corporation common stock?

1980	*10 %*
1981	*5 %*
1982	*-12 %*
1983	*2 %*
1984	*40 %*
1985	*10 %*
1986	*25 %*
1987	*-10 %*

END-OF-CHAPTER PROBLEMS

1. You are considering an investment in the common stocks of one of two companies: Upscale Incorporated or Tradition Corporation. After a considerable amount of research, you have decided on the following probability distribution of possible states of the economy for the next year, along with the returns you expect from an investment in each company should a particular state of the economy exist.

State of the Economy	Probability of Each State(%)	Return for Upscale(%)	Return for Tradition (%)
Boom	10	100	20
Normal	80	15	15
Recession	10	-70	10

What is the expected return, standard deviation of returns, and coefficient of variation for each company's stock? Which investment appears to be riskier? Why?

2. Calculate the expected return, variance, standard deviation, and coefficient of variation of the following probability distribution of returns for Paper Products, Incorporated.

State of the Economy	Probability of State (%)	Return for Paper Products for Each State (%)
Recession	10	-50
Below Average	15	5
Average	50	20
Above Average	20	50
Boom	5	80

3. Calculate the expected return, variance, standard deviation, and coefficient of variation of the following probability distribution of returns for Gemini Novelties Corporation.

State of the Economy	Probability of State (%)	Return for Gemini Novelties for Each State (%)
Recession	5	5
Below Average	15	10
Average	60	30
Above Average	15	50
Boom	5	100

4. You are considering purchasing the common stocks of one of two companies: United Incorporated or Outbacker Corporation. After a considerable amount of research, you have decided on the following probability distribution of possible states of the economy for the next year, along with the returns you expect from an investment in each company should a particular state of the economy exist.

State of the Economy	Probability of Each State	Return for United	Return for Outbacker
Boom	10	100	20
Normal	80	15	15
Recession	10	-70	10

a. What is the expected return, standard deviation, and coefficient of variation of returns for each company?

b. A friend has told you that she feels that Outbacker is the riskier of the two investments. Do your calculations substantiate this claim? Why or why not?

5. Calculate the arithmetic mean, geometric mean, variance, standard deviation, and coefficient of variation of the following set of historical returns for Tall Pines Corporation:

1979	25%
1980	10%
1981	-5%
1982	-10%
1983	5%
1984	65%
1985	27%
1986	10%
1987	-7%

Which measure of central tendency provides a more accurate measure of the average return an investor would have realized over the past nine years: the arithmetic mean or the geometric mean? Why?

6. After observing the historical returns for Tall Pines Corporation in question 5, you consult a friend who is a security analyst regarding the potential return for the company's stock for next year. He provides you with the following probability distribution of returns based on his expectations about the state of the economy:

State of the Economy	Probability of State (%)	Return for Tall Pines for Each State (%)
Recession	5	-15
Below Average	15	10
Average	60	20
Above Average	15	35
Boom	5	50

a. Calculate the expected return for Tall Pines based on your friend's estimates.

b. Does the expected return correspond with the stock's geometric mean return over the past nine years?

c. According to your calculations, there is approximately a 95.5 percent probability that the actual return on Tall Pines stock next year will be within what range?

7. Use the following information to answer parts a and b of this question:

	Bradley	**Willard**
1979	25%	20%
1980	10%	8%
1981	-5%	1%
1982	-10%	-5%
1983	5%	6%
1984	65%	34%
1985	27%	18%
1986	10%	10%
1987	-7%	-3%

a. Calculate the arithmetic mean, geometric mean, variance, standard deviation, and coefficient of variation for the two firms.

b. Which of the two firms' stocks was more risky (volatile) over the time period you examined? Why? (Use your results from part a to substantiate your answer.)

Chapter Nine
The Capital Asset Pricing Model

The four preceding chapters dealt with the concepts of security valuation, risk, and returns. You learned that the value of an investment depends on (1) its expected returns, (2) the timing of the returns, and (3) the relative riskiness of the return stream. The Capital Asset Pricing Model (CAPM) is a concept from portfolio theory that brings together these three factors by providing a framework within which the relationship between risk and return can be analyzed. This chapter presents the basic framework of the CAPM and introduces you to a PROFIT+ routine designed to incorporate the CAPM into the pricing of common stocks. For a more thorough review of portfolio theory, you should consult your financial management textbook. (For example, consult Chapter Six in either *Fundamentals of Financial Management*, 4th ed., by Eugene F. Brigham, or *Essentials of Managerial Finance*, 8th ed., by J. Fred Weston and Eugene F. Brigham.)

PORTFOLIO RISK, REGRESSION, AND BETA

Diversification allows investors to reduce the risk associated with their investment portfolios. However, it is virtually impossible to diversify away all of the risk associated with investing. Some element of risk is always present.

Company-Specific and Market Risk

For investments in common stocks, the risk that can be eliminated through diversification is called *diversifiable*, or *company-specific*, risk. This type of risk is caused by factors that are unique to individual firms—unsuccessful marketing programs, death of a key manager, strikes, legal actions, etc. It is highly unlikely that events such as these will affect all companies in an investor's portfolio at the same time; so when bad events do strike one firm, they tend to be offset by the good events being enjoyed by others. Therefore, company-specific risk can be reduced, or eliminated, through diversification.

The type of risk that cannot be diversified away is frequently called *market*, or *nondiversifiable*, risk. It is caused by the effects that national and world events have on all firms. Such factors as inflation, recession, changes in tax laws, high interest rates, wars, and other political disputes tend to affect all firms at the same time, making it impossible for diversification to eliminate the investment risks they precipitate.

Since one type of risk can be eliminated, but another cannot, with which type should investors holding portfolios of investments be concerned? The answer is the risk that still remains after diversification has had its effect—that is, market risk. Since company risk can be diversified away, the riskiness of a well-diversified portfolio is primarily determined by its market risk—the extent to which the portfolio tends to be affected by fluctuations in the overall market. Because of these facts, the *relevant risk* of an individual stock is the amount of market risk it contributes to a well-diversified portfolio.

Beta

A stock's market risk can be measured by its *beta coefficient*, or simply its beta. Betas measure the volatility of individual stocks in relationship to an *average stock* in the overall market. An average stock is one that tends to move up and down in the same pattern as some stock market indicator, such as *The New York Stock Exchange Index*, *The Standard and Poor's 500 Index*, or *The Dow Jones Industrial Average*. A stock that moves *exactly* with the index in question is said to have a beta of 1.0. For example, if the market moves up or down by 5 percent, we would expect a stock whose beta is 1.0 would fluctuate by the same amount. If a stock is less volatile than the market, its beta will be less than 1.0; and if it is more volatile, its beta will be greater than 1.0.

If you were to construct a portfolio of stocks, all of which had betas equal to 1.0, you would expect your portfolio to possess a level of risk equal to that of the market. On the other hand, if you wanted your portfolio to be less risky than the market, you could construct it of stocks whose betas were less than 1.0, and vice versa, if you desired a portfolio riskier than the market. In fact, the riskiness of a diversified portfolio can be calculated by determining the weighted average of the betas of the stocks included in the portfolio.

The concept of beta coefficients was first put forth by William F. Sharpe in his article, "Capital Asset Prices: A Theory of Market Equilibrium under Conditions of Risk," published in the September 1964 issue of the *Journal of Finance*. Betas, which are now calculated by Value Line, Merrill Lynch, Pierce, Fenner and Smith, and other organizations, can be determined by statistically analyzing an individual stock's returns in comparison with those of the market. The way in which this is done is to construct the regression line that best fits the relationship between the two series of returns. Such a line will take the form

$$k_j = A_j + B_j k_m + E \tag{9.1}$$

where
k_j = the return for the jth stock
A_j = the Y-intercept of the regression line for the jth stock
B_j = the slope of the regression line for the jth stock
k_m = the return for the market.
E = the random error.

Random error accounts for the deviations of the actual results from the results predicted by the equation. It is B_j that is of interest to us at this point, since the slope of the regression line is the beta of the stock we are examining.

The Least-Squares Method

Although regression lines can be roughly estimated by constructing a scatter plot relating the returns of a particular stock to those of the market and then drawing the best-fit line by eye, the technique used in practice to determine the betas of stock is called the *least-squares method*. Your PROFIT+ software package includes a routine for computing the least-squares regression line between two series. The following paragraphs discuss the arithmetic performed by this routine.

Equation 9.1, given above, is a specific expression of the more generalized equation for a regression line given in Equation 9.2:

$$Y = A + BX + E \tag{9.2}$$

where
Y = the dependent variable
X = the independent variable
A = the Y-intercept
B = the slope of the regression line
E = the random error term.

Y is the variable to be modeled, or predicted, and depends on the value of X in the equation. The following equations explain how each of these values is calculated by your PROFIT+ software:

$$B = \text{slope} = \frac{SS_{xy}}{SS_{xx}} \tag{9.3}$$

$$A = \text{Y-intercept} = \bar{Y}. - B\bar{X}. \tag{9.4}$$

$$SS_{xy} = \sum_{i=1}^{n} X_i Y_i - \frac{\sum_{i=1}^{n} X_i \sum_{i=1}^{n} Y_i}{n} \tag{9.5}$$

$$SS_{xx} = \sum_{i=1}^{n} X_i^2 - \frac{\sum_{i=1}^{n} X_i^2}{n} \tag{9.6}$$

where
n = number of observations in the series
SS = the sum of the squares.

In addition to providing the best-fit regression line, PROFIT+'s Least-Squares Regression routine also calculates several other related values. The first is the model's "coefficient of determination" (represented by R^2). This value, which is reported as a decimal, expresses the proportion of the entire variance in the dependent variable (Y) that is explained by the independent variable (X). An R^2 of 0.70, for example, implies that the model, by relating the value of Y to the value of X, is able to explain 70 percent of the variance in Y. The formula for calculating R^2 is given in Equation 9.7:

$$R^2 = 1 - \frac{SSE}{SS_{yy}} \tag{9.7}$$

$$SS_{yy} = \sum_{i=1}^{n} Y_i^2 - \frac{\sum_{i=1}^{n} Y_i^2}{n} \tag{9.8}$$

$$SSE = SS_{yy} - B(SS_{xy}) \tag{9.9}$$

where SSE = the sum of the squared errors.

PROFIT+ also provides a measure of the extent to which the two variables, X and Y, tend to move together. This measure is called the *Pearson product moment correlation coefficient* (R) and is calculated as follows:

$$R = \frac{SS_{xy}}{(SS_{xx}SS_{yy})^{.5}} \tag{9.10}$$

R can take on any value from +1.00 to -1.00; the former indicates perfect positive correlation (X and Y move exactly together in the same direction) between the two variables, and the latter perfect negative correlation (X and Y move exactly together, but in opposite directions). You can find more detailed discussions of the least-squares regression analysis and the coefficients of correlation and determination in most business statistics textbooks.

Exhibit 9.1 shows that the PROFIT+ Capital Asset Pricing Model program, Option G on the Main Menu, includes as Choice 1 on its submenu a routine for calculating the beta of a stock. In addition, it reports the Y-intercept of the regression equation, the equation's R and R^2, and the arithmetic means for the returns of the stock in question and for those of the market.

Exhibit 9.2 shows how the PROFIT+ Beta Calculation routine can be used to answer the following sample problem:

Exhibit 9.1

PROFIT+ PROFIT+

CAPITAL ASSET PRICING MODEL

This routine involves three steps. They may be undertaken separately, or in conjunction with each other.

1. Beta Calculation (Simple Linear Regression Analysis)
2. Security Market Line Calculation
3. Common Stock Valuation
4. All three of the above in sequence

Use ↑↓ to make your selection and press [RETURN]
or
type the number preceding your selection.

[F1]=HELP [F2]=REVIEW [ESC]=MENU

Exhibit 9.2

PROFIT+ PROFIT+

BETA CALCULATION (SIMPLE REGRESSION)

Number of Observations 10

	Market Return % (X Variable)	Stock's Return % (Y Variable)		Market Return % (X Variable)	Stock's Return % (Y Variable)
1:	9.200	12.000	2:	6.000	10.000
3:	-5.000	-8.000	4:	10.700	14.000
5:	8.500	11.500	6:	-14.000	-20.000
7:	53.000	62.000	8:	20.800	24.600
9:	10.000	15.000	10:	16.700	22.000

Beta	Y Intercept	R	R Square	X Mean	Y Mean
+1.210	0.287	0.995	0.990	11.590	14.310

[F1]=HELP [F2]=REVIEW [F3]=CALC [F5]=REDO [F9]=PRINT [ESC]=MENU

Sample Problem: Using the least-squares regression method, calculate the best-fit regression line that models the returns for Kooler Incorporated's common stock in terms of those for the market over the past ten years. What is Kooler's beta? How much of the variance in the returns for Kooler is explained by the variance in the market? (Hint: What is the model's R^2?) What is the coefficient of correlation (R) between the two series? The necessary data is provided below.

Year	*Kooler's Return (%)*	*Market Return (%)*
1978	12.0	9.2
1979	10.0	6.0
1980	-8.0	-5.0
1981	14.0	10.7
1982	11.5	8.5
1983	-20.0	14.0
1984	62.0	53.0
1985	24.6	20.8
1986	15.0	10.0
1987	22.0	16.7

The Security Market Line

At the core of the CAPM is the security market line, a line that shows the relationship between risk and the required rate of return for individual securities. The equation for the line is

$$k_i = k_{rf} + b_i(k_m - k_{rf}) \tag{9.11}$$

where k_i = the required return for the ith stock

k_{rf} = the risk-free rate of return, usually approximated as the return on U.S. Treasury securities

k_m = the required return on the market portfolio of *all* stocks, but usually measured by the return on a well-known stock market indicator series (this is also the required return for a stock with a beta of 1.00)

b_i = the beta coefficient for the ith stock

$(k_m - k_{rf})$ = the market risk premium

$b_i(k_m - k_{rf})$ = the risk premium for the ith stock.

Exhibit 9.3

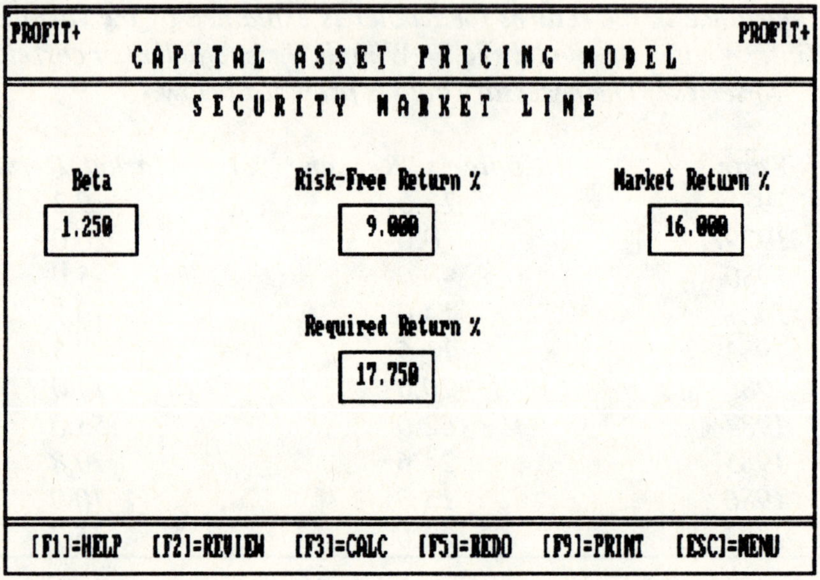

A close examination of the security market line, along with the aid of the definitions of its components, shows you that the return for a stock is derived from two factors: (1) the risk-free rate of return, and (2) a risk premium for the stock in question. The risk premium for a stock is determined by multiplying the stock's beta times the market risk premium (the risk premium for an average, or beta = 1.0, stock). Thus, if a stock is of the same risk as the market, multiplying its beta, 1.0, times the market risk premium will result in a risk premium for the stock that is identical to that of the market, and a required return equal to that of the market. If a stock is of greater risk than the market, its beta will be greater than one, its risk premium will be greater than that of the market, and its required return will be greater than the market's (an outcome that is consistent with the concept that a greater return should be required from an investment with greater risk). Similarly, a stock that is less risky than the market will have a beta that is less than one, and thus, will lead to a required return that is less than that of the market.

Choice 2 on the PROFIT+ Capital Asset Pricing Model submenu is a routine that makes use of the security market line to determine the required return for a stock. Exhibit 9.3 shows how the routine can be used to obtain the answer to the following sample problem:

Sample Problem: Sommers Corporation common stock has a beta of 1.25. What return should investors require of the stock if the risk-free rate is 9 percent, and the return for the market is 16 percent?

Putting It All Together: Back to Common Stock Valuation

In Chapter Seven, during the discussion of common stock valuation, you always had a required return for the stock in question given to you. Now that you have studied this chapter, however, you have acquired the knowledge that is necessary to determine what that required return should be. In other words, you can now proceed with the following steps to determine the value of a share of common stock:

1. Use the least-squares regression method to determine the beta of the stock.

2. Use the beta you calculated in step 1 as an input in the security market line to determine the stock's required return.

3. Use the required return calculated in step 2 as an input in either the constant growth or supernormal growth dividend valuation model to estimate the value of the stock.

Choice 4 on the PROFIT+ Capital Asset Pricing Model submenu provides a routine for performing steps 1 through 3 above in sequence. The routine automatically uses the beta resulting from step 1 as an input in step 2, and the required return calculated in step 2 as an input in the common stock valuation model that you choose. (Choice 3 on the Capital Asset Pricing Model submenu takes you directly to the Common Stock Valuation submenu that was discussed in Chapter Seven. It is included on the Capital Asset Pricing Model for your convenience, but examples of its use were already presented in Chapter Seven.)

Exhibits 9.4, 9.5, 9.6, and 9.7 demonstrate how Choice 4 on the Capital Asset Pricing Model submenu can be used in conjunction with the sample problem that follows. In Exhibit 9.4, the first decision you must make after selecting Choice 4 involves whether you wish to use the constant growth dividend valuation model or the supernormal growth model. After this initial choice, the stock's beta is calculated in Exhibit 9.5, its required return is determined in Exhibit 9.6, and its value is estimated in Exhibit 9.7.

Sample Problem: You have been given the task of estimating the value of a share of Pederson Corporation common stock. After quite a bit of effort, you have obtained the following information that will help with your task. Use this information in conjunction with PROFIT+ to estimate the value of the stock.

Year	*Pederson's Return (%)*	*Market Return (%)*
1980	*5.0*	*2.0*
1981	*12.0*	*8.7*
1982	*16.3*	*11.7*
1983	*-12.0*	*-8.0*
1984	*47.0*	*33.0*
1985	*22.7*	*16.8*
1986	*33.3*	*22.6*
1987	*25.2*	*15.8*

Risk-free rate *5%*
Market return *16.0%*
Pederson's latest dividend *$2.35*
Pederson's projected constant growth rate *10.0%*

Exhibit 9.4

PROFIT+ PROFIT+

CAPITAL ASSET PRICING MODEL

You have chosen option 4 from the Capital Asset Pricing Model menu. Before continuing, you must specify which common stock valuation model you desire PROFIT+ to use in its calculations. Two choices are available:

1. Valuation of a zero growth or a constant growth stock

2. Valuation of a supernormal growth stock.

Use ↑↓ to make your selection and press [RETURN]
or
type the number preceding your selection.

[F1]=HELP [F2]=REVIEW [ESC]=MENU

Exhibit 9.5

PROFIT+ PROFIT+

B E T A   C A L C U L A T I O N   (S I M P L E   R E G R E S S I O N)

Number of Observations: 8

Market Return % (X Variable)	Stock's Return % (Y Variable)	Market Return % (X Variable)	Stock's Return % (Y Variable)
1: 2.000	5.000	2: 8.700	12.000
3: 11.700	16.300	4: -8.000	-12.000
5: 33.000	47.000	6: 16.800	22.700
7: 22.600	33.300	8: 15.800	25.200

Beta	Y Intercept	R	R Square	X Mean	Y Mean
+1.429	0.359	0.997	0.993	12.825	18.688

[F1]=HELP [F2]=REVIEW [F3]=CALC [F5]=REDO [F9]=PRINT [ESC]=MENU [PGDN]=SML

Exhibit 9.6

PROFIT+ PROFIT+

C A P I T A L   A S S E T   P R I C I N G   M O D E L

S E C U R I T Y   M A R K E T   L I N E

Beta	Risk-Free Return %	Market Return %
1.429	9.500	16.000

Required Return %: 18.789

[PGUP]=BETA CALCULATION [PGDN]=STOCK VALUATION

[F1]=HELP [F2]=REVIEW [F3]=CALC [F5]=REDO [F9]=PRINT [ESC]=MENU

Exhibit 9.7

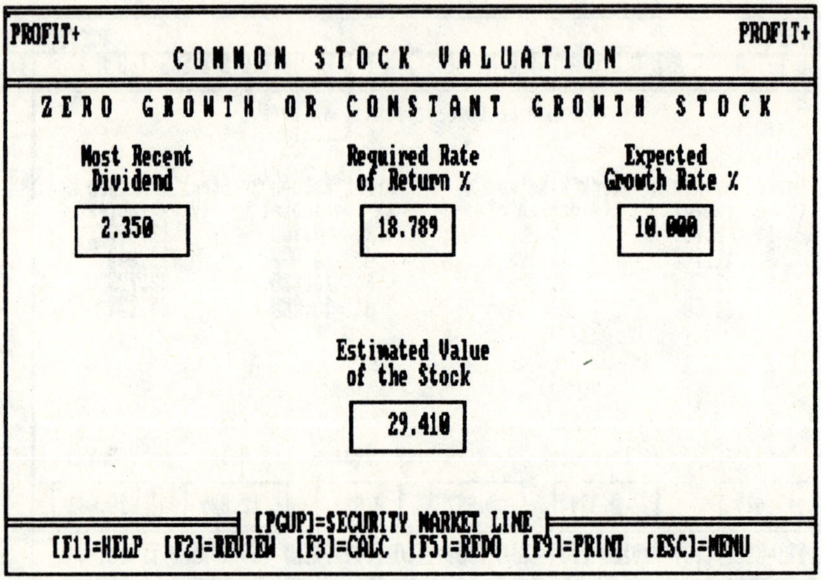

SUMMARY

Although the concepts discussed in this chapter—beta and simple linear regression analysis, the security market line, and common stock valuation—appear to be rather straightforward, you should understand that much more is involved with the actual use of the concept of the CAPM than was discussed in this chapter. Betas and the security market line have an important place in both the theory and application areas of finance, but they are not perfect measures, and you should know their limitations. To gain this knowledge, you should study this subject in your financial management textbook.

END-OF-CHAPTER PROBLEMS

1. The table given below shows the annual rates of return for Imagination common stock and for an appropriate stock market index. From this information, determine the beta for Imagination stock. What is the correlation coefficient of returns between the two series? What percentage of the variation in the returns for Imagination is explained by the variations in returns for the market?

Year	Market's Return (%)	Imagination's Return (%)
1981	10.0	8.0
1982	12.5	9.2
1983	-6.0	-2.5
1984	1.5	.2
1985	35.0	27.6
1986	27.0	19.8
1987	10.0	4.1

2. Below you will find a table listing the returns on the common stock of Continental Cube and those for the overall market for a five-year period.

Year	Continental Cube (%)	The Market (%)
1983	38.6	23.8
1984	-24.7	-7.2
1985	12.3	6.6
1986	8.2	20.5
1987	40.1	30.6

a. What were the mean returns and the standard deviations for both series over the period?

b. Which series was more risky (more volatile) during this period?

c. What is the beta for the market?

d. What is the beta for Continental Cube common stock?

e. How does your answer to part d confirm your answer to part b?

3. Use the information in the following table to answer questions a through c below.

Year	Brown Corp. (%)	Greene Corp. (%)	Market (%)
1981	-10.1	-2.2	-1.7
1982	12.7	6.5	4.3
1983	34.6	25.3	23.8

Year	Brown Corp. (%)	Greene Corp. (%)	Market (%)
1984	-28.7	-8.1	-7.2
1985	8.3	7.5	6.6
1986	4.2	23.7	20.5
1987	36.1	32.9	30.6

a. What is the beta for each stock?

b. Which regression equation explains the greatest proportion of variance in the stock's returns by variance in the market's returns?

c. Which stock is of greater risk to a well-diversified investor? Why?

4. Assuming that the risk-free return is 8.5 percent and the return for the market is 15.2 percent, use the PROFIT+ Security Market Line routine to determine the required rate of return for each of the following stocks:

Stock	Beta
ABC	0.50
DEF	0.75
GHI	1.00
JKL	1.25
MNO	1.50
PQR	2.00

5. Use the PROFIT+ Security Market Line routine to calculate the required return on Vigil Corporation stock under each of the following conditions:

Beta	Risk-free Rate%	Market's Return%
1.00	8.8	16.0
1.00	7.0	16.0
1.00	10.5	16.0
1.50	8.8	16.0
1.50	7.0	16.0
1.50	10.5	16.0
1.00	8.8	14.0
1.00	7.0	14.0
1.00	10.5	14.0
2.00	8.8	16.0
2.00	7.0	16.0
2.00	10.5	16.0

6. Sedcore Industries common stock has a beta of 0.91. If the risk-free rate is 8 percent and the required return for the market is 15 percent, what should be the required return for Sedcore stock?

7. Walton Products common stock has a beta of 1.30. The present rate on long-term U.S. Treasury securities is 11.5 percent and the required return for the market is 17.6 percent. Walton's latest dividend was $3.35 per share, and security analysts project that the dividend will grow at a constant rate of 7 percent in the foreseeable future.

a. Given the above information, what return should investors require of Walton Products common stock?

b. Given your answer to part a, and the additional information provided above, what should be the value of a share of Walton's stock? (Note: You will have to use two separate PROFIT+ routines to answer this question.)

c. How would your answers to parts a and b change if Walton's beta was 0.90, rather than 1.30?

d. How would your answers to parts a and b change if required return for the market was 15 percent, rather than 17.6 percent? (Remember to change beta back to 1.30.)

8. Given the following information, what is the appropriate value of a share of Joecorp common stock?

Year	Joecorp's Return (%)	Market's Return (%)
1980	4.0	2.0
1981	14.0	8.7
1982	15.2	11.7
1983	-11.1	-8.0
1984	44.5	33.0
1985	21.6	16.8
1986	30.3	22.6
1987	22.0	15.8

Risk-free rate	9.5%
Market return	16.0%
Joecorp's latest dividend	$2.35
Joecorp's projected constant growth rate	10.0%

9. Given the information that follows, answer questions a through d below:

a. What is the appropriate value of a share of Jazmine common stock?

b. How would the value of Jazmine's stock change if the projected constant growth rate was 10 percent, rather than 8 percent?

c. How would the value of Jazmine's stock change if the projected constant growth rate was 6 percent, rather than 8 percent?

d. How would your answers to parts a, b, and c change if the risk-free rate was 10 percent, rather than 9 percent?

Year	Jazmine's Return (%)	Market's Return (%)
1980	2.2	2.0
1981	9.5	8.7
1982	12.2	11.7
1983	-9.1	-8.0
1984	34.9	33.0
1985	17.8	16.8
1986	23.6	22.6
1987	17.1	15.8

Risk-free rate	9.0%
Market return	15.0%
Jazmine's latest dividend	$1.75
Jazmine's projected constant growth rate	8.0%

10. As an assistant to a security analyst, you have been given the assignment of determining the appropriate price of a share of Westcon Incorporated's common stock. The stock's latest dividend was $1.44 per share, and your boss projects that it will grow at an annual rate of 25 percent for the next five years, after which it will decrease to a constant rate of 9 percent and remain at that level for the foreseeable future. By referring to the appropriate publications, you have determined that the current risk-free return is 12 percent, and the required return for the market is 16.8 percent. In addition, you have accumulated the following table of data for Westcon stock and for the market. What is an appropriate price for the stock?

Year	Westcon's Return (%)	Market's Return (%)
1980	4.0	2.0
1981	14.0	8.7
1982	15.2	11.7
1983	-11.1	-8.0
1984	44.5	33.0
1985	21.6	16.8
1986	30.3	22.6
1987	22.0	15.8

Chapter Ten
Financial Statement Analysis

You cannot be an effective financial manager without first having a knowledge of the financial health of your company. Understanding your firm's financial health not only helps you take advantage of its strengths, but also assists you in identifying any weaknesses so that they can be alleviated. Furthermore, since you, as financial manager, are responsible for your firm's financial health, keeping abreast of that health provides you (and your superiors) with a measure by which to assess your performance. Although this knowledge can be gained in many ways, one of the most logical involves the analysis of the documents businesses use to express their financial position and performance—the balance sheet and the income statement.

This chapter discusses the concept of financial statement analysis—specifically, ratio analysis—and the PROFIT+ routine designed to facilitate the task.

RATIO ANALYSIS

Consider the following situation: Firm A earned $5000 this year, while Firm B earned $50,000. Which firm is better managed? Which firm is more efficient? Which firm is more profitable? Which firm earned the greater profit? If you approached these questions correctly, you should have been able to answer only one of them—the last one. There is no way that you can confidently answer the first three questions without first gaining some additional information. For example, you could probably better answer the first three questions if you knew such facts as the relative sizes of the two firms—their asset bases, their annual sales, or other such measures. Once you have learned some of these factors, you can start making some comparisons. For instance, if you knew that both firms had generated $100,000 in sales for the year, you would probably answer that Firm B was the more profitable and maybe the more efficient. If you knew instead that Firm A's sales had been $10,000 and Firm B's $1 million, your answers would favor Firm A. The point is that financial analysis requires that comparisons be made, and this is where ratio analysis can help.

Comparisons is the key word in ratio analysis. Not only are ratios themselves comparisons, but also the only way in which they can be a viable tool of financial analysis is to use them for making additional comparisons. Once you have calculated a set of financial ratios for a company, these ratios cannot be evaluated in isolation. They must be compared with standards for the industry (if such standards can be obtained or generated), with the historical pattern of ratios for the firm in question, and with the overall economic and financial environment in which the firm operates. Only then does ratio analysis hold the potential for being a useful tool.

Keeping Ratio Analysis in Perspective

Before learning about PROFIT+'s financial analysis software, you should remember that ratios are only a "tool" of financial analysis. As with most other tools, ratios must be used with care. Ratios can help you identify potential problem areas but should seldom, if ever, be used to make sweeping generalizations about the financial condition of a firm. They point the direction for further research, and only after this research has been undertaken should you make the final conclusions about the financial health of the firm being analyzed.

To proceed with ratio analysis without first understanding its limitations could lead you to draw some erroneous conclusions about the financial condition of the firm being analyzed. Although a complete discussion of the limitations of ratio analysis is beyond the scope of this guide, the following list of factors (taken from Chapter 7 of *Essentials of Managerial Finance,* 8th ed., by J. Fred Weston and Eugene F. Brigham) will give you an introduction to the most important limitations to keep in mind:

1. Developing industry standard ratios for large firms can be quite difficult, since many such firms operate in a number of very different industries.

2. Using average industry ratios for comparison (when they are available) may not be a desired standard of performance, since many firms strive to do better than average.

3. Ratios can be distorted due to seasonal differences in financial statement accounts and deliberate attempts by management to use "window dressing" techniques to make a company's financial position appear better than it really is.

4. Different firms in the same industry can employ varying operating and accounting practices. This practice can lead to difficulties in comparing the firms with one another.

5. Generalizing whether an individual ratio is "good" or "bad" can be quite difficult. For a particular ratio, sometimes being higher than the norm can indicate good things about a company's financial position, while it might be an indicator of bad things under another set of circumstances.

6. Since a firm can have some ratios that look "bad" while others appear "good," arriving at a conclusion about the overall financial condition of the business can be difficult.

7. The balance sheets of many firms have been severely distorted by inflation. In addition, since inflation affects both depreciation charges and inventory costs, profits are also affected. These facts simply imply the need for additional care when undertaking time series or cross-sectional ratio analysis.

8. Some firms use "window dressing" techniques to make their financial statements appear better to financial analysts. Many of these techniques affect financial statements only in the near term; thus, the firm's long-term financial condition is not substantially altered, a fact of which the analyst needs to be aware.

THE PROFIT+ FINANCIAL STATEMENT ANALYSIS PROGRAM

The PROFIT+ Financial Statement Analysis routine is Option H on the Main Menu. Once into this routine, you will be required to enter balance sheet and income statement information, after which PROFIT+ will calculate both common size financial statements and 13 financial ratios. The following paragraphs describe the calculations that PROFIT+ makes to provide the output from this program. They also include some brief discussions of the reasons for computing individual ratios. For complete examples of using ratio analysis, however, you should refer to the sample analyses included in your financial management textbook. (Chapter 7 of *Fundamentals of Financial Management*, 4th ed., by Eugene F. Brigham, Chapter 7 of *Essentials of Managerial Finance*, 8th ed., by J. Fred Weston and Eugene F. Brigham, and Chapter 8 of *Finance: An Introduction*, 2nd ed., by Herbert B. Mayo all provide such discussions.)

Common Size Financial Statements

Balance sheets and income statements that are expressed in percentages are frequently called *common size* statements. In common size balance sheets, all asset, liability, and equity accounts are expressed as percentages of total assets or total liabilities and net worth. Common size income statements usually express all income statement items as a percentage of net sales. Your PROFIT+ software generates common size statements in this manner.

In effect, common size statements are simply financial statements expressed as ratios—the ratios being the individual percentage figures. Common size statements are used to get a picture of the overall structure of a firm's financial statements from year to year. By expressing items as percentages, absolute dollar figures are eliminated, and you can concentrate on identifying any relative changes that have taken place among various accounts. For example, a series of common size balance sheets for a firm could help you identify any substantial changes that have taken place in the company's asset mix and financing patterns over the years.

Although more sophisticated software programs allow their users to design financial statement formats that suit their particular needs, PROFIT+ prepares common size financial statements and calculates financial ratios based on the standard income statement and balance sheet formats given in Exhibits 10.1 and 10.2, respectively. Most financial analysis problems you will encounter in introductory (and even second-level) financial management classes either will match, or can easily be adapted to, these formats.

Exhibit 10.1

Income Statement
for the Year Ending XX/XX/19XX

Sales..
- Cost of Goods Sold..........................
Gross Profit..................................
- Operating Expenses ....
Operating Income (EBIT) ....
- Interest Expense ....
Pretax Income ....
- Income Taxes ....
Net Income after Taxes.......................
- Preferred Stock Dividends ....
Net Inc. after Pref. Dividends ....

Exhibit 10.2

Balance Sheet
as of XX/XX/19XX

ASSETS

Cash ....
Marketable Securities.......................
Accounts Receivable........................
Inventories...................................
Other Current Assets ....
Total Current Assets......................
Gross Fixed Assets..........................
- Accumulated Depreciation...............
Net Fixed Assets.............................
Other Assets ....
Total Assets..................................

CLAIMS

Accounts Payable ....
Notes Payable ....
Accruals.......................................
Other Current Liabilities...................
Total Current Liabilities...................
Long-Term Debt ....
Total Liabilities............................
Preferred Stock.............................
Common Stockholders' Equity ....
Total Liability and Equity................

Ratios Calculated by PROFIT+

To include within one software package, or one textbook, all of the financial ratios that can be of use under varying circumstances to financial analysts is difficult. Instead of even attempting to provide anything close to an all-inclusive set, PROFIT+ follows the pattern established in introductory financial management texts—it includes a representative set of ratios designed to measure several of the most important aspects of a firm's financial position. PROFIT+'s ratios can be divided into four groups:

1. Liquidity Ratios—those designed to measure a firm's ability to meet its maturing obligations.

2. Asset Management Ratios—sometimes called activity ratios, these attempt to measure how effectively management is using a firm's assets.

3. Debt Management Ratios—(or leverage ratios) are designed to help determine the extent to which a firm employs debt financing, and its ability to meet the interest expenses that accompany this type of financing.

4. Profitability Ratios—help to measure the overall operating performance of the firm (the ability of the firm to generate profits from sales, on assets, and on owners' investment in the business).

Liquidity Ratios PROFIT+ computes two liquidity ratios. The first, the current ratio, is calculated by dividing current assets by current liabilities.

$$\text{Current Ratio} = \frac{\text{Current assets}}{\text{Current liabilities}}$$

The current ratio determines whether the assets normally converted into cash during the current operating period (current assets) are of sufficient value to cover obligations that will be encountered during the same period (current liabilities).

A quick examination of the current ratio should tell you that, under some circumstances, it might not be an adequate measure of the true liquidity position. If a firm has a high level of uncollectible receivables, or has large amounts of inventories that cannot be sold, the current ratio can make a firm appear liquid when it is not. One way to help overcome this deficiency is to calculate the quick (or acid test) ratio. It deducts the least liquid current asset, inventory, from current assets and then divides the remainder by current liabilities.

$$\text{Quick or Acid Test Ratio} = \frac{\text{Current assets - Inventories}}{\text{Current liabilities}}$$

Calculating the acid test ratio, the second liquidity ratios computed by your PROFIT+ software, provides a check on the current ratio. It helps you determine a firm's ability to meet its short-term obligations without having to rely on the sale of additional inventories, which may or may not be liquid.

Activity (Asset Management) Ratios Four activity or asset management ratio are calculated by PROFIT+. Each of these ratios helps you determine whether the level of a particular asset or assets is appropriate, too high, or too low given the current and expected levels of operations.

Inventory turnover or utilization is the first asset management ratio that PROFIT+ computes. Although it can be calculated in several ways, PROFIT+ determines the ratio by dividing annual sales by inventories.

$$\text{Inventory Turnover or Utilization} = \frac{\text{Sales}}{\text{Inventories}}$$

PROFIT+ uses this method because it is the one used by Dun & Bradstreet, a major source of industry standard ratios. Where more detailed financial information is available, inventory turnover can be calculated by dividing cost of goods sold by average inventories. Since the value for sales includes markups, using cost of goods sold in the numerator allows the ratio to be computed solely on a cost basis. Using average inventories (sum of end-of-month inventories divided by 12) in the denominator helps smooth out distortions caused by fluctuating inventories.

The second asset management ratio computed by PROFIT+ is the average collection period (ACP). This ratio helps you determine the average number of days a firm must wait before it receives cash from a sale. In addition to being compared with the firm's industry average and its historical trend, ACP should also be evaluated in light of the credit terms the company offers. If the firm requires customers to pay their bills within 30 days and the ACP is 48 days, customers, on the average, are not heeding the company's credit terms. PROFIT+ calculates ACP by dividing receivables by average sales per day.

$$\text{ACP} = \frac{\text{Receivables}}{\text{Average sales per day}} = \frac{\text{Receivables}}{\text{Annual sales/360}}$$

Fixed asset utilization or turnover is the third activity ratio that PROFIT+ computes. This ratio, which is calculated by dividing sales by net fixed assets, can assist you in determining whether a firm is making efficient use of its fixed assets.

$$\text{Fixed Asset Utilization or Turnover} = \frac{\text{Sales}}{\text{Net fixed assets}}$$

PROFIT+'s final asset management ratio is total asset utilization or turnover. It is computed by dividing sales by total assets.

$$\text{Total Asset Utilization or Turnover} = \frac{\text{Sales}}{\text{Total assets}}$$

This ratio examines the efficiency with which the firm is using its entire asset base to generate sales.

Debt Management Ratios PROFIT+ computes three ratios designed to help measure the extent to which a firm uses debt financing or leverage. Although many firms can use leverage to the advantage of their shareholders—that is, they use it to "lever" shareholder returns to higher levels—too much debt can lead to serious financial difficulties and even bankruptcy. Thus, an important component of a firm's overall financial position is its ability to manage its debt.

The first debt management ratio calculated by your PROFIT+ software is the debt ratio, which measures the proportion of assets that are financed with debt (both current and long-term debt). It is calculated by dividing total debt by total assets.

$$\text{Debt Ratio} = \frac{\text{Total debt}}{\text{Total assets}}$$

PROFIT+'s second debt management ratio, the debt-to-equity ratio, is obtained by dividing total debt by total stockholders' equity.

$$\text{Debt-to-Equity} = \frac{\text{Total debt}}{\text{Total equity}}$$

Although this ratio is simply a transformation of the debt ratio [D/E = Debt Ratio/(1 - Debt Ratio)], it is frequently used by financial analysts and thus is provided by PROFIT+. Both this ratio and the debt ratio increase as a firm makes greater use of debt to finance its operation. Although these maximums will never be reached, the upper limit for the debt ratio is 100 percent, whereas the debt-to-equity ratio has an infinite upper limit.

The times-interest-earned ratio (TIE) is the third debt management ratio computed by PROFIT+. This ratio helps determine the "cushion" a firm has in its ability to meet the annual interest charges on its debt. The TIE ratio, which is calculated by dividing operating income (also known as earnings before interest and taxes or EBIT) by annual interest charges, lets you measure the extent to which operating earnings can decline before the firm is unable to meet these interest charges.

$$\text{Times-Interest-Earned} = \frac{\text{EBIT}}{\text{Interest charges}}$$

Profitability Ratios PROFIT+ computes four ratios designed to measure the profitability of a business. The first of these, profit margin on sales, shows the percentage of sales that remains as profits after all expenses (including income taxes) have been deducted. It is calculated by dividing net income after taxes and preferred dividends by sales.

$$\text{Profit Margin} = \frac{\text{Net income after preferred dividends}}{\text{Sales}}$$

Basic earning power is the second profitability ratio that your PROFIT+ software generates. Keeping in mind that assets are financed with both debt and equity, this ratio computes the ability of assets to provide returns to both of these two categories of investors. To do this, taxes and interest (creditors' returns) are added back to after-tax profits to obtain earnings before interest and taxes, and this figure is divided by total assets.

$$\text{Basic Earning Power} = \frac{\text{Earnings before interest and taxes}}{\text{Total assets}}$$

Return on total assets, also computed by PROFIT+, is another ratio designed to measure the overall profitability of a firm's assets. It differs from basic earning power in that its numerator is net income after taxes and preferred dividends, rather than EBIT.

$$\text{Return on Total Assets} = \frac{\text{Net income after preferred dividends}}{\text{Total assets}}$$

The final profitability ratio that your PROFIT+ software calculates is return on common equity. This ratio is designed to measure the results from operations by the returns they generate for the residual owners of the firm—the common stockholders. Return on common equity is calculated by dividing net income after taxes and dividends on preferred stock by common stockholders' equity.

$$\text{Return on Common Equity} = \frac{\text{Net income after preferred dividends}}{\text{Common stockholders' equity}}$$

Exhibits 10.3 through 10.7 show how the PROFIT+ Financial Statement Analysis routine can be used to calculate common size financial statements and ratios for the following sample problem. Exhibits 10.3 and 10.4 are the data entry screens, while Exhibits 10.5 through 10.7 contain the output. (Note: In the sample problem on the next page, the only request is that you calculate common size financial statements and ratios. You are not asked to analyze the results. For such an analysis, you could discuss the results in class or refer to the discussion that appears in Chapter 7 of *Fundamentals of Financial Management*, 4th ed., by Eugene F. Brigham. This is the same sample problem discussed in that chapter; however, the financial statements here have been stated in a simpler form.)

PROFIT+ allows you to change portions of your financial statement data and recalculate common size statements and ratios under new assumptions. If you change items on the balance sheet, pay special attention to keeping the statement in balance. (PROFIT+ will catch these errors and inform you of them, but exercising caution will eliminate the need for any error messages.)

Sample Problem: Below are the balance sheet and income statement for National Metals Company for 1985. Using your PROFIT+ software, compute common size financial statements and financial ratios for the firm.

National Metals Company
Balance Sheet
as of December 31, 1985
(in $1000s)

ASSETS

Cash	$ 50
Marketable Securities	0
Accounts Receivable	350
Inventories	300
Other Current Assets	0
Total Current Assets	700
Gross Fixed Assets	1,800
- Accumulated Depreciation	500
Net Fixed Assets	1,300
Other Assets	0
Total Assets	$2,000

CLAIMS

Accounts Payable	$ 60
Notes Payable	100
Accruals	140
Other Current Liabilities	0
Total Current Liabilities	300
Long-Term Debt	800
Total Liabilities	1,100
Preferred Stock	0
Common Stock and Paid-In Capital	150
Retained Earnings	50
Total Common Stock Equity	900
Total Liabilities and Equity	$2,000

National Metals Company
Income Statement
or the Year Ending December 31, 1985
(in $1000s)

Sales	*$3,000*
- Cost of Goods Sold	*2,544*
Gross Profit	*456*
- Operating Expenses	*190*
Operating Income (EBIT)	*266*
- Interest Expense	*66*
Pretax Income	*200*
- Income Taxes	*80*
Net Income after Taxes	*$ 120*

Exhibit 10.3

PROFIT+ PROFIT+

FINANCIAL STATEMENT ANALYSIS

BALANCE SHEET

ASSETS		CLAIMS	
CURRENT ASSETS		CURRENT LIABILITIES	
Cash....................	50.00	Accounts Payable........	60.00
Marketable Securities...	0.00	Notes Payable (S-T).....	100.00
Accounts Receivable.....	350.00	Accruals................	140.00
Inventories.............	300.00	Other Cur. Liabilities..	0.00
Other Current Assets....	0.00	Total Cur. Liab.	300.00
Total Current Assets..	700.00		
FIXED AND OTHER ASSETS		L-T DEBT AND EQUITY	
Gross Fixed Assets......	1800.00	Long-Term Debt..........	800.00
- Acc'd. Depreciation...	500.00	Total Liabilities.....	1100.00
Net Fixed Assets......	1300.00	Preferred Stock.........	0.00
Other Assets............	0.00	Common Shldrs.' Equity..	900.00
Total Assets.........	2000.00	Total Claims.........	2000.00

[F1]=HELP [F2]=REVIEW [F5]=REDO [F9]=PRINT [PGDN]=INC. STMT. [ESC]=MENU

Exhibit 10.4

PROFIT+ PROFIT+

F I N A N C I A L   S T A T E M E N T   A N A L Y S I S

INCOME STATEMENT

Sales..........................	3000.00
- Cost of Goods Sold..........	2544.00
Gross Profit...................	456.00
- Operating Expenses..........	190.00
Operating Income (EBIT)........	266.00
- Interest Expense............	66.00
Pretax Income..................	200.00
- Income Taxes................	80.00
Net Income after Taxes.........	120.00
Preferred Stock Dividends......	0.00
Income after Pref. Dividends...	120.00

[PGUP]=BALANCE SHEET [PGDN]=COMMON-SIZE BALANCE SHEET
[F1]=HELP [F2]=REVIEW [F5]=REDO [F9]=PRINT [ESC]=MENU

Exhibit 10.5

PROFIT+ PROFIT+

F I N A N C I A L   S T A T E M E N T   A N A L Y S I S

COMMON-SIZE BALANCE SHEET

ASSETS		CLAIMS	
CURRENT ASSETS		CURRENT LIABILITIES	
Cash....................	2.50 %	Accounts Payable........	3.00 %
Marketable Securities...	0.00 %	Notes Payable (S-T).....	5.00 %
Accounts Receivable.....	17.50 %	Accruals................	7.00 %
Inventories.............	15.00 %	Other Cur. Liabilities..	0.00 %
Other Current Assets....	0.00 %	Total Cur. Liab.	15.00 %
Total Current Assets..	35.00 %		
FIXED AND OTHER ASSETS		L-T DEBT AND EQUITY	
Gross Fixed Assets......	90.00 %	Long-Term Debt..........	40.00 %
- Acc'd. Depreciation...	25.00 %	Total Liabilities.....	55.00 %
Net Fixed Assets......	65.00 %	Preferred Stock.........	0.00 %
Other Assets............	0.00 %	Common Shldrs.' Equity..	45.00 %
Total Assets..........	100.00 %	Total Claims..........	100.00 %

[PGUP]=INCOME STATEMENT [PGDN]=COMMON-SIZE INCOME STATEMENT
[F1]=HELP [F2]=REVIEW [F9]=PRINT [ESC]=MENU

Exhibit 10.6

PROFIT+ PROFIT+

FINANCIAL STATEMENT ANALYSIS

COMMON-SIZE INCOME STATEMENT

Sales..........................	100.00	%
- Cost of Goods Sold...........	84.80	%
Gross Profit...................	15.20	%
- Operating Expenses...........	6.33	%
Operating Income (EBIT)........	8.87	%
- Interest Expense.............	2.20	%
Pretax Income..................	6.67	%
- Income Taxes.................	2.67	%
Net Income after Taxes.........	4.00	%
Preferred Stock Dividends......	0.00	%
Income after Pref. Dividends...	4.00	%

[PGUP]=COMMON-SIZE BALANCE SHEET [PGDN]=RATIOS
[F1]=HELP [F2]=REVIEW [F9]=PRINT [ESC]=MENU

Exhibit 10.7

PROFIT+ PROFIT+

FINANCIAL STATEMENT ANALYSIS

FINANCIAL RATIOS

LIQUIDITY RATIOS

Current Ratio............	2.33 X
Quick (Acid Test) Ratio..	1.33 X

DEBT MANAGEMENT RATIOS

Debt Ratio................	55.00 %
Debt to Equity Ratio.......	122.22 %
Times Interest Earned......	4.03 X

ASSET UTILIZATION RATIOS

Inventory Turnover.......	10.00 X
Avg. Collection Period...	42.00 days
Fixed Asset Turnover.....	2.31 X
Total Asset Turnover.....	1.50 X

PROFITABILITY RATIOS

Net Profit Margin..........	4.00 %
Basic Earning Power........	13.30 %
Return on Total Assets.....	6.00 %
Return on Common Equity....	13.33 %

[PGUP]=COMMON-SIZE INCOME STATEMENT [PGDN]=BALANCE SHEET
[F1]=HELP [F2]=REVIEW [F9]=PRINT [ESC]=MENU

SUMMARY

As you complete your study of this chapter, you should remember some of the cautions given at its beginning. Ratio analysis is a useful tool of financial analysis, *if* it is used properly. You must not be lulled into believing that this type of financial analysis is straightforward. It is not. Ratio analysis has many limitations; to use it properly, you must realize these limitations so that they can be overcome, or at least included as factors in your analysis. If you will keep these points in mind, and if you will learn not just how ratios are calculated, but also *why*, then you will be on your way toward understanding how this type of financial analysis can be of use to you as a financial manager.

END-OF-CHAPTER PROBLEMS

1. Below you will find the 1986 and 1987 financial statements for Reference, Incorporated, along with a set of industry standard ratios for 1987.

a. Restate these financial statements on a common size basis, and compute the 13 financial ratios calculated by PROFIT+ for both years.

b. Using your results from part a, analyze the financial strengths and weaknesses of the company drawing on both how the ratios changed from one year to the next and on how Reference's 1987 ratios compare with those of the industry.

c. How would Reference's financial ratios have been affected if it had sold $100 million worth of inventory at cost just prior to December 31, 1987 and had used the proceeds ($100 million) to reduce long-term debt? Since the inventory is sold at cost, no profits are generated, and since the debt is paid off at the end of the year, interest expense is not affected. (Note: You can answer this portion of the problem simply by changing the accounts affected—inventories and long-term debt.)

Reference, Incorporated
Balance Sheets as of December 31
(in $1000s)

ASSETS	1986	1987
Cash	$ 8,745	$8,011
Marketable Securities	5,642	3,057
Accounts Receivable	120,917	89,320
Inventories	398,723	415,574
Total Current Assets	534,027	515,962
Gross Fixed Assets	476,333	553,493
-Accumulated Depreciation	107,920	157,192
Net Fixed Assets	368,413	396,301
Total Assets	$902,440	$912,263

CLAIMS		
Accounts Payable	$156,121	$129,858
Notes Payable	19,727	5,898
Accruals	58,987	184,287
Total Current Liabilities	234,835	320,043
Long-Term Debt	149,581	175,540
Total Liabilities	384,416	495,583
Preferred Stock	290,705	179,321
Common Stock and Paid-in Capital	100,000	100,000
Retained Earnings	127,319	137,359
Total Common Stock Equity	227,319	237,359
Total Liability and Equity	$902,440	$912,263

Reference, Incorporated
Income Statements
for the Years Ending December 31
(in $1000s)

	1986	1987
Sales	$1,339,000	$1,093,000
- Cost of Goods Sold	937,300	765,100
Gross Profit	401,700	327,900
- Operating Expenses	279,851	249,200
Operating Income(EBIT)	121,849	78,700
- Interest Expense	20,085	16,395
Pretax Income	101,764	62,305
- Income Taxes	37,492	27,325
Net Income after Taxes	64,272	34,980
- Preferred Stock Dividends	12,732	13,736
Income Available to Common Stockholders	$ 51,540	$ 21,244

1987 INDUSTRY AVERAGE RATIOS

Current	2.0 times
Acid Test	0.9 times
Inventory Turnover	3.6 times
Average Collection Period	30.0 days
Fixed Asset Turnover	2.8 times
Total Asset Turnover	1.9 times
Debt-to-Assets	47.0 %
Debt-to-Equity	88.6 %
Times-Interest-Earned	6.5 times
Profit Margin	5.0 %
Basic Earning Power	14.0 %
Return on Assets	9.5 %
Return on Common Equity	17.9 %

2. Below are the balance sheets and income statements for Volkman, Incorporated, for 1986 and 1987, along with industry average ratios for 1987. Use this information to undertake a financial analysis of the company. Remember to include a thorough discussion of the firm's financial strengths and weaknesses. Look both at the changes in ratios from one year to the next and at how Volkman's 1987 ratios compare with those of the industry.

Volkman, Incorporated
Balance Sheets as of December 31
(in $1000s)

	1987	1986
ASSETS		
Cash	$ 1,260.0	$ 840.0
Marketable Securities	74.2	43.4
Accounts Receivable	281.4	82.6
Inventories	8,153.6	6,517.0
Total Current Assets	9,769.2	7,483.0
Gross Fixed Assets	8,689.0	2,859.6
- Accumulated Depreciation	2,200.0	1,300.0
Net Fixed Assets	6,489.0	1,559.6
Total Assets	$16,258.2	$ 9,042.6
CLAIMS		
Accounts Payable	$ 1,096.2	$ 959.0
Accruals	1,143.8	947.8
Total Current Liabilities	2,240.0	1,906.8
Long-Term Debt	4,275.6	789.6
Total Liabilities	6,515.6	2,696.4
Common Stockholders' Equity	9,742.6	6,346.2
Total Claims	$16,258.2	$9,042.6

Volkman, Incorporated
Income Statements
for the Years Ending December 31
(in $1000s)

	1987	1986
Sales	$32,363.8	$25,799.2
- Cost of Goods Sold	18,443.6	14,882.0
Gross Profit	13,920.2	10,917.2
- Operating Expenses	10,444.0	8,366.4
Operating Income (EBIT)	3,476.2	2,550.8
- Interest Expense	443.8	247.8
Pretax Income	3,032.4	2,303.0
- Income Taxes	1,440.6	977.2
Net Income after Taxes	$ 1,591.8	$ 1,325.8

1987 INDUSTRY AVERAGE RATIOS

Current	4.0 times
Acid Test	0.4 times
Inventory Turnover	5.0 times
Average Collection Period	3.0 days
Fixed Asset Turnover	5.0 times
Total Asset Turnover	3.0 times
Debt-to-Assets	50.0 %
Times-Interest-Earned	5.0 times
Profit Margin	3.5 %
Return on Assets	10.5 %
Return on Common Equity	21.0 %

3. Below are the balance sheet and income statement for United Timepieces, Incorporated, for 1987, along with industry average ratios for 1987. Use this information to undertake a ratio analysis of the company. Remember to include a thorough discussion of the firm's financial strengths and weaknesses.

United Timepieces, Incorporated
Balance Sheet as of December 31, 1987
(in $1000s)

ASSETS

Cash	$ 160.0
Accounts Receivable	670.0
Inventories	480.0
Total Current Assets	1,310.0
Gross Fixed Assets	700.0
- Accelerated Depreciation	115.0
Net Fixed Assets	585.0
Total Assets	$1,895.0

CLAIMS

Accounts Payable	$ 260.0
Notes Payable	170.0
Accruals	230.0
Total Current Liabilities	660.0
Long-Term Debt	510.0
Total Liabilities	1,170.0
Common Stockholders' Equity	725.0
Total Claims	$1,895.0

United Timepieces, Incorporated
Income Statement
for the Year Ending December 31, 1987
(in $1000s)

Sales	$3,200.0
-Cost of Goods Sold	2,800.0
Gross Profit	400.0
- Operating Expenses	285.0
Operating Income (EBIT)	115.0
- Interest Expense	50.0
Pretax Income	65.0
- Income Taxes	26.0
Net Income after Taxes	$ 39.0

1987 INDUSTRY AVERAGE RATIOS

Current	2.0 times
Acid Test	1.2 times
Inventory Turnover	6.7 times
Average Collection Period	35.0 days
Total Asset Turnover	2.0 times
Debt-to-Assets	58.0 %
Times-Interest-Earned	3.0 times
Profit Margin	2.0 %
Return on Assets	4.0 %
Return on Common Equity	9.5 %

Chapter Eleven
Sources and Uses of Funds

THE CASH FLOW CYCLE

As a business operates, funds (i.e., cash) flow in and out of the firm on a daily basis. Sales lead to reduced inventories and increased receivables. As receivables are collected, cash is increased, and, if the selling prices of the inventories have exceeded the associated costs, profits are generated. These profits, in turn, are used to pay dividends and/or to help finance expansion. Expansion can also be financed (that is, additional cash can also be acquired) through the use of debt and equity financing. All of these, and a variety of other *funds flows*, are often referred to as the cash flow cycle, and are frequently depicted in pictorial form. (For an example of a graphical representation of the cash flow cycle, see Figure 7.1 in either of the following texts: *Fundamentals of Financial Management*, 4th ed., by Eugene F. Brigham, or *Essentials of Managerial Finance*, 8th ed., by J. Fred Weston and Eugene F. Brigham.)

STATEMENT OF CHANGES IN FINANCIAL POSITION

The statement of changes in financial position is designed to reflect the cash flow cycle for a given period of time (usually one year) in numerical form. In general, this statement shows where a firm obtained funds and how these funds were used. The statement of changes in financial position is just as important a financial statement to understand as the balance sheet and the income statement because it helps its users answer questions such as: What major fixed asset acquisitions were made during the year? How were these acquisitions financed? Was this financing internal, external, or both? Did the firm primarily use debt or equity financing? What relative mix of short-term and long-term debt did the firm use? Have current assets built up during the year, or have they been drawn down? All of these specific questions can be grouped into three general categories that the statement of changes in financial position is designed to answer:

1. What did the firm do with funds that were available during the year?

2. Where did the firm get the funds that were available during the year?

3. Did the firm's operations during the year lead to an increase or decrease in its liquidity position as reflected in the balance of its cash and near-cash (marketable securities) accounts?

Answers to these questions are of obvious importance to all parties concerned with the firm's operations—managers, shareholders, and creditors alike. Exhibit 11.1 contains a basic statement of changes in financial position for Marley Corporation.

The upper portion of the statement in Exhibit 11.1 identifies funds generated and used by operations: Marley Corporation's operations produced $52 million of funds during the year and used $90 million; thus, $38 million more funds were needed to support operations than were produced by those operations. The greatest single use of funds was the increase in fixed assets, so Marley must be rather heavily involved with expanding its fixed asset base.

The second part of the statement shows how Marley acquired the additional $38 million it needed for operations: this was accomplished through financing activities—$8 million from additional notes payable and $48 million from the sale of additional debentures. Also, the firm repaid $4 million of its mortgage bonds during the year.

Next, the statement shows that Marley paid $20 million in common and preferred dividends.

When all of the preceding sources and uses are totaled and are netted against one another, Marley's liquidity position as measured by its cash and marketable securities accounts decreased by $6 million.

Exhibit 11.1

Marley Corporation
Statement of Changes in Financial Position
for the Year Ending 12/31/87
(in millions of Dollars)

Sources:	
Net income before preferred dividends	$24
Depreciation	20
Increase in accounts payable	6
Increase in accrued taxes	2
Total sources from operations	$52
Uses:	
Increase in accounts receivable	$ 7
Increase in inventories	17
Increase in fixed assets	66
Total uses from operations	$90
Net funds from operations	($38)
Financing Activities:	
Increase in notes payable	$ 8
Increase in debentures	48
Repayment of mortgage bonds	(4)
Net funds from financing	$52
Less: Common and preferred dividends	20
Decrease in cash and marketable securities	($ 6)

Preparing a Statement of Changes in Financial Position

The first step in preparing a statement of changes in financial position is to determine how each balance sheet account changed during the year and then classify each change as either a source or a use of funds. The following rules should be adhered to during the classification process:

Sources of Funds

1. any increase in a liability or equity account

2. any decrease in an asset account

Exhibit 11.2

Marley Corporation
Changes in Balance Sheet Accounts during 1987
(in millions of dollars)

			Change	
	12/31/87	12/31/86	Source	Use
Cash	$10	$11	$ 1	
Marketable Securities	0	55		
Accounts Receivable	70	63		$ 7
Inventories	60	43		17
Gross Plant and Equipment	360	294		66
Accumulated Depreciation	100	80	20	
Accounts Payable	12	6	6	
Notes Payable	20	12	8	
Accrued Wages	2	2		
Accrued Taxes	26	24	2	
Mortgage Bonds	100	104		4
Debentures	60	12	48	
Common Stock	10	10		
Paid-In Capital	20	20		
Retained Earnings	150	146	4	
Totals			$94	$94

Uses of Funds

1. any decrease in a liability or equity account
2. any increase in an asset account

Exhibit 11.2 shows end-of-year balance sheets for Marley Corporation for 1986 and 1987, along with changes classified as either sources or uses of funds.

In Exhibit 11.2 total sources equal total uses. If you are classifying balance sheet changes as either sources or uses and the totals of each category are not equal, you have made an error and need to check your work. Exhibit 11.2 also shows that the increase in accumulated depreciation is treated as a source of funds, because depreciation is a noncash charge against income and must be added back to net income to arrive at an estimate of the actual funds generated from operations. In other words, depreciation charges *do not* generate additional funds, they simply hide income

Exhibit 11.3

PROFIT+ PROFIT+

SOURCES AND USES OF FUNDS ANALYSIS

	Year 2	Year 1	Source	Use
Cash........................	10.00	11.00	1.00	
Marketable Securities.......	0.00	5.00	5.00	
Accounts Receivable.........	70.00	63.00		7.00
Inventories.................	60.00	43.00		17.00
Gross Plant and Equipment...	360.00	294.00		66.00
Accumulated Depreciation..	100.00	80.00	20.00	
Accounts Payable............	12.00	6.00	6.00	
Notes Payable...............	20.00	12.00	8.00	
Accrued Wages...............	2.00	2.00		
Accrued Taxes...............	26.00	24.00	2.00	
Mortgage Bonds..............	100.00	104.00		4.00
Debentures..................	60.00	12.00	48.00	
Common Stock................	10.00	10.00		
Paid-in Capital.............	20.00	20.00		
Retained Earnings...........	150.00	146.00	4.00	
Totals..			94.00	94.00

[F1]=HELP [F2]=REVIEW [F3]=CALC [F5]=REDO [F9]=PRINT [ESC]=MENU

(i.e., funds) to which the firm actually has access. (The funds are hidden for tax purposes. For a more complete discussion of how depreciation is treated on a statement of changes in financial position, see Chapter 7 in either *Fundamentals of Financial Management*, 4th ed., by Eugene F. Brigham, or *Essentials of Managerial Finance,* 8th ed., by J. Fred Weston and Eugene F. Brigham.)

The sources and uses from Exhibit 11.2 are then used, along with information on net income and dividend payments, to produce the formal statement of changes in financial position shown in Exhibit 11.1. The procedure at this point simply involves the proper arrangement of sources and uses into the appropriate categories.

The PROFIT+ Sources and Uses Routine

Option I, Sources and Uses of Funds, on the PROFIT+ Main Menu classifies balance sheet changes as either sources or uses of funds. In other words, when you input comparative balance sheets, PROFIT+ properly categorizes the changes in each account as a source or a use. You can then use this information to manually prepare a formal statement of changes in financial position. (Due to the wide variety of potential sources and uses, and depending on how a particular balance sheet account actually changed, PROFIT+ does not have the capacity to prepare the formal statement of changes in financial position. However, the sources and uses routine performs the bulk of the necessary calculations so that you are left with a relatively simple task as you prepare the formal statement.)

Exhibit 11.3 shows how the PROFIT+ Sources and Uses of Funds routine can be used to classify the balance sheet changes shown for Marley Corporation in Exhibit 11.2.

END-OF-CHAPTER PROBLEMS

1. From the comparative balance sheets given below for Loren Corporation, use the PROFIT+ Sources and Uses of Funds routine to classify each account change as a source or a use of funds:

Loren Corporation
Comparative Balance Sheets for 1986 and 1987
(in millions of dollars)

	12/31/87	**12/31/86**
Cash	$60	$66
Marketable Securities	0	30
Accounts Receivable	420	378
Inventories	360	258
Gross Plant and Equipment	2,160	1,764
Accumulated Depreciation	600	480
Accounts Payable	72	36
Notes Payable	120	72
Accrued Wages	12	12
Accrued Taxes	156	144
Mortgage Bonds	600	624
Debentures	360	72
Common Stock	60	60
Paid-In Capital	120	120
Retained Earnings	900	876

2. Use your results from problem 1, along with the fact that Loren's net income before $120 million of common dividends was $144 million, to manually prepare a formal statement of changes in financial position for 1987.

3. Use the information given on the next page to classify the changes in Volkman, Incorporated's balance sheet as either sources or uses of funds.

4. Use your results from problem 3, along with the fact that Volkman's net income for 1987 was $1,591,800, to manually prepare a formal statement of changes in financial position for 1987. (The firm paid no dividends.)

Volkman, Incorporated
Balance Sheets as of December 31
(in $1000s)

	1987	1986
ASSETS		
Cash	$ 1,260.0	$ 840.0
Marketable Securities	74.2	43.4
Accounts Receivable	281.4	82.6
Inventories	8,153.6	6,517.0
Total Current Assets	9,769.2	7,483.0
Gross Fixed Assets	8,689.0	2,859.6
- Accumulated Depreciation	2,200.0	1,300.0
Net Fixed Assets	6,489.0	1,559.6
Total Assets	$ 16,258.2	$9,042.6
CLAIMS		
Accounts Payable	$ 1,096.2	$ 959.0
Accruals	1,143.8	947.8
Total Current Liabilities	2,240.0	1,906.8
Mortgage Bonds	4,275.6	789.6
Total Liabilities	6,515.6	2,696.4
Common Stock	1,304.6	1,000.0
Paid-in Capital	3,500.0	2,000.0
Retained Earnings	4,938.0	3,346.2
Total Claims	$16,258.2	$9,042.6

5. Use the information given on the next page to classify the changes in Cassidy Corporation's balance sheet as either sources or uses of funds.

6. Use your results from problem 5, along with the fact that Cassidy's net income before $180,000 of common dividends was $256,000, to manually prepare a formal statement of changes in financial position for 1987.

Cassidy Corporation
Comparative Balance Sheets for 1986 and 1987
(in $1000s)

	12/31/87	12/31/86
Cash	$ 80	$ 66
Marketable Securities	10	30
Accounts Receivable	630	378
Inventories	540	258
Gross Plant and Equipment	3,240	1,764
Accumulated Depreciation	900	480
Accounts Payable	108	36
Notes Payable	180	72
Accrued Wages	18	12
Accrued Taxes	234	144
Mortgage Bonds	1,100	624
Debentures	576	72
Common Stock	150	60
Paid-in Capital	280	120
Retained Earnings	954	876

7. Use the following financial statements for Bradco, Incorporated, to classify changes in balance sheet accounts as either sources or uses of funds, then use your results to manually prepare a formal statement of changes in financial position for 1987.

Bradco, Incorporated
Income Statements for the Years Ending 12/31
(in $1000s)

	1986	1987
Sales	$1,339,000	$1,093,000
- Cost of Goods Sold	937,300	765,100
Gross Profit	401,700	327,900
-Operating Expenses	279,851	249,200
Operating Income (EBIT)	121,849	78,700
- Interest Expense	20,085	16,395
Pretax Income	101,764	62,305
- Income Taxes	37,492	27,325
Net Income after Taxes	64,272	34,980

	1986	1987
- Preferred Stock Dividends	12,732	13,736
Inc. Avail. to Common Stockholders	51,540	21,244
- Common Stock Dividends	20,000	11,204
Addition to Retained Earnings	$ 31,540	$ 10,040

Bradco, Incorporated
Balance Sheets as of December 31
(in $1000s)

ASSETS	1986	1987
Cash	$ 8,745	$ 8,011
Marketable Securities	5,642	3,057
Accounts Receivable	120,917	89,320
Inventories	398,723	415,574
Total Current Assets	$534,027	$515,962
Gross Fixed Assets	476,333	553,493
- Accumulated Depreciation	107,920	157,192
Net Fixed Assets	$368,413	396,301
Total Assets	$902,440	$912,263

CLAIMS		
Accounts Payable	$156,121	$129,858
Notes Payable	19,727	5,898
Accruals	58,987	184,287
Total Current Liabilities	234,835	320,043
Long-Term Debt	149,581	175,540
Total Liabilities	384,416	495,583
Preferred Stock	290,705	179,321
Common Stock	10,000	10,000
Paid-in Capital	90,000	90,000
Retained Earnings	127,319	137,359
Total Common Stock Equity	227,319	237,359
Total Liability and Equity	$902,440	$912,263

Chapter Twelve
Financial Forecasting

Chapter Eight of *Essentials of Managerial Finance*, 8th ed., by J. Fred Weston and Eugene F. Brigham, begins with the following paragraph:

> Firms need assets to make sales, and if sales are to grow, assets must also increase. A sales expansion requires a prior investment in new current assets, and, if the firm is operating at full capacity, fixed assets must also be added. Capital will be needed to finance these new assets. Some of the required capital can be obtained by retaining earnings, but if the growth rate is high, even a very profitable firm will need external capital. It is important that firms have reasonably accurate estimates of their forecasted capital requirements. Such estimates are required so that plans may be made to obtain funds before they are needed.

What this paragraph says is that most growth does not take place on its own. It must be planned for, and financing needs must be anticipated, or a firm may find itself lacking the funds necessary for growth. Thus, a very important part of the financial management process is financial forecasting—projecting the firm's future need for funds. This chapter deals with two basic techniques that can be used both to help forecast financial needs and to help you understand what is involved with the task of financial forecasting.

SALES FORECASTING

Financial forecasts must be based on the level of sales projected for future years. Almost all types of forecasts—employment levels, production levels, etc.—are based on sales projections. Firms expend a great deal of time, money, and effort to make (what they hope are) reasonably accurate sales forecasts. For large companies with many divisions both in this country and abroad, the process can become quite involved, even to the point of requiring sophisticated, computerized planning models. In making their projections, these models take into consideration the relationships between a firm's sales and many economic, demographic, and political factors. This guide, or your PROFIT+ software, does not attempt to discuss the process of sales forecasting. Entire courses, and even series of courses, are devoted to the topic (generally in the marketing curriculum), making it both impossible and impractical to do more than mention its importance here. However, you must realize that the financial forecasting techniques discussed in this chapter are based on sales forecasts. Thus, if projected levels of sales are inaccurate, so too will be the results of methods designed to help forecast financial needs.

FINANCIAL FORECASTING TECHNIQUES

Most introductory financial management textbooks introduce students to two techniques that can be of use in the financial forecasting process. The first, a rather simple technique called the percent of sales method, is based on a rather strict set of assumptions about the relationships that exist among the future levels of sales and a firm's balance sheet accounts. The method, however, is a very good one for making some preliminary estimates of future financial needs. It also is quite useful for demonstrating the basic factors involved with financial forecasting.

The second forecasting technique with which this chapter deals is simple linear regression, the technique that we used in Chapter Nine to calculate the betas of common stocks. Here you will learn how it can be used to help estimate the relationships between specific asset and liability accounts and sales.

Percent of Sales Method

In its simplest form, the percent of sales method is based on the following assumptions:

1. Most balance sheet accounts are directly related to sales.

2. The firm is operating efficiently. That is, the current levels of all assets are optimal for the current sales level.

Given these assumptions, the percent of sales method estimates a firm's financial requirements by expressing the various balance sheet items as percentages based on current and expected sales.

On occasion when using the percent of sales method, it is useful to relax assumption 2 a bit, especially as it relates to the relationship between fixed assets and sales. Only if the firm is operating at full capacity will fixed assets have to be increased in direct proportion to sales; therefore, fixed (and sometimes selected other assets) are not varied with sales when using this forecasting technique. One advantage of the percent of sales method is that it is flexible enough to handle such assumptions.

The following steps outline the basic procedures involved with the percent of sales method when all assets are projected to vary directly with sales:

1. Calculate the increase in sales expected for next year. Base this on the difference between this year's sales and the sales level forecasted for next year.

2. Assuming that total assets will increase proportionately with sales, calculate the increase in assets projected for next year. Do this by multiplying the ratio of this year's assets to this year's sales times the expected increase in sales. The result is your estimate of financing needs for the coming year.

3. Calculate the amount(s) of any spontaneous sources of financing expected for next year. Spontaneous financing occurs when some liability accounts are expected to increase in proportion to sales. For example, generating more sales usually means purchasing more inventories. Increased levels of inventories generally lead to increased trade credit from suppliers, which shows up on the balance sheet as increased accounts payable. Other common sources of spontaneous financing include increases in various types of accruals, such as accrued wages and taxes. To determine the anticipated amount of spontaneous financing, multiply the current ratio of spontaneous sources to current sales times the expected change in sales. This amount will help meet some of your financing needs.

4. Calculate the projected addition to retained earnings for the coming year. Do this by multiplying next year's expected sales by the projected profit margin, and then multiplying the result by (1 - D), where D is the firm's dividend payout ratio. Retained earnings will also help provide some of next year's financial needs.

5. The final step in the process is to calculate external funds required (EFR), or what is also called *additional funds needed* (AFN). This is the amount that the financial manager is especially interested in determining, since it is not generated by the growth alone. In other words, AFN must be anticipated so that the financial manager can make plans for acquiring the necessary funds.

For a more thorough discussion of the technique, along with a detailed numerical example, refer to Chapter 8 of *Essentials of Managerial Finance*, 8th ed., by J. Fred Weston and Eugene F. Brigham, or to Chapter 8 of *Fundamentals of Financial Management,* 4th ed., by Eugene F. Brigham.

Another way in which to describe the percent of sales method is to express it as a formula. Below you will find this formula first stated in words and then in the form of a mathematical equation.

Additional Funds Needed	=	Required increase in assets	-	Spontaneous increase in liabilities	-	Increase in retained earnings

$$AFN = \frac{A}{S}(\Delta S) - \frac{L}{S}(\Delta S) - M(1 - D)S_1 \qquad \textbf{(12.1)}$$

where A = this year's total assets
L = total amount of this year's spontaneous liabilities
M = next year's projected profit margin
D = next year's projected dividend payout ratio
ΔS = change in sales
S_1 = projected sales for next year

Your PROFIT+ software includes a routine (Option J, Financial Forecasting, on the Main Menu) that uses the percent of sales method to determine the external funds needed to finance a given level of growth. When you choose Option J, you will see the Financial Forecasting submenu shown in Exhibit 12.1. The percent of sales method is the first choice on this submenu. When it is selected, the routine requires that you enter complete balance sheet data. It reports the results in the form of a pro forma balance sheet with AFN as the balancing figure.

Exhibits 12.2, 12.3, 12.4, and 12.5 show how the PROFIT+ percent of sales routine can be used to solve the sample problem on page 179.

Exhibit 12.1

PROFIT+ PROFIT+

FINANCIAL FORECASTING

This routine offers two options:

1. Percent of sales forecasting

2. Simple linear regression forecasting

Use ↑↓ to make your selection and press [RETURN]
or
type the number of your selection.

[F1]=HELP [F2]=REVIEW [ESC]=MENU

Exhibit 12.2

PROFIT+ PROFIT+

PERCENT OF SALES FORECASTING

THIS YEAR'S BALANCE SHEET

ASSETS		CLAIMS	
CURRENT ASSETS		CURRENT LIABILITIES	
Cash....................	10.00	Accounts Payable........	50.00
Marketable Securities...	0.00	Notes Payable (S-T).....	0.00
Accounts Receivable.....	85.00	Accruals................	25.00
Inventories.............	100.00	Other Cur. Liabilities..	0.00
Other Current Assets....	0.00	Total Cur. Liab.	75.00
Total Current Assets..	195.00	L-T DEBT AND EQUITY	
		Long-Term Debt..........	70.00
FIXED AND OTHER ASSETS		Total Liabilities.....	145.00
Net Fixed Assets........	150.00	Preferred Stock.........	0.00
Other Assets............	0.00	Common Shldrs.' Equity..	200.00
Total Assets..........	345.00	Total Claims..........	345.00

[PGDN]=OPTIONS AND ADDITIONAL INPUTS

[F1]=HELP [F2]=REVIEW [F3]=CALC [F5]=REDO [F9]=PRINT [ESC]=MENU

Sample Problem: Given the following information for Willard Company, use the percent of sales method to arrive at an estimate of the firm's external financing requirements for the coming year. (Assume that all assets, including fixed assets, will vary directly with sales.)

Willard's sales for 1987 were $500 million; its capacity limit. Its profit margin on sales was 4 percent, and it intends to pay out 50 percent of profits as dividends. The company's marketing department forecasts that sales for 1988 will be $750 million.

The Willard Company
Balance Sheet
December 31, 1987
(millions of dollars)

Assets		***Liabilities***	
Cash	*$ 10*	*Accounts Payable*	*$ 50*
Receivables	*85*	*Accrued Taxes and Wages Payable*	*25*
Inventories	*100*	*Mortgage Bonds*	*70*
Fixed Assets (net)	*150*	*Common Stock*	*100*
		Retained Earnings	*100*
Total Assets	*$345*	*Total Liabilities and and Net Worth*	*$345*

Exhibit 12.3

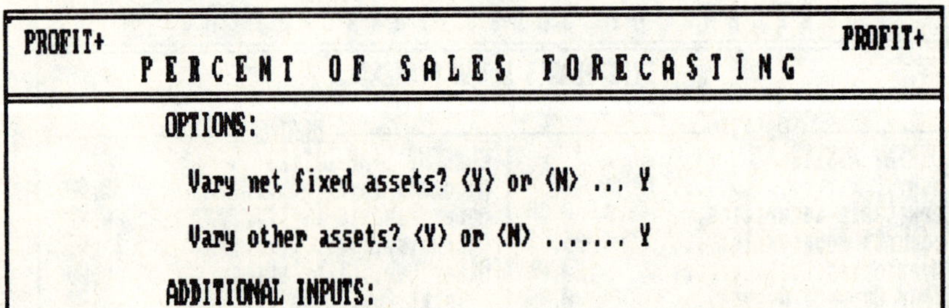

Exhibit 12.4

PROFIT+ PROFIT+

PERCENT OF SALES FORECASTING

THIS YEAR'S BALANCE SHEET
ITEMS THAT VARY WITH SALES EXPRESSED AS A % OF THIS YEAR'S SALES

ASSETS		CLAIMS	
CURRENT ASSETS		CURRENT LIABILITIES	
Cash....................	2.00 %	Accounts Payable........	10.00 %
Marketable Securities...	0.00 %	Notes Payable (S-T).....	n.a.
Accounts Receivable.....	17.00 %	Accruals................	5.00 %
Inventories.............	20.00 %	Other Cur. Liabilities..	n.a.
Other Current Assets....	0.00 %	Total Cur. Liab.	n.a.
Total Current Assets..	39.00 %	L-T DEBT AND EQUITY	
		Long-Term Debt..........	n.a.
FIXED AND OTHER ASSETS		Total Liabilities.....	n.a.
Net Fixed Assets........	30.00 %	Preferred Stock.........	n.a.
Other Assets............	. %	Common Shldrs.' Equity..	n.a.
Total Assets..........	69.00 %	Total Claims..........	n.a.

This Year's Sales = 500.00

[PGUP]=OPTIONS AND ADDT'L INPUTS [PGDN]=NEXT YEAR'S PRO FORMA BALANCE SHEET
[F1]=HELP [F2]=REVIEW [F5]=REDO [F9]=PRINT [ESC]=MENU

Exhibit 12.5

PROFIT+ PROFIT+

PERCENT OF SALES FORECASTING

NEXT YEAR'S PRO FORMA BALANCE SHEET AND ADDITIONAL FUNDS NEEDED CALCULATION

ASSETS		CLAIMS	
CURRENT ASSETS		CURRENT LIABILITIES	
Cash....................	15.00	Accounts Payable........	75.00
Marketable Securities...	0.00	Notes Payable (S-T).....	0.00
Accounts Receivable.....	127.50	Accruals................	37.50
Inventories.............	150.00	Other Cur. Liabilities..	0.00
Other Current Assets....	0.00	Total Cur. Liab.	112.50
Total Current Assets..	292.50	L-T DEBT AND EQUITY	
		Long-Term Debt..........	70.00
FIXED AND OTHER ASSETS		Total Liabilities.....	182.50
Net Fixed Assets........	225.00	Preferred Stock.........	0.00
Other Assets............	0.00	Common Shldrs.' Equity..	215.00
Total Assets..........	517.50	Funds Available.......	397.50
		Additional Funds Needed.	120.00
		Total Claims Including Additional Funds.....	517.50

[PGUP]=THIS YR'S BAL. SHEET-% OF SALES [PGDN]=THIS YR'S BAL. SHEET
[F1]=HELP [F2]=REVIEW [F5]=REDO [F9]=PRINT [ESC]=MENU

PROFIT+ gives you the opportunity to change some of your assumptions and recalculate AFN. For example, if you want to determine how a lower profit margin would affect external funds requirements, you simply have to alter that input and recalculate. PROFIT+ also allows you to control the assumptions regarding whether to vary fixed and other assets with sales.

Simple Linear Regression

Although the percent of sales method provides a good means by which to explain the overall process of financial planning, the assumptions on which it is based can limit its practical use. For example, the percent of sales method assumes that all assets are increasing in direct proportion to sales. Although this assumption might be true under some circumstances, the more likely case is that assets increase as sales increase, but not necessarily in a directly proportional manner. For instance, growth can enable a firm to afford more sophisticated inventory management methods that allow the business to reduce inventories as a percentage of sales. Thus, growth could lead to economies of scale for inventories. That is, at higher levels of sales, a proportionately lower investment in inventories is necessary because more efficient management techniques (use of the computer, for example) are employed.

To avoid complications caused by situations such as the one just discussed, we need a forecasting method that takes into consideration the fact that some (maybe even most) assets do not increase in direct proportion to sales. It is in this area that simple linear regression can be of assistance. Simple regression gives you a tool for determining the historical relationships between sales growth and the growth of asset and spontaneous liability accounts. This not only allows you to see whether such relationships are, indeed, directly proportional (as assumed by the percent of sales technique), but also yields formulas that can be used for forecasting asset and spontaneous liability levels when directly proportional relationships are not discovered. The technique results in a straight-line equation that shows the relationship between a dependent variable (the Y-variable) and an independent variable (the X-variable). Such an equation takes the following form:

$$Y = A + BX + E \qquad \textbf{(12.2)}$$

When used to determine the relationship between the levels of asset or spontaneous liability accounts (the Y-variable) and sales (the X-variable), the method results in an equation that can be used to forecast future assets and liabilities based on sales projections. For example, if simple linear regression analysis has shown that the relationship over the past ten years between inventories and sales for a firm can be expressed by the equation

$$\text{Inventories} = \$1{,}000 + .10(\text{Sales}),$$

and next year's sales are projected to be \$110,000, inventories for the coming year can be estimated in the following manner:

$$\begin{aligned} \text{Inventories} &= \$1{,}000 + .10(\$110{,}000) \\ &= \$1000 + \$11{,}000 \\ &= \$12{,}000 \end{aligned}$$

Reviewing Chapter Nine will help you recall how a simple least-squares regression line is calculated. Other things being equal, the higher the R-square, the more confidence you can have in the ability of a regression equation to predict the future level of a particular asset or spontaneous liability account. However, be cautioned that regression equations are based on historical data. So if any changes are anticipated in the future that could alter historical relationships, their use in forecasting is significantly reduced. The procedure for using regression analysis to forecast future financial needs is basically the same as that used in the percent of sales method. That is, you must first determine the increase in assets necessary to support the forecasted sales growth, then deduct from that amount any spontaneous financing and projected retained earnings. The difference between the two methods lies in the way in which asset and spontaneous liability increases are estimated. Whereas the percent of sales method makes these projections using constant percentage relationships, simple linear regression analysis requires that you develop separate regression equations for each asset and liability account and use these in producing your estimates.

To use your PROFIT+ software to generate simple linear regression models to help with financial forecasting, select Option J from the Main Menu, and then choose the second alternative, Simple Linear Regression Analysis, from the Financial Forecasting submenu. When developing your models, remember that sales is always the X-variable, and the asset or spontaneous liability account in question is the Y-variable. In the sample problem that follows, a regression line is estimated for only one asset—inventories. In actual practice, you would have to follow this procedure for all asset and spontaneous liability accounts. Exhibit 12.6 shows how PROFIT+ can be used to solve the following sample problem:

Sample Problem: (Note: This problem is a continuation of the Willard Company example encountered earlier in this chapter.) Based on the values of Willard's inventories and sales from 1977 to 1987, calculate the least-squares regression line that best describes the relationship between inventories and sales. What is the R-square for your regression model?

Historical Data on Inventory and Sales for
the Willard Company from 1977 to 1987
(in millions of dollars)

Year	***Inventory***	***Sales***
1977	*$ 44*	*$175*
1978	*48*	*200*
1979	*53*	*215*
1980	*57*	*185*
1981	*60*	*235*
1982	*66*	*265*
1983	*73*	*300*
1984	*70*	*280*
1985	*78*	*350*
1986	*90*	*420*
1987	*100*	*500*

Exhibit 12.6

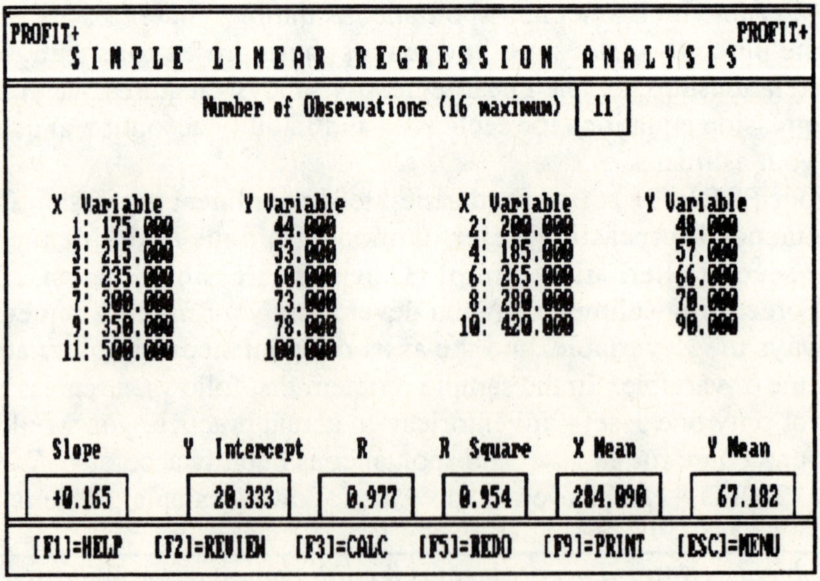

SUMMARY

This chapter has shown you how the PROFIT+ Financial Forecasting routines can be of assistance in financial forecasting. You should realize, however, that making projections such as those we dealt with in this chapter is far from an exact science that has been reduced to a few mathematical equations. Any type of forecasting requires various assumptions to be made about future conditions, and any projections are only as good as these assumptions. Because of this, it is becoming increasingly common to generate a set of forecasts based on varying assumptions, and then to develop contingency plans for dealing with the various outcomes. Computerized spreadsheets, such as "Lotus 1-2-3," "Multiplan," and "Symphony" have been of great help in this area due to the ease with which their users can ask "what if?" questions. So, too, have been several specialized financial planning software packages. Your experiences with PROFIT+ and its capabilities that allow you to ask "what if?" questions will help you better appreciate the extent to which the computer can be of assistance in the planning process.

END-OF-CHAPTER PROBLEMS

1. Spring Teas Corporation supplies quality teas and brewing equipment to offices and restaurants. Its 1987 balance sheet is given below.

In 1987 the firm's sales were $80 million, on which it earned $2.268 million in after-tax profits. The firm paid $907,200 in dividends to its common stockholders in 1987. Spring Teas Corporation is operating at full capacity, and management considers the current relationships between assets and sales as optimal.

Spring Teas Corporation
Balance Sheet for the Year Ending December 31, 1987
(in millions of dollars)

Cash	$ .80	Accounts Payable	$ 2.00
Receivables	6.00	Notes Payable	4.00
Inventories	13.20	Accruals	2.00
Total Current Assets	20.00	Total Current Liabilites	8.00
Gross Fixed Assets	10.08	Long-Term Debt	1.36
- Acc'd Depreciation	2.00	Common Stock	3.36
Net Fixed Assets	8.08	Retained Earnings	15.36
Total Assets	$28.08	Total Liab. & Equity	$28.08

a. If the company projects that 1988 sales will increase by $20 million, what will the firm's external capital requirements be if the present profit margin and dividend payout ratio are maintained? Express your results as a pro forma balance sheet using "additional funds needed" as the balancing account.

b. How would your answer to part a change if the firm were able to increase its after-tax profit margin to 5 percent in 1988? (Note: Remember! You do not have to start all over to answer this one! PROFIT+ lets you ask "what if?" questions.)

c. How would your answer to part a be affected if 1988 sales were expect to increase by $2 million rather than $20 million? By $40 million rather than $20 million? (Note: Remember to change the profit margin back to its initial value when answering this question.)

2. Forrest Innovation's 1987 balance sheet and income statement are shown on the next pages. While the firm's management believes that all other assets will vary directly with sales, it feels that sufficient fixed assets are available to support the level of sales projected for 1988. The company's planners project that next year's profit margin will be the same as this year's and that the 1987 dividend payout ratio will be maintained in 1988.

Forrest Innovation, Incorporated
Balance Sheet as of December 31, 1987
(in $1000s)

ASSETS

Cash	$ 160.0
Accounts Receivable	670.0
Inventories	480.0
Total Current Assets	1,310.0
Gross Fixed Assets	700.0
- Accumulated Depreciation	115.0
Net Fixed Assets	585.0
Total Assets	$1,895.0

CLAIMS

Accounts Payable	$260.0
Notes Payable	170.0
Accruals	230.0
Total Current Liabilities	660.0
Long-Term Debt	510.0
Total Liabilities	1,170.0
Common Stockholders' Equity	725.0
Total Claims	$1,895.0

Forrest Innovation, Incorporated
Income Statement
for the Year Ending December 31, 1987
(in $1000s)

Sales	$3,200.0
- Cost of Goods Sold	2,800.0
Gross Profit	400.0
- Operating Expenses	285.0
Operating Income (EBIT)	115.0
- Interest Expense	60.0
Pretax Income	55.0
- Income Taxes	23.0
Net Income after Taxes	32.0
- Common Stock Dividends	16.0
Addition to Ret. Earnings	$ 16.0

a. Assuming that 1988 sales are projected to be $4 million, what additional funds will Forrest Innovation need to finance the increased sales?

b. How would your answer to part a change if Forrest Innovation's net profit margin dropped to 6 percent, rather than remained at its 1987 level?

c. How would your answer to part a change if the firm increased its dividend payout ratio in 1988 to 75 percent? (Keep the net profit margin at its initial level.)

d. How would your answers to parts a, b, and c change if 1988 sales were forecast to be $5 million, rather than $4 million?

3. How would your answers to question 2 change if Forrest Innovation was operating at full capacity and had to add additional fixed assets in direct proportion to the increase in sales projected in the problem? (Note: Do not rework the problem! Use PROFIT+'s "what if?" capabilities.)

4. Time-Saverz Corporation supplies efficiency software to telemarketing firms. Its 1987 balance sheet is given below:

Time-Saverz Corporation
Balance Sheet for the Year Ending December 31, 1987
(in millions of dollars)

Cash	$10.80	Accounts Payable	$ 4.00
Receivables	7.20	Notes Payable	3.00
Inventories	18.00	Accruals	2.50
Total Current Assets	36.00	Total Current Liabilities	9.50
Gross Fixed Assets	8.00	Long-Term Debt	10.50
- Accumulated Depreciation	2.00	Common Stock	11.00
Net Fixed Assets	6.00	Retained Earnings	11.00
Total Assets	$42.00	Total Liabilities & Equity	$42.00

In 1987 the firm's sales were $50 million, on which it earned $2.5 million, or 5 percent, in after-tax profits. The firm's 1987 dividend payout ratio was 20 percent. Time-Saverz Corporation is operating at full capacity, and management considers the current relationships between assets and sales to be optimal.

a. If the company projects that 1988 sales will increase by $15 million, what will the firm's external capital requirements be if the 1987 profit margin and dividend payout ratio are maintained in 1988?

b. How would your answer to part a change if the firm were able to increase its after-tax profit margin to 6 percent in 1988?

c. How would your answer to part a be affected if 1988 sales were expect to increase by $5 million rather than $15 million? By $25 million rather than $15 million? (Note: Remember to change the profit margin back to 5 percent.)

5. The following table gives historical data on Springfield Chicken Products Corporation's accounts receivable, inventories, and sales. (In your calculations remember to treat sales as the independent variable and the asset accounts as the dependent variable.)

Springfield Chicken Products Corporation
Historical Data on Receivables, Inventories, and Sales
(in millions of dollars)

Year	Receivables	Inventories	Sales
1978	$ 2.00	$ 8.40	$50.0
1979	3.50	9.50	55.0
1980	4.44	10.24	62.0
1981	4.78	10.80	67.0
1982	4.99	11.40	72.0
1983	5.35	11.60	75.0
1984	5.60	12.20	80.0
1985	5.94	12.56	83.0
1986	6.80	14.70	90.0
1987	7.20	14.90	94.0

a. Using simple linear regression, determine the best-fit lines describing the relationships between accounts receivable and sales, and inventories and sales.

b. How well does sales seem to explain the variances in receivables and inventories? (Hint: Check the R-square of each equation.)

c. Use the two equations developed in part a to project 1988 receivables and inventories for Springfield Chicken Products Corporation. 1988 sales are projected to be $90 million. (Note: You will have to make these projections by hand.)

6. The following table gives historical data on Spring Tea Corporation's cash, inventories, and sales.

Spring Teas Corporation
Historical Data on Cash, Inventories, and Sales
(in millions of dollars)

Year	Cash	Inventories	Sales
1978	$1.75	$ 6.40	$40.0
1979	3.20	7.20	46.0
1980	4.04	8.24	49.0
1981	4.50	8.60	52.0
1982	4.68	9.60	56.0
1983	4.90	11.20	60.0
1984	5.10	12.08	68.0
1985	5.24	12.76	74.5
1986	5.60	13.08	76.0
1987	6.00	13.20	80.0

a. Using simple linear regression, determine the best-fit lines describing the relationships between cash and sales, and inventories and sales.

b. How well does sales seem to explain the variances in cash and inventories? (Note: Check the R-square of each equation to answer this question.)

c. Use the two equations developed in part a to project 1988 cash and inventories for Spring Teas Corporation. (Use the sales projection from question 1.)

d. How do the simple regression projections compare with the percent of sales estimates of cash and inventories in question 1? Why do they differ?

e. In a case such as this, which method do you feel yields better results: simple regression or percent of sales? Why?

Chapter Thirteen
Economic Order Quantity

CURRENT ASSET MANAGEMENT

The management of a firm's current assets—cash, marketable securities, accounts receivable, and inventories—is an ongoing, day-to-day process. Current assets probably demand the greatest amount of time in asset management, since their daily changes are caused by, and are the reflections of, the ongoing operations of the business. Since normal business activity causes current assets to fluctuate a great deal, their levels must be continually monitored.

Allowing too great an amount of funds to build up in current assets can have a detrimental effect on the profitability of the firm, while investing too little in these vital assets can cause lost sales or even illiquidity. Thus, like so many other decisions that have economic impacts, current asset management involves balancing the benefits of having the assets on hand with the costs of investing in the assets.

Current asset management is such an important task that much time and effort have been expended in developing quantitative models to help with the process. Although many of the models actually used in practice are beyond the scope of most introductory financial management classes, some of the more basic techniques are presented at this level. This chapter, and the two following it, discuss three aspects of current asset management in which the computer has applications. In this chapter, you will learn about the economic order quantity model used in inventory management. In Chapter Fourteen, the topic of credit policy analysis will be discussed, while Chapter Fifteen will deal with cash budgeting.

INVENTORY MANAGEMENT

The primary task involved with inventory management is the determination of what is the "right" amount of inventory to have on hand. In other words, inventory management is concerned with seeking the optimal inventory level—one that is not so low as to result in lost sales or lost production time, but also not so high that profitability suffers because unnecessary costs are incurred.

Economic Order Quantity

One popular method for determining the optimal inventory level makes use of models that calculate economic order quantity (EOQ). The rationale behind these models is that the inventory of any item is composed of two amounts:

1. a "safety stock" that is held as a buffer against interruptions in supply and/or periods of abnormal demand for the item, and

2. a "working stock" that fluctuates with both the amount of inventory ordered and the usage, or sales, rate of the item.

Although models for determining the optimum safety stock are not discussed in this chapter, you should have at least a basic understanding of the factors that have an impact on their level. In general, firms will carry higher safety stocks as

1. demand forecasts become more uncertain,

2. the costs of missing sales increase, and

3. the chances of delays in receiving shipments become greater.

On the other hand, smaller safety stocks usually occur when the costs of carrying additional inventories are relatively high.

EOQ models are directly related to an item's working stock, since they determine the optimum amount of inventory to order at any one time. The greater the order size for a particular item, the higher its working stock will be. Likewise, smaller, more frequent orders lead to lower working stocks. To calculate EOQ, the models solve for the order quantity that minimizes the total costs associated with inventories. Inventory costs are of two types: those that rise as the quantity of inventory ordered increases, and those that fall with increased order quantity. Examples of the former include storage costs, the opportunity cost of funds invested in inventories, insurance charges, and obsolescence. Costs such as those involved with ordering, foregone profits on sales lost due to stockouts, and the expenses involved with production interruptions caused by inventory shortages all fall as order quantity increases.

PROFIT+ includes a routine that uses the EOQ model discussed in most introductory financial management textbooks—the basic EOQ model. The model is referred to as being basic because of the assumptions made in its development, namely:

1. Sales can be forecasted perfectly.
2. Sales are evenly distributed throughout the year.
3. Orders are received with no delays whatever.

These assumptions may appear to be rather rigid, but you should remember that a major reason for holding safety stocks is to provide a buffer for times when your assumptions are incorrect. (Furthermore, more complex models have been developed that allow their users to take into consideration such factors as seasonal variations in sales and the costs of outages and shipment delays.)

The basic EOQ model takes the following form:

$$EOQ = \sqrt{\frac{2FS}{CP}} \tag{13.1}$$

where	EOQ	=	optimum quantity to be ordered each time an order is placed
	F	=	fixed costs of placing and receiving an order
	S	=	annual sales in units
	C	=	carrying cost expressed as a percentage of inventory value
	P	=	purchase price our firm must pay per unit of inventory.

In this formula, the costs that rise as order size increases are lumped together and referred to as carrying costs, and the fixed costs of placing and receiving an order are the only costs considered to decline as order size increases (they decline since greater order size means fewer orders placed per year). Where necessary, more detailed models exist for including other types of costs.

Number of Orders per Year

You can calculate the number of orders that will be placed per year for an item by dividing total annual usage by EOQ.

$$\text{Number of Orders/Year} = \frac{\text{Usage (or sales) in units}}{\text{EOQ}} \tag{13.2}$$

Order Frequency

Once the number of orders per year has been calculated, you can determine how frequently orders will be placed by dividing the approximate number of days in a year (360) by the number of orders per year.

$$\text{Order Frequency} = \frac{360}{\text{Number of orders/Year}} \tag{13.3}$$

Average Inventory

EOQ is a prime determinant of both the average inventory and the average investment in any item of inventory. Just after an order is received, the amount of inventory on hand is equal to the EOQ, and it will decline to zero just before the next order arrives. If you assume a constant usage (or sales) rate, average inventory can be calculated by dividing EOQ by 2.

$$\text{Average Inventory} = \frac{\text{EOQ}}{2} \tag{13.4}$$

Since EOQ is expressed in numbers of units of inventory, you can easily obtain the average dollar investment in inventory by multiplying average inventory by the purchase price per item of inventory.

When a safety stock of a particular item is normally held, average inventory must be increased by that amount. Thus, the formula for determining average inventory where safety stocks are present is

$$\text{Average Inventory} = \frac{\text{EOQ}}{2} + \text{Safety stock.} \tag{13.5}$$

Reorder Point

In most cases, it takes anywhere from several days to several weeks to receive an order of inventory once it has been placed. Given this fact, any inventory management scheme should include an estimate of the reorder point for each item of inventory. The reorder point is the inventory level at which another order (of an amount = EOQ) must be placed. It is calculated by multiplying the order lead time (the number of days it takes to receive an order) times the average daily usage or sales of the item (total annual usage or sales/360).

$$\text{Reorder Point} = (\text{Order lead time in days}) \times (\text{Average daily usage}) \qquad \textbf{(13.6)}$$

THE PROFIT+ ECONOMIC ORDER QUANTITY ROUTINE

Option K, Economic Order Quantity, on the PROFIT+ Main Menu is a routine for calculating EOQ, average units of inventory, average investment in inventory, number of orders per year, order frequency, and reorder point. To compute each of these items, PROFIT+ uses Equations 13.1 through 13.6. As usual, your PROFIT+ software also gives you the opportunity to ask "what if?" questions that change these initial assumptions.

Exhibit 13.1 shows how the PROFIT+ Economic Order Quantity routine can be used to solve the following sample problem:

Sample Problem: Waldo Hemingway, inventory manager for Colonial Books Company, has obtained the following information on inventory item #2978:

Annual sales	*2500 units*
Purchase price per unit....................................	*$1.56*
Carrying cost as a percent of purchase price	*20%*
Cost per order placed.	*$30.00*
Desired safety stock (currently on hand)	*200 units*
Order lead time...	*7 days*

a. *What is the EOQ for item #2978?*

b. *What is the average number of units of the item that Colonial Books will have on hand at any one time?*

c. What is Colonial Books' average dollar investment in this item of inventory?

d. How many orders should the firm place for this item each year? How frequently does this mean the company will be placing orders for item #2978?

e. What is the reorder point for the item? (i.e., Colonial Books should place an order for the EOQ of the item when the number of items in stock falls to what level?)

SUMMARY

This chapter has given you a basic model that can be of use in inventory management. Perhaps even more important than the model itself are the factors that have been included in its development. Having a basic knowledge of these factors should help you acquire a better understanding of the considerations that are involved with inventory management. Once you have gained this knowledge, you can more easily comprehend models that are more sophisticated and deal with more complex, real-world inventory management problems.

Exhibit 13.1

```
PROFIT+                                                      PROFIT+
              E C O N O M I C   O R D E R   Q U A N T I T Y

Unit Sales per Year ...... 2500        Fixed Costs per Order ....       30.00
Carrying Costs as a                    Safety Stock in Units ....         200
  % of Inventory Value ...     20.00   Order Lead Time in Days ..           7
Purchase Price per Unit ..      1.56

           Economic Order Quantity (EOQ) ......          694
           Average Units of Inventory .........          547
           Average Investment in Inventory ....       853.32
           Number of Orders per Year ..........            4
           Reorder Point in Units .............          249

      An order for     694  units should be placed every  99 days.

 [F1]=HELP  [F2]=REVIEW  [F3]=CALC  [F5]=REDO  [F9]=PRINT  [ESC]=MENU
```

END-OF-CHAPTER PROBLEMS

1. The following facts have been obtained for an item of inventory that your firm stocks:

Annual sales	240,000 units
Carrying cost as a percent of purchase price	30 %
Purchase price per unit	$2.40
Fixed costs of placing an order..............................	$50.00
Desired safety stock (currently on hand)....................	4000 units
Order lead time	5 days

a. What is the EOQ for this item?

b. What should be the average inventory of this item?

c. What should be your firm's average dollar investment in this item of inventory?

d. How many orders for the item should be placed each year?

e. What is the order frequency for the item?

f. At what inventory level should a reorder be made?

g. How would each of the following affect your answers to parts a through f above? (Note: Treat each of these changes separately. They are not meant to have a cumulative effect. Remember to use PROFIT+'s "what if?" capabilities to answer these questions.)

i. Annual sales are expected to be 500,000 units

ii. Carrying costs are 20 percent

iii. The item's purchase price is $5

iv. Safety stock is 2500 units

2. PPT Company is expecting the demand for its model A24 orange peeler to double next year and is attempting to determine how this change will affect its current inventory management policies for the item. The information necessary to help the company answer this question is given on the next page. Using this information, determine how each of the following factors will be affected by the changes expected to accompany the increased demand: EOQ, average inventory, average investment in inventory, number of orders per year, order frequency, and reorder point.

	This Year	Next Year
Sales (in units)	5000	10,000
Purchase price per unit	$9.90	$8.50
Carrying cost as a % of purchase price	22 %	22 %
Fixed cost per order placed	$40.00	$40.00
Desired safety stock	250.0	500.0
Order lead time	21 days	14 days

3. The following information has been obtained for an item of inventory that Newline Products Corporation sells:

Annual sales	50,000 units
Carrying cost as a percent of purchase price	25 %
Purchase price per unit	$6.35
Fixed costs of placing an order	$75.00
Desired safety stock (currently on hand)	1500 units
Order lead time	14 days

a. What is the EOQ for this item?

b. What should be the average inventory of this item?

c. What should be your firm's average dollar investment in this item of inventory?

d. How many orders for the item should be placed each year?

e. What is the order frequency for the item?

f. At what inventory level should a reorder be made?

g. How would each of the following affect your answers to parts a through f above? (Note: Treat each of these changes separately. They are not meant to have a cumulative effect.)

i. Annual sales are expected to be 70,000 units

ii. Carrying costs are 30 percent

iii. The item's purchase price is $8.00

iv. Safety stock is 2,000 units

4. The Chocolate Milk Company purchases and then sells (as chocolate milk) 5 million pounds of cocoa per year. Ordering costs, which include storage facility removal charges of $1,000, are $1,500 per order. Annual carrying costs are 5 percent of the purchase price per pound of $1.12. The company maintains a safety stock of 100,000 pounds. The order lead time is 35 days.

a. What is the EOQ?

b. What should be the average inventory?

c. What should be the firm's average dollar investment in cocoa?

d. How many orders for cocoa should be placed each year?

e. How often should an order for cocoa be placed?

f. At what inventory level should a reorder be made?

5. You have gathered the following information regarding a particular product that your firm sells:

Annual sales	20,000 units
Carrying cost as a percent of purchase price	10 %
Purchase price per unit	$57.60
Fixed costs of placing an order	$150.00
Desired safety stock (currently on hand)	200 units
Order lead time	14 days

a. What is the EOQ for this product?

b. What should be the average inventory of this product?

c. What should be your firm's average dollar investment in this product?

d. How many orders for the product should be placed each year?

e. What is the order frequency for the product?

f. At what inventory level should a reorder be made?

g. How would each of the following affect your answers to parts a through f above? (Note: Treat each of these changes separately. They are not meant to have a cumulative effect.)

i. Annual sales are expected to be 30,000 units
ii. Carrying costs are 15 percent
iii. The product's purchase price is $50
iv. Safety stock is 500 units

6. Balls and Bats Sporting Goods Company sells 4,500 baseballs per year. The optimal safety stock (which is currently on hand) is 100 balls. Each ball cost Balls and Bats $4.12, inventory carrying costs are 5 percent, the cost of placing an order with the factory is $15, and the order lead time is 7 days.

a. What is the EOQ for the baseballs?

b. What should be the average inventory of the baseballs?

c. What should be your firm's average dollar investment in the baseballs?

d. How many orders for the baseballs should be placed each year?

e. What is the order frequency for the baseballs?

f. At what inventory level should a reorder be made?

7. The following inventory data have been accumulated for G. Swales Company: annual sales are 450,000 units; the purchase price per unit is $7.50; carrying costs are 18 percent of the purchase price; cost per order placed is $20; the desired safety stock (presently on hand) is 25,000 units; and 10 days is the order lead time.

a. What is the EOQ for this product?

b. What should be the average inventory of this product?

c. What should be your firm's average dollar investment in this product?

d. How many orders for the product should be placed each year?

e. What is the order frequency for the product?

f. At what inventory level should a reorder be made?

g. How would each of the following affect your answers to parts a through f above? (Note: Treat each of these changes separately. They are not meant to have a cumulative effect.)

i. Annual sales are expected to be 530,000 units

ii. Order costs are $50

iii. The product's purchase price is $7

iv. Safety stock is 50,000 units

v. Order lead time is 21 days

8. The following relationships for inventory costs have been determined for product number 11233ZZ used by the Mochan Corporation:

Annual sales	120,000 units
Carrying cost as a percent of purchase price	15 %
Purchase price per unit	$2.00
Fixed costs of placing an order	$40.00
Desired safety stock (currently on hand)	10,000 units
Order lead time	7 days

a. What is the most economical order quantity?

b. What should be the average inventory of this product?

c. What should be your firm's average dollar investment in this product?

d. How many orders for the product should be placed each year?

e. What is the order frequency for the product?

f. At what inventory level should a reorder be made?

g. If annual unit sales double, what is the percent increase in EOQ? What is the elasticity of EOQ with respect to sales (i.e., the percent change in EOQ divided by the percent change in sales)?

h. Keeping all other factors at their initial values, if the fixed costs per order double, what is the elasticity of EOQ with respect to cost per order?

i. Keeping all other factors at their initial values, if the carrying cost declines by 50 percent, what is the elasticity of EOQ with respect to carrying costs?

j. Keeping all other factors at their initial values, if the purchase price per unit declines by 50 percent, what is the elasticity of EOQ with respect to purchase price?

k. Of what value is it to managers to know the answers to parts g through j?

Chapter Fourteen
Credit Policy Analysis

According to *Essentials of Managerial Finance*, 8th ed., by J. Fred Weston and Eugene F. Brigham, approximately 20 percent of the typical manufacturing firm's assets are invested in accounts receivable, which are created when a business sells on credit. Therefore, financial managers must stay attuned to their firms' receivables management policies.

Receivables, or credit, management is a many-faceted endeavor that is just as much related to the marketing policies of the firm as it is to the firm's financial policies. Because of this, it is beyond the scope of this guide to review all the fundamentals of credit management. Instead, this chapter focuses on analyzing the projected effects on net income of changes in credit policy variables.

CREDIT POLICY VARIABLES

One of the primary factors that determines whether a firm sells its products is its credit policy. A firm's credit policy results from managements' decisions regarding four credit policy variables:

1. The credit period, or length of time that customers have before they must pay for their purchases.

2. The firm's credit standards; that is, its decision regarding the minimum financial quality of customers to whom it will extend credit.

3 . The firm's collection policy, or how aggressively it seeks payment on overdue accounts.

4 . Cash discounts extended for early payment.

In general, easing any or all of these credit policy variables will stimulate sales. On the other hand, these increased sales will come at a cost. Loosening credit standards, for example, will stimulate more sales because more customers can be approved for credit. These additional customers will be of lower financial quality, however, and will most likely raise bad debt expenses, receivables carrying costs (the average receivable will be outstanding longer), and collection expenses. Whether the decision to relax credit standards will prove to be a good one depends on whether the additional revenues generated by the higher sales outweigh the increased costs of extending credit to lower-quality customers. To restate this in more general terms, the primary question in evaluating a proposed change in credit policy is this: Will increased revenues resulting from the change be more than the increased costs, thus causing net income to increase, or will the greater costs overshadow any increased revenues?

CREDIT POLICY ANALYSIS

Exhibit 14.1 summarizes the general idea behind credit policy analysis. It is taken from Table 12-2 and the accompanying discussion in *Essentials of Managerial Finance,* 8th ed., by J. Fred Weston and Eugene F. Brigham, and is based on the information in the next several paragraphs.

Column 1 shows the projected 1988 income statement for Mitchell Office Equipment Company under the assumption that the firm's present credit policy is maintained throughout the year. Excess capacity exists, so sales could be increased without adding either new plant or general overhead expense. Column 2 shows the expected effects of easing credit policy by extending the credit period, offering larger discounts, relaxing credit standards, and easing collection efforts. Specifically, Mitchell is analyzing the effects of changing its credit terms from 1/10, net 30, to 2/10, net 40, relaxing its credit standards, and putting less pressure on slow-paying customers. Column 3 shows the projected 1988 income statement incorporating the expected effects of the relaxed credit policy. In general, the analysis shows that while the looser policy will lead to increased sales and lower collection costs, it will also cause increases in discounts and several other types of costs. The overall projected net effect is that the change will increase Mitchell's net

Exhibit 14.1

Mitchell Office Equipment Company
Analysis of Suggested Credit Policy Change
(in millions of dollars)

	Projected 1988 Income Statement under Present Policy (1)	Effect of Change (2)	Projected 1988 Income Statement Under New Policy (3)
Gross Sales	$400.0	+ $130.0	$530.0
Less Discounts	2.0	+ 4.0	6.0
Net Sales	$398.0	+ $126.0	$524.0
Less Production Costs, including Overhead	280.0	+ 91.0	371.0
Gross Profit before Credit Costs	$118.0	+ $ 35.0	$153.0
Less Credit-Related Costs:			
Carrying Costs	3.3	1.6	4.9
Credit Analysis and Collection Expenses	5.0	- 3.0	2.0
Bad Debt Losses	10.0	+ 21.8	31.8
Opportunity Cost	0	+ .2	.2
Gross Profit	$ 99.7	+ $ 14.4	$114.1
Less Taxes (40%)	39.9	+ 5.7	45.6
Net Income	$ 59.8	+ 8.7	$ 68.5

costs. The overall projected net effect is that the change will increase Mitchell's net income by $8.7 million. The subsequent paragraphs explain how the figures in the table were determined.

If the present credit policy is maintained, annual sales will be $400 million. Under the current policy, 50 percent of paying customers pay on day 10 and take the cash discount, 40 percent pay on the thirtieth day, and 10 percent pay on day 40. Mitchell's average collection period under the present policy is (0.50)(10) + (0.40)(30) + (0.10)(40) = 21 days.

Mitchell presently spends $5 million per year to analyze and collect bad debts, but in spite of these efforts, 2.5 percent of sales will never be collected. Thus, bad debt losses under the present policy are (0.025) ($400,000,000) = $10 million. The firm's cash collections will also be reduced by the amount of cash discounts taken. Since 50 percent of customers who pay (100% - 2.5% = 97.5% of all customers pay) take the 1 percent cash discount, discounts equal ($400,000,000)(0.50)(0.975)(0.01) = $1,950,000, or approximately $2 million. Total sales are multiplied by (1 - bad debt ratio) to get collected sales, and collected sales are then multiplied by the discount.

The annual carrying cost for receivables is obtained by multiplying the average amount of receivables times the variable cost percentage times the cost of money used to carry receivables. The average amount of receivables is equal to the average collection period (ACP) times sales per day. Mitchell's average collection period is 21 days (as calculated above), its variable cost ratio is 70 percent (the percentage is multiplied times sales to get production costs), and the cost of funds invested in receivables is 20 percent. Given this information, Mitchell's cost of carrying receivables under its present credit policy is calculated as follows:

$$\text{Cost of Carrying Receivables} = \text{ACP} \times \text{Sales per day} \times \text{Variable cost ratio} \times \text{Cost of funds}$$

$$= (21) \times \frac{\$400{,}000{,}000}{360} \times (0.70) \times (0.20)$$

$$= \$3{,}266{,}667$$

or approximately $3.3 million

Only variable costs enter into the calculation, since they are the only costs that must be financed as a result of a change in the credit policy. If a new customer purchases $100 worth of goods, Mitchell will only have $70 invested ($100 x .70 variable cost ratio) in them. Thus, it will have to finance only $70 although its receivables increase by $100.

Mitchell's proposed new policy includes a greater discount, a longer payment period, a relaxed collection effort, and decreased credit standards. Management projects that these changes will cause sales to increase to $530 million per year.

Estimates are that, under the new policy, 60 percent of customers that pay will take the 2 percent cash discount, and that bad debt losses will increase to 6 percent; therefore, discounts will be (\$530,000,000)(0.60)(0.94)(0.02) = \$5,978,400 or approximately \$6 million. Bad debt expenses will be (\$530,000,000)(0.06) = \$31,800,000. Twenty percent of paying customers will pay on the fortieth day, while the remaining 20 percent will pay on day 50. This means that the average collection period under the proposed new policy will be (0.60)(10) + (0.20)(40) + (0.20)(50) = 24 days. The cost of carrying receivables under the new policy will increase to approximately \$4.9 million due to the longer average collection period and the higher level of sales. The carrying cost calculation is as follows:

$$\text{Carrying Costs} = (24) \times \frac{530{,}000{,}000}{360} \times (0.70) \times (0.20) = \$4.9 \text{ million}$$

Opportunity costs will arise if the new policy is instituted, because Mitchell will have to wait longer to receive the profit from the goods it sells. The dollar amount of this opportunity cost is determined by multiplying the old sales per day times the change in ACP times the contribution margin (i.e., 1 - variable cost ratio) times the cost of funds invested in receivables.

$$\text{Opportunity Cost} = \frac{\text{Old Sales}}{360} \times \begin{matrix}\text{Change}\\ \text{in}\\ \text{ACP}\end{matrix} \times (1 - v) \times \begin{matrix}\text{Cost}\\ \text{of}\\ \text{funds}\end{matrix}$$

$$= \frac{\$400{,}000{,}000}{360} \times (3) \times (0.30) \times (0.20)$$

$$= \$0.2 \text{ million.}$$

Mitchell's management expects that the lower credit standards and a more lenient collection policy will reduce the firm's annual credit analysis and collection expenditures to \$2 million from their present \$5 million level. In contrast to this decreased cost, however, will be the increased bad debt losses of (\$530,000,000)(0.06) = \$32 million.

As can be seen from Exhibit 14.1, when all of these effects are taken together, the net projected impact of the proposed change in credit policy is that net income should increase by \$8.7 million. The change, therefore, should be instituted if management is reasonably confident in these projections.

Exhibit 14.2

PROFIT+ PROFIT+

CREDIT POLICY ANALYSIS

	Present Policy	New Policy
Gross Sales	400.0	530.0
Cash Discount Percentage (%)	1	2
Bad Debts Percentage (%)	2.5	6.0
Current Policy:		
Percentage of Paying Customers Paying on Day 10 ..	50	
Percentage of Paying Customers Paying on Day 30 ..	40	
Percentage of Paying Customers Paying on Day 40 ..	10	
New Policy:		
Percentage of Paying Customers Paying on Day 10 ..		60
Percentage of Paying Customers Paying on Day 40 ..		20
Percentage of Paying Customers Paying on Day 50 ..		20
Cost of Carrying Receivables (%)	20	20
Credit Analysis and Collection Expenses	5.0	2.0
Variable Cost Ratio (%)	70	70
Tax Rate (%)	40	40

[PGDN]=PROJECTED INCOME STATEMENTS

[F1]=HELP [F2]=REVIEW [F5]=REDO [F9]=PRINT [ESC]=MENU

THE PROFIT+ CREDIT POLICY ANALYSIS ROUTINE

Option L, Credit Policy Analysis, on the PROFIT+ Main Menu is a routine designed to undertake analyses similar to the one discussed in the preceding paragraphs. Exhibits 14.2 and 14.3 show how the routine can be used to produce the results that were discussed above.

SUMMARY

While quantitative discussions such as the one contained in this chapter appear to be rather straightforward, there are many factors that complicate such an analysis in real-world situations. The most important of these factors is the uncertainty involved with the projections of the effects that changing credit policy will have on the firm. As with so many other decisions in business, the reliability of the output from the credit policy analysis depends on the accuracy of the projections used to generate it.

Exhibit 14.3

PROFIT+ PROFIT+

CREDIT POLICY ANALYSIS

PROJECTED INCOME STATEMENTS

	Present Policy	Effect of Change	New Policy
Gross Sales	400.0	130.0	530.0
Less Discounts	2.0	4.0	6.0
Net Sales	398.0	126.0	524.0
Production Costs, including Overhead	280.0	91.0	371.0
Gross Profit before Credit Costs	118.0	35.0	153.0
Credit-related Costs:			
Cost of Carrying Receivables	3.3	1.6	4.9
Credit Analysis and Collection Expenses ..	5.0	-3.0	2.0
Bad Debt Losses	10.0	21.8	31.8
Opportunity Cost of Credit Policy Change .		0.2	0.2
Gross Profit	99.7	14.4	114.1
Taxes	39.9	5.7	45.6
Net Income	59.8	8.7	68.5

[PGUP]=INPUT DATA

[F1]=HELP [F2]=REVIEW [F5]=REDO [F9]=PRINT [ESC]=MENU

END-OF-CHAPTER PROBLEMS

1. Your boss has given you the following information regarding a change in the firm's credit policy that he is considering. You have been asked to generate a projected income statement for next year for both the present and the new credit policy, and to show the difference between the two projections. What advice would you give your boss regarding the proposed change? Use your PROFIT+ Credit Policy Analysis routine to assist you with this analysis.

	Present Policy	New Policy
Gross Sales..	$300	$350
Cash Discount Percentage	2	3
Bad Debts Percentage	3	5
Current Policy:		
Percentage of Paying Customers Paying on Day 10.....	40	
Percentage of Paying Customers Paying on Day 30.....	40	
Percentage of Paying Customers Paying on Day 40.....	20	

	Present Policy	New Policy
New Policy:		
Percentage of Paying Customers Paying on Day 10.....		60
Percentage of Paying Customers Paying on Day 40.....		25
Percentage of Paying Customers Paying on Day 50.....		15
Cost of Carrying Receivables (%)	15	15
Credit Analysis and Collection Expenses	10	8
Variable Cost Ratio (%)	70	70
Tax Rate (%)	40	40

2. Use the information in the following table to answer the following questions:

a. What effect would the new credit policy have on the firm's bad debt expenses?

b. What effect would the new credit policy have on the cost of carrying receivables?

c. Should the new policy be instituted? Why or why not?

	Present Policy	New Policy
Gross Sales	$15	$17
Cash Discount Percentage	1	2
Bad Debts Percentage	2	3.5
Current Policy:		
Percentage of Paying Customers Paying on Day 10....	15	
Percentage of Paying Customers Paying on Day 30....	60	
Percentage of Paying Customers Paying on Day 40....	25	
New Policy:		
Percentage of Paying Customers Paying on Day 10....		50
Percentage of Paying Customers Paying on Day 30....		20
Percentage of Paying Customers Paying on Day 45....		30
Cost of Carrying Receivables (%)	14	14
Credit Analysis and Collection Expenses	2	1.7
Variable Cost Ratio (%)	67	67
Tax Rate (%)	38	38

3. Microlize Microchips Corporation is considering changing its credit terms from 1/15, net 30, to 2/15, net 30, to speed collections. Currently, 40 percent of Microlize's paying customers take the 1 percent discount and pay on day 15, 30 percent pay on day 30, and the remaining 30 percent pay on day 40. Under the proposed terms, management estimates that 65 percent of paying customers will take advantage of the 2 percent discount, 20 percent will pay on day 30, while the remaining 15 percent will pay on day 40. Since the change does not involve an easing of credit standards, bad debt losses should remain at their present 1.5 percent of sales. Credit analysis and collection expenses under both policies should also remain a constant $1 million. Management estimates that in addition to speeding collections, the increased discount should raise sales to $40 million from their present $37 million level. The firm's variable cost ratio is 70 percent, its cost of funds invested in receivables is 15 percent, and its average tax rate is 38 percent.

a. What are the projected discount costs before and after the change?

b. What is the dollar cost of carrying receivables before and after the change?

c. What is the dollar opportunity cost associated with the change?

d. What is the bad debt loss before and after the change?

e. What is the projected incremental profit from the change in credit terms?

f. Should Microlize institute the change? Why or why not?

g. If the sales projection under the new terms is lowered to $37.5 million, should Microlize change its credit policy? Why or why not?

4. Justin Corporation is considering changing its credit terms from 1/10, net 30, to 2/10, net 40, and relaxing its credit standards in order to promote sales. Currently, 40 percent of Justin's paying customers take the 1 percent discount and pay on day 10, 30 percent pay on day 30, and the remaining 30 percent pay on day 40. Under the proposed terms, management estimates that 55 percent of paying customers will take advantage of the 2 percent discount and pay on day 10, 15 percent will pay on day 40, while the remaining 30 percent will pay on day 50. Under the change, bad debt losses should increase from their present 1.5 percent of sales to 4 percent of sales. Credit analysis and collection expenses under the old policy were $3 million, but relaxing of standards should reduce them to $1.5 million. Management estimates that the increased discount, when coupled with the longer net period and relaxed credit standards, should raise sales to $100 million from their present $80 million level. The firm's variable cost ratio is 68 percent, its cost of funds invested in receivables is 12 percent, and its average tax rate is 40 percent.

a. What are the projected discount costs before and after the change?

b. What is the dollar cost of carrying receivables before and after the change?

c. What is the dollar opportunity cost associated with the change?

d. What is the bad debt loss before and after the change?

e. What is the projected incremental profit from the change in credit terms?

f. Should Justin institute the change?

g. If the sales projection under the new terms is lowered to $90 million, should Justin change its credit policy?

h. Under the assumption that sales under the new terms are at the original $100 million level, should Justin change its credit policy if management increased the projected bad debt percentage under the new policy to 6 percent?

i. Under the original set of assumptions, just how low would the sales projection under the new policy have to be to make the change unattractive?

5. Catelyn O'Hare, credit manager for Markco Corporation, is considering changing her firm's credit terms from 1/15, net 40, to 3/10, net 30. Currently, 20 percent of Markco's paying customers take the 1 percent discount and pay on day 15, 50 percent pay on day 40, and the remaining 30 percent pay on day 60. Under the proposed terms, O'Hare estimates that 65 percent of paying customers will take advantage of the 3 percent discount and pay on day 10, 25 percent will pay on day 30, while the remaining 10 percent will pay on day 40. Under the change, bad debt losses should remain at their present 1.5 percent of sales. Credit analysis and collection expenses under the old policy were $2 million and will remain at approximately that level under the new terms. O'Hare estimates that the increased discount should raise sales to $50 million from their present $45 million level, even though the net period will be decreased. O'Hare has also determined that the firm's variable cost ratio is 70 percent, its cost of funds invested in receivables is 15 percent, and its average tax rate is 40 percent.

a. What are the projected discount costs before and after the change?

b. What is the dollar cost of carrying receivables before and after the change?

c. What is the dollar opportunity cost associated with the change?

d. What is the bad debt loss before and after the change?

e. What is the projected incremental profit from the change in credit terms?

f. Should O'Hare proceed with the change? Why or why not?

g. Assume that O'Hare has just received additional information from Markco's director of marketing that leads her to believe that sales will only increase to $47 million if the proposed credit policy is instituted. Will this information have any effect on her decision regarding the change? Why or why not?

6. Idea Retrieval, Inc., expects to have sales of $20 million this year under its present operating (including credit) policies. Its variable cost ratio is 75 percent, and its cost of funds invested in receivables is 15 percent. The firm's present credit policy is net 30 (no discount for early payment). However, its average collection period is 40 days (50 percent of paying customers pay on day 30, and the remaining 50 percent pay on day 50), and its bad debts loss percentage is 2 percent. The company spends $100,000 per year on credit analysis and collecting bad debts. Its average tax rate is 40 percent.

Kelly John Swift, Idea Retrieval's credit manager, is considering two alternative proposals, outlined below, for changing the firm's credit policy. Find the expected change in net income, taking into consideration anticipated changes in carrying costs for accounts receivable, the probable bad debt losses, and the discounts likely to be taken for each proposal. Which, if either, of the proposed changes should be instituted?

Proposal A: Lengthen the credit period by going from net 30 to net 40. The credit analysis and collection expenses will remain constant. Under this proposal, Swift projects that sales will increase by $2 million, and the bad debts percentage will increase to 2.5 percent. Swift also estimates that the average collection period will increase to 50 days (50 percent of paying customers will pay on day 40, and 50 percent will pay on day 60).

Proposal B: Shorten the credit period by going from net 30 to net 25. Again, credit analysis and collection expenses will remain constant. Swift estimates that this change will cause sales to decrease by $2 million, will result in a decline in the bad debts percentage to 1.5 percent, and will reduce the average collection period from 40 to 30 days (50 percent of paying customers doing so on day 25, and 50 percent paying on day 35).

Chapter Fifteen
Cash Budgeting

CASH BUDGETING

One of the primary cash management tools used by financial managers is the cash budget. It is a statement that shows a firm's projected cash inflows and outflows over a given period of time, along with estimates of how much borrowing will have to be done to maintain the optimum cash balance and/or how much surplus cash will be available for temporary (or permanent) investment. In this chapter, you will review the basics of cash budgeting and then learn how the PROFIT+ Cash Budgeting routine can assist in preparing the types of cash budgets that are encountered in the typical introductory financial management class.

A Sample Cash Budget

The best way to understand what is included in a cash budget is to go through the process of preparing one. The following paragraphs include a discussion of how Melnyk Toy Company, a leading producer of games, dolls, stuffed animals, and toys, prepared its cash budget for the last six months of 1987. This example is taken from Chapter 9 of *Essentials of Managerial Finance*, 8th ed., by J. Fred Weston and Eugene F. Brigham.

Melnyk's products are sold year-round, but most of the company's sales are generated in September, when retailers are stocking up for Christmas. All sales are made on terms that allow a 2 percent cash discount for payments made within 20 days. If the discount is not taken, the full amount must be paid in 40 days.

However, like most other companies, Melnyk finds that some of its customers delay payment up to 90 days. Experience shows that payment is made on 20 percent of sales during the month in which the sale is made. On 70 percent of sales, payment is made during the first month following the sale, and on 10 percent of sales, payment is made during the second month after the sale.

Instead of producing at a constant rate throughout the year, Melnyk manufactures its games and toys immediately before they are required for delivery. Raw materials, component parts, and other materials amount to 70 percent of sales and are purchased the month prior to that in which the firm expects to sell the finished products. Its own purchase terms allow Melnyk to delay payment on its purchases for one month. Therefore, if July sales are forecast at $10 million, purchases during June will amount to $7 million, and this amount will actually be paid in July.

Other cash expenditures such as wages and rent are given in the lower part of Exhibit 15.1. The company must also make tax payments of $2 million on September 15 and December 15, while payment for a new plant must be made in October. Assuming the company needs to keep a minimum cash balance of $2.5 million at all times and that it has $3 million on July 1, what are Melnyk's financial requirements and/or estimated cash surpluses for the period July through December? The firm's monthly cash requirements are shown in Exhibit 15.1. The top portion of the exhibit provides a worksheet for calculating estimated collections on sales and payments on purchases. The first line in the worksheet gives the sales forecast for the period May through December; May and June sales are necessary to determine the collections for July and August. Next, estimates of cash collections are given. The first line of this section shows that 20 percent of the sales during any given month are collected that month (less the 2 percent cash discount). The second line shows the collections on the prior month's sales: 70 percent of the sales in the preceding month. The third line gives collections from sales two months earlier: 10 percent of sales in that month. Finally, the collections are added to determine the total projected cash receipts from sales during each month.

Following the collections worksheet, the cash budget itself is constructed. Receipts from collections are given on the top line. Next, payments during each month are summarized. The difference between cash receipts and cash payments is the net cash gain or loss during the month. For example, in July there is a projected net cash loss of $2.14 million. The initial cash on hand at the beginning of the month is added to the net cash gain or loss during the month to obtain the cumulative cash that would be on hand if no financing (i.e., borrowing) were done. At the end of July, for instance, Melnyk would have cumulative cash totaling $860,000. The cumulative cash is next subtracted from the target cash balance, $2.5 million, to determine the firm's borrowing requirements or surplus cash, whichever the case may be. (If cumulative cash is less than the target balance, the

Exhibit 15.1
Melnyk Toy Company: Worksheet and Cash Budget (thousands of dollars)

	May	June	July	Aug.	Sept.	Oct.	Nov.	Dec.
I. Worksheet								
Sales (gross)[a]	$5,000	$5,000	$10,000	$15,000	$20,000	$10,000	$10,000	$5,000
Collections:								
During month of sales (20% less 2% discount)	980	980	1,960	2,940	3,920	1,960	1,960	980
During first month after sale month (70%)		3,500	3,500	7,000	10,500	14,000	7,000	7,000
During second month after sale month (10%)			500	500	1,000	1,500	2,000	1,000
Total collections	$ 980	$4,480	$ 5,960	$10,440	$15,420	$17,460	$10,960	$8,980
Purchases (70% of next month's gross sales)	$3,500	$7,000	$10,500	$14,000	$ 7,000	$ 7,000	$ 3,500	
Payments (1-month lag)		$3,500	$ 7,000	$10,500	$14,000	$ 7,000	$ 7,000	$3,500
II. Cash Budget								
(1) Collections (from worksheet)			$ 5,960	$10,440	$15,420	$17,460	$10,960	$8,980
(2) Payments:								
(3) Purchases (from worksheet)			$ 7,000	$10,500	$14,000	$ 7,000	$ 7,000	$3,500
(4) Wages and salaries			750	1,000	1,250	750	750	500
(5) Rent			250	250	250	250	250	250
(6) Other expenses			100	150	200	100	100	50
(7) Taxes					2,000			2,000
(8) Payment for plant construction						5,000		
(9) Total payments			$ 8,100	$11,900	$17,700	$13,100	$ 8,100	$6,300
(10) Net cash gain (loss) during month (Line 1 − Line 9)			($ 2,140)	($ 1,460)	($ 2,280)	$ 4,360	$ 2,860	$2,680
(11) Cash at start of month if no borrowing is done (started July with $3,000; calculated thereafter)[b]			3,000	860	(600)	(2,880)	1,480	4,340
(12) Cumulative cash (= cash at start + gains or − losses = Line 10 + Line 11)			$ 860	($ 600)	($ 2,880)	$ 1,480	$ 4,340	$7,020
(13) Target cash balance (assumed)			2,500	2,500	2,500	2,500	2,500	2,500
(14) Total loans outstanding required to maintain $2,500 target cash balance if Line 13 exceeds Line 12: Line 13 − Line 12[c]			$ 1,640	$ 3,100	$ 5,380	$ 1,020	—	—
(15) Surplus cash if Line 12 exceeds Line 13: Line 12 − Line 13[c]			—	—	—	—	$ 1,840	$4,520

[a] Although the budget period is July through December, sales and purchases data for May and June are needed to determine collections and payouts during July and August.

[b] The amount shown on Line 11 for the first budget period month, the $3,000 balance on July 1, is assumed to be on hand initially. The values shown for each of the following months on Line 11 represent the cumulative cash as shown on Line 12 for the preceding month; for example, the $860 shown on Line 11 for August is taken from Line 12 in the July column.

[c] When the target cash balance of $2,500 (Line 13) is subtracted from the cumulative cash balance (Line 12), a resulting negative figure is shown on Line 14 as a required loan, while a positive figure is shown on Line 15 as surplus cash.

firm must borrow, whereas if it is greater than the target, there will be surplus cash.) In July, Melnyk expects to have cumulative cash of $860,000, as shown on line 12. Since its target cash balance is $2.5 million, the firm is projecting that it will have to borrow $1.64 million ($2,500,000 - $860,000 = $1,640,000) by the end of July to bring the cash balance up to the target level. If this amount is borrowed, loans outstanding will total $1.64 million at the end of July.

This same procedure is used in the following months. Sales will expand seasonally in August. With the increased sales will come increased payments for purchases, wages, and other items. Receipts from sales will go up also, but the firm still will be left with a $1.46 million net cash outflow (loss) for the month. The cumulative borrowing requirements at the end of August will be $3.1 million: the cumulative cash (-$600,000) plus the target cash balance ($2,500,000). The $3.1 million is also equal to the $1.64 million needed at the end of July plus the $1.46 million cash loss for August. Thus, loans outstanding will total $3.1 million at the end of August.

Sales peak in September, and the cash deficit during this month is projected to amount to another $2.28 million. The total borrowing requirements through September will increase to $5.38 million ($1.64 million from July, $1.46 million from August, and $2.28 million in September). Sales, purchases, and payments for past purchases are projected to decline sharply in October; collections should be the highest of any month because they reflect the high September sales. As a result, Melnyk projects a healthy $4.36 million cash gain during October. This gain can be used to pay off borrowing, so loans outstanding will decline by $4.36 million, to $1.02 million ($5.38 million - $4.36 million = $1.02 million).

Melnyk is projecting yet another cash gain in November, which will permit it to eliminate completely the need for borrowing. In fact, the company is expected to have $1.84 million in surplus cash (the cash gain of $2.86 million less the repayment of the remaining $1.02 million in loans outstanding) by the month's end, while another cash gain in December will increase the cash surplus to $4.52 million. With such a large amount of extra cash, Melnyk's treasurer will want to invest in interest-bearing securities or put the funds to use in some other way. Your financial management textbook discusses the types of investments that management might choose when it comes to using surplus cash.

Before proceeding with a discussion of PROFIT+'s cash budgeting software, it is important to make six points with respect to the cash budget that was developed for Melnyk Company:

1. To simplify the explanation, Melnyk's cash budget does not reflect interest on loans or income from the investment of surplus cash. Refinements to include these items could be added quite easily.

2. If cash inflows and outflows are not uniform during the month, we could be seriously understating or overstating Melnyk's financial needs. For example, if all payments must be made on the fifth of each month but collections come in uniformly throughout the month, then we would need to borrow much larger amounts than those shown in Exhibit 15.1. Preparing cash budgets on a daily basis can help identify such a problem.

3. Since depreciation is a noncash charge, it does not appear on the cash budget.

4. The target cash balance would probably be adjusted over time, rising and falling with seasonal patterns and with longer-term changes in the scale of the firm's operations.

5. If Melnyk had been a larger, multidivisional firm, then cash budgets developed by each division would have been consolidated into one overall corporate cash budget so as to make the most efficient use of cash by channeling it from divisions with excesses to those with deficits.

6. Finally, the cash budget represents a forecast; therefore, all the values in the exhibit are expected values. If actual sales, purchases, and so on are different from the forecasted levels, then our projected cash deficits and surpluses will also be incorrect.

Although all of the preceding points are important, it is the last one—that the cash budget is a forecast—that leads to the real worth of PROFIT+'s Cash Budgeting routine.

THE PROFIT+ CASH BUDGETING ROUTINE

PROFIT+ includes a routine (Option M, Cash Budgeting, on the Main Menu) for working with cash budgeting problems similar to the Melnyk Toy Company example. The routine is composed of two screens. On the first, you enter several basic assumptions regarding the budget that you are preparing: length of the budgetary period (three to six months); sales two months prior to the budgetary period; sales one month prior to the budgetary period; cash discount percentage; collection projections; and purchases as a percentage of next month's sales. The second screen is essentially a cash budgeting spreadsheet on which you must enter sales forecasts, expense estimates, the beginning cash balance, and the target cash

Exhibit 15.2

PROFIT+ CASH BUDGET PROFIT+

ASSUMPTIONS:

Length of Budgetary Period in Months (3 - 6) 6

Sales 2 Months Prior to Budgetary Period 5000

Sales 1 Month Prior to Budgetary Period 5000

Cash Discount Percentage (%) 2

Collections -- Percentage Collected During Month of Sale (%) 20
Percentage Collected 1 Month Following Sale (%) ... 70
Percentage Collected 2 Months Following Sale (%) .. 10

Purchases as a Percentage of Next Month's Sales (%) 70

[PGDN]=CASH BUDGET

[F1]=HELP [F2]=REVIEW [F3]=CALC [F5]=REDO [F9]=PRINT [ESC]=MENU

Exhibit 15.3

PROFIT+ CASH BUDGET PROFIT+

	MONTH 1	MONTH 2	MONTH 3	MONTH 4	MONTH 5	MONTH 6
Sales	10000	15000	20000	10000	10000	5000
Collections:						
Month of Sale	1960	2940	3920	1960	1960	980
1 mon. following	3500	7000	10500	14000	7000	7000
2 mon. following	500	500	1000	1500	2000	1000
Tot. Collections	5960	10440	15420	17460	10960	8980
Payments:						
Purchases	7000	10500	14000	7000	7000	3500
Wages & Salaries	750	1000	1250	750	750	500
Rent	250	250	250	250	250	250
Miscellaneous	100	150	200	100	100	50
Taxes	0	0	2000	0	0	2000
Other	0	0	0	5000	0	0
Total Payments	8100	11900	17700	13100	8100	6300
Net Gain / Loss (-) ..	-2140	-1460	-2280	4360	2860	2680
Beginning Cash	3000	860	-600	-2880	1480	4340
Cummulative Cash	860	-600	-2880	1480	4340	7020
Target Cash Balance ..	2500	2500	2500	2500	2500	2500
Tot. Loans Outstd. ...	1640	3100	5380	1020	0	0
Surplus Cash	0	0	0	0	1840	4520

[PGUP]=ASSUMPTIONS

[F1]=HELP [F2]=REVIEW [F3]=CALC [F5]=REDO [F9]=PRINT [ESC]=MENU

balance for each month. After these entries, PROFIT+ completes the budget. You are then free to subject the budget to sensitivity analysis by changing any of your assumptions and entries.

Exhibits 15.2 and 15.3 show how the PROFIT+ Cash Budgeting routine can be used to complete the cash budget for Melnyk Toy Company that was discussed earlier in this chapter.

SUMMARY

In this chapter you have reviewed the topic of cash budgeting and have learned how to use PROFIT+'s Cash Budgeting routine. Although PROFIT+'s routine is designed for a problem that is structured in a particular manner, it gives you a very practical, and easily understood, introduction to the basics of cash budgeting.

END-OF-CHAPTER PROBLEMS

1. Use the information in the following table to develop a cash budget for the first three months of 1988 for the Automation Corporation:

Sales for November 1987	$45,000
Sales for December 1987	$50,000
Cash Discount Percentage	2 %
Collection Estimates:	
Percentage collected during the month of sale	30 %
Percentage collected 1 month following sale	60 %
Percentage collected 2 months following sale	10 %
Purchases as a Percentage of Next Month's Sales	68 %

	January	February	March
Sales Forecasts:	$50,000	$60,000	$40,000
Payment Forecasts:			
Wages and salaries	5,000	5,000	5,000
Rent	3,500	3,500	4,000
Miscellaneous	1,000	1,000	1,000
Taxes	7,500		
Other	6,700		
Beginning Cash Balance	1,600		
Target Cash Balance	2,000	2,000	2,000

2. Use the information in the following table to prepare a cash budget for the first four months of 1988 for Telephone Marketing, Incorporated, and then modify the budget you have prepared to answer parts a through d of this question:

a. In an effort to speed up collections, Telephone's management is considering offering a 2 percent cash discount for early payment. If this is done, it is projected that 40 percent of a month's sales will be collected during the month of the sale (less the 2 percent discount), 50 percent will be collected the month following the sale, and 10 percent will be collected the second month following the sale. If instituted, how would this change affect the firm's borrowing needs for the first four months of 1988? Explain your results.

b. Telephone Marketing's management believes that the firm can reduce the purchases percentage to 55 percent of the following month's sales by switching suppliers. Disregarding the changes made in part a, how would switching suppliers affect the firm's borrowing needs during the budgetary period?

c. Some newly acquired information leads Telephone Marketing's marketing manager to believe that the sales forecast for March should be $400,000 rather than $300,000. Assuming the initial set of circumstances, how would these increased sales affect the firm's borrowing needs over the budgetary period?

d. After careful examination of the initial budget that was prepared, Telephone Marketing's cash manager believes that the target cash balance for March can be reduced to $35,000, and for April to $20,000. How will making these changes affect the company's borrowing needs for the first four months of 1988?

Sales for November 1987	$800,000
Sales for December 1987..............................	$980,000
Cash Discount Percentage..............................	0 %
Collection Estimates:	
Percentage collected during the month of sale	10 %
Percentage collected 1 month following sale........	60 %
Percentage collected 2 months following sale.......	30 %
Purchases as a Percentage of Next Month's Sales	62 %

	Jan.	Feb.	Mar.	Apr.
Sales Forecasts	$650,000	$450,000	$300,000	$200,000
Payment Forecasts:				
Wages and Salaries	200,000	200,000	130,000	130,000
Rent	40,000	40,000	30,000	30,000
Miscellaneous	122,000	122,000	82,000	70,000

	Jan.	Feb.	Mar.	Apr.
Taxes			47,400	
Other	87,000	87,000	74,000	74,000
Beg. Cash Balance	22,000			
Target Cash Balance	40,000	40,000	45,000	35,000

3. The Charles Corporation is planning to request a line of credit from its bank. The firm offers a 2 percent cash discount for early payment. Charles' credit and collection department has generated the following collection estimates: collected during the month of sale, 10 percent; collected the month following the sale, 75 percent; collected the second month following the sale, 15 percent. The following sales forecasts have been made by the marketing department:

May 1988	$ 375,000
June	375,000
July	750,000
August	1,100,000
September	1,550,000
October	800,000
November	800,000
December	185,000

Purchases amount to 60 percent of the following month's sales and are typically paid for during the month following that in which they are made. Wages and salaries are estimated to be as follows:

July 1988	$125,000
August	160,000
September	205,000
October	130,000
November	130,000
December	68,500

Rent payments will be $18,200 per month; depreciation charges are $75,000 per month; miscellaneous expenses will be $5,300 per month; income tax payments of $132,000 will be due in both September and December; and a progress payment of $390,000 on a new employees' health club must be paid in October. Beginning cash, as of July 1 will be $280,000, and a minimum cash balance of $200,000 should be maintained throughout the budgetary period.

a. Prepare a monthly cash budget for the last six months of 1988.

b. Approximately how large a line of credit should Charles Corporation request?

c. How much, when, and for what period of time will Charles have surplus cash to invest? What types of securities would suit these investments?

d. Suppose a recession occurs, and sales fall 20 percent below those that were forecast; however, the firm continues to incur all expenses, except purchases, according to the plans reflected in the budget you have prepared. What effect would this have on Charles' borrowing needs?

e. In addition to the decreased sales mentioned in part d, suppose that the recession also causes customers to delay payments so that sales are collected in the following manner: during the month of sale, 5 percent; during the month following the sale, 50 percent; during the second month following the sale, 45 percent. How would this change, in combination with the decreased sales, affect the firm's borrowing needs?

4. The Consolidated Moldings Corporation is planning to request a line of credit from its bank. The firm offers a 1 percent cash discount for early payment. Consolidated's credit manager has given you the following collection estimates: collected during the month of sale, 20 percent; collected the month following the sale, 60 percent; collected the second month following the sale, 20 percent. The marketing department reports the following sales forecasts:

November 1987	$ 30,000
December	20,000
January 1988	60,000
February	100,000
March	80,000
April	40,000
May	20,000
June	20,000

Purchases amount to 70 percent of the following month's sales and are typically paid for during the month following that in which they are made. Wages and salaries are estimated to be as follows:

January 1988	$ 7,000
February	11,000
March	9,000
April	5,000
May	3,000
June	3,000

Rent payments will be $1,200 per month; depreciation charges are $3,000 per month; miscellaneous expenses will be $300 per month; income tax payments of $11,000 will be due in both January and April; and other expenses will be $700 per month. Beginning cash as of January 1 will be $8,000, and a minimum cash balance of $10,000 should be maintained throughout the budgetary period.

a. Prepare a monthly cash budget for the first six months of 1988 for Consolidated Moldings.

b. Approximately how large a line of credit should Consolidated Moldings Corporation request from its bank?

c. If you prepared your budget correctly, it should show total loans outstanding in March of $36,380. If you were discussing the budget with a loan officer at Consolidated's bank, what would you tell the loan officer the company was planning to do in March with respect to its line of credit?

d. If your budget is prepared correctly, it should show a net cash gain of $24,760 for May. According to the budget, what plans exist for the use of this gain?

e. "Bits" MacIntosch, Consolidated's computer guru, believes that he can develop a cash management program that will enable the firm to reduce its target cash balance to $5,000 per month. If his program works, what effect will the lower target cash balance have on the company's borrowing needs?

5. Derrik Lender, your supervisor and the vice-president for finance of Gyles Corporation, is preparing a request for a line of credit from Midstates Bank. Gyles offers a 2 percent cash discount for early payment. The company's collection department has given him the following collection estimates: collected during the month of sale, 20 percent; collected the month following the sale, 65 percent; collected the second month following the sale, 15 percent. Rick Medium, director of marketing research, recently sent Lender the following sales forecasts:

May 1988	$140,000
June	140,000
July	125,000
August	160,000
September	215,000
October	130,000
November	130,000
December	69,000

Lender estimates that purchases amount to 55 percent of the following month's sales and are typically paid for during the month following that in which they are made. Accounting reports that wages and salaries should be as follows:

July 1988	$35,000
August	38,000
September	47,000
October	32,000
November	32,000
December	22,500

Rent payments will be $12,000 per month; depreciation charges are $19,000 per month; miscellaneous expenses will be $15,000 per month; income tax payments of $22,000 will be due in both September and December; and a progress payment of $65,000 on a new air displacer plant must be paid in November. Beginning cash as of July 1 will be $41,000, and a minimum cash balance of $35,000 should be maintained throughout the budgetary period. Lender has requested that you develop a monthly cash budget for the last six months of 1988, and then answer the following questions:

a. Approximately how large a line of credit should Gyles Corporation request?

b. If a proposed import tariff is put into effect, purchases as a percentage of the following month's sales could increase to 60 percent. How would this increase affect Gyles' financing needs and surplus cash position?

c. Jean Locator, the firm's property manager, is attempting to negotiate a new lease that would reduce rent expense to $10,000 per month. What effect would this change have on the company's financing needs and surplus cash position? (Answer this question independently of part b.)

d. Recent information from Gyles' bank hints that the compensating balance the firm must maintain may be reduced to $25,000 from its present $35,000 level. Since this requirement has been the sole determinant of Gyles' target cash balance, what effect would reducing the target cash balance have on the firm's financing needs and surplus cash position? (Answer this question independently of parts b and c.)

e. As you complete your analysis, Lender rushes into your cubical and informs you that Plant Superintendent Bildemfast just phoned with some bad news. It seems that the vintage lathe on the number two production line broke down and will require $8500 in repairs for which payment must be made during June. Lender wants to know immediately how this additional expenditure will affect Gyles' borrowing needs for the budgetary period. What is your answer? (Once again, do not consider the other changes that you have made in the original budget.)

Chapter Sixteen
Effective Rates on Short-Term Financing

SHORT-TERM FINANCING

In Chapter Fifteen, the cash budget was used to help estimate the firm's borrowing needs over the budgetary period. The example that was discussed in that chapter showed that Melnyk Toy Company would need to have some funds borrowed during four of the six months covered by the budget to meet its target cash balance. Financing such as that needed by Melnyk, that is, loans obtained for periods of time less than a year, are considered to be short-term financing. This chapter reviews the basic types of short-term financing used by businesses, discusses how effective rates of interest can be determined for each type, and introduces you to a PROFIT+ routine that calculates these effective rates.

THE COST OF SHORT-TERM FINANCING

Numerous factors cause the cost of short-term financing to vary over time, among lenders and borrowers, and on different types of short-term loans. As short-term interest rates vary, the cost of various types of loans made by financial institutions also varies. In addition, since various lenders operate under different sets of philosophies, both interest rates and lending terms vary among lenders. Finally, since all borrowers are not of the same financial strength, lending rates vary among borrowers—higher rates for those that are of greater risk, and lower rates for those of lesser risk.

This chapter's focus is on how different types of lending arrangements impact the effective cost of short-term loans. The *effective cost,* also called the *effective annual rate* or *annual percentage rate* (APR), is the annual rate of interest on a loan, rather than the stated, or nominal, rate. The effective rate on a loan answers the question, "If this loan were made for one year, what annual simple interest rate would my firm be paying?" As you will learn from the following paragraphs, two loans can have the same nominal rate of interest, but different lending terms can cause their effective rates to be quite dissimilar. Being able to calculate the effective rates of short-term loans gives management a means by which it can evaluate various types of financing alternatives on a common basis in terms of their interest rates.

How Effective Rates Are Calculated

The first step in determining the effective rate of interest on a loan is to calculate the *periodic rate.* This is simply the interest rate paid for the term of the loan. In general, the periodic rate is calculated using the following formula:

$$\text{Periodic Rate} = \frac{\text{Interest paid}}{\text{Funds available for the full term of the loan}} \qquad \textbf{(16.1)}$$

where interest paid is calculated using the simple interest formula I = Prt. (Equation 4.1—Refer to Chapter Four of this guide for a brief review of using the simple interest formula.)

Unless the loan with which you are dealing has a maturity of one year (in which case the periodic rate is equal to the effective rate), you must annualize the periodic rate to obtain the effective rate of interest. To do this, you use the following annualization formula:

$$\text{Effective Rate} = (1.0 + \text{periodic rate})^m - 1.0 \qquad \textbf{(16.2)}$$

where m = the number of loan periods there are in one year (if, for example, you are dealing with a two-month loan, m = 12/2 = 6, two-month periods in one year).

How you determine the effective rates of interest for three types of bank (or other financial institution) lending arrangements, and for trade credit (credit between businesses) is discussed in the following paragraphs.

Regular, or Simple, Interest

A simple interest loan is one on which interest is charged on the amount borrowed for the full term of the loan, and on which interest is paid when the loan matures. At the loan's onset, the borrower receives the entire amount borrowed (the principal), and at maturity the borrower repays the principal along with the interest. Consider, for example, a $5,000 loan made for three months at 10 percent simple interest. Interest on the loan would be ($5,000)(0.10)(3/12) = $125. The borrower would receive $5,000 at the beginning of the loan, and would repay $5,125 at the end of three months when the loan matures. Expressed as a time line, the loan would appear as follows:

3 months

$5,000 ———————————————— $5,125

The effective rate can be calculated as follows by using Equations 16.1 and 16.2:

$$\text{Periodic Rate} = \frac{\$125}{\$5{,}000} = 0.025$$

$$\begin{aligned}\text{Effective Rate} &= (1.0 + 0.025)^4 - 1.0\\ &= .1038 = 10.38\%\end{aligned}$$

Here "m," the number of lending periods per year, was obtained by dividing the number of months per year by the term of the loan (12/3 = 4).

Using PROFIT+ to Calculate the Effective Rate on a Simple Interest Loan Option N, Effective Rates on Short-Term Financing, on the PROFIT+ Main Menu gives you the ability to calculate effective rates for all four of the types of short-term financing discussed in this chapter. When you select this option, you will be presented with the Effective Rates on Short-Term Loans submenu shown in Exhibit 16.1. As you can see from this exhibit, Choice 1 on the submenu allows you to calculate the effective rate of "Simple interest or discount interest loans with or without a compensating balance." You will learn about discount interest and compensating balances later in this chapter, but for now, refer to Exhibit 16.2 to examine how Choice 1 can be used to solve the simple interest problem that we just worked. In that problem the principal was $5,000, the interest rate was 10 percent, and the term of the loan was three months. In Exhibit 16.2 no compensating balance percentage was entered, and "N" was answered to the question, "Is the loan discounted?"

Discount Interest

With one rather important exception, discount interest loans are quite similar to simple interest loans. The exception is that interest is determined using the simple interest equation, and then is deducted from the loan's principal *in advance*. This means that the borrower receives (and has use of) less than the full principal of the loan. On a three-month, $5,000 loan, at 10 percent interest, on a discount basis, interest due would be ($5,000)(0.10)(3/12) = $125. This interest would be deducted from principal, and the borrower would receive $5,000 - $125 = $4,875. Expressed as a time line, this loan would appear as follows:

```
                                        3 months
  /-------------------------------------------/
$4,875                                     $5,000
```

The effective rate can be calculated as follows by using Equations 16.1 and 16.2:

$$\text{Periodic Rate} = \frac{\$125}{\$4{,}875} = 0.0256$$

$$\text{Effective Rate} = (1.0 + 0.0256)^4 - 1.0$$

$$= .1066 = 10.66\%$$

The effective rate on this discounted loan is greater than that on the simple interest loan that we discussed earlier, even though the principal, the nominal rate, and the term of the loan are identical in both examples. This is because, with discount interest, the borrower does not have the use of the $5,000 principal for the full term of the loan. Interest is figured on the $5,000, but the borrower only gets the use of $4,875. This causes the periodic rate, and consequently the effective rate, to be higher for discount interest.

Exhibit 16.1

```
PROFIT+                                                    PROFIT+
   E F F E C T I V E   R A T E S   O F   S H O R T - T E R M   L O A N S

   YOU MAY CALCULATE THE EFFECTIVE RATE OF INTEREST (APR) ON THREE TYPES
   OF SHORT-TERM LOANS:

    ►1.  Simple interest or discount interest loans with or without a
         compensating balance

     2.  Add-on interest loans

     3.  Trade Credit

              Use ↑↓ to make your choice and press [RETURN]
                                  or
                 type the number preceeding your choice.

              [F1]=HELP   [F2]=REVIEW   [ESC]=MENU
```

Exhibit 16.2

```
PROFIT+                                                    PROFIT+
   E F F E C T I V E   R A T E S   O F   S H O R T - T E R M   L O A N S
 SIMPLE INTEREST OR DISCOUNT INTEREST, WITH OR WITHOUT A COMPENSATING BALANCE

     Loan Principal ............................ 5000
     Interest (or Discount) Rate (%) ..........      10.00
     Term of the Loan in Months ...............          3
     Compensating Balance (%) .................       0.00
     Is the loan discounted? (Y) or (N) .......          N


     Interest (Discount) .......................$   125.00

     Compensating Balance ......................$     0.00

     Effective Rate (APR) (%) .................      10.38

 [F1]=HELP  [F2]=REVIEW  [F3]=CALC  [F5]=REDO  [F9]=PRINT  [ESC]=MENU
```

Exhibit 16.3

```
PROFIT+                                                     PROFIT+
       E F F E C T I V E   R A T E S   O F   S H O R T - T E R M   L O A N S

SIMPLE INTEREST OR DISCOUNT INTEREST, WITH OR WITHOUT A COMPENSATING BALANCE

     Loan Principal ............................. 5000
     Interest (or Discount) Rate (%) ..........       10.00
     Term of the Loan in Months ...............           3
     Compensating Balance (%) .................        0.00
     Is the loan discounted? <Y> or <N> ........          Y

     Interest (Discount) ......................$    125.00

     Compensating Balance .....................$      0.00

     Effective Rate (APR) (%) .................      10.66

 [F1]=HELP  [F2]=REVIEW  [F3]=CALC  [F5]=REDO  [F9]=PRINT  [ESC]=MENU
```

Using PROFIT+ to Calculate the Effective Rate on a Discount Interest Loan In Exhibit 16.1, Choice 1 on the Effective Rates on Short-Term Loans submenu allows the effective rate to be calculated for both simple interest and discount interest loans. Exhibit 16.3 shows how this PROFIT+ routine can be used to calculate the effective rate on the discount interest example that we just worked. Once again, the loan principal is $5,000, the interest rate is 10 percent, and the term of the loan is three months. No compensating balance is required, but the loan is discounted; therefore, "Y" is given as the answer to the question, "Is the loan discounted?"

Compensating Balances

Both simple and discount interest loans can be made under terms that require a *compensating balance* (a minimum checking account balance that a firm must maintain with a commercial bank, generally equal to 10 to 20 percent of the principal of the loan). On either type of loan, a compensating balance will raise the effective rate of interest because it reduces the actual amount of funds that the firm has available for use during the full term of the loan. For an example of this effect, we will return to the example of a simple interest loan that was discussed earlier ($5,000, 10 percent, three-month). We will add the additional assumption that the bank re-

Exhibit 16.4

```
PROFIT+                                                         PROFIT+
    E F F E C T I V E   R A T E S   O F   S H O R T - T E R M   L O A N S

SIMPLE INTEREST OR DISCOUNT INTEREST, WITH OR WITHOUT A COMPENSATING BALANCE

      Loan Principal ............................. 5000
      Interest (or Discount) Rate (%) ..........      10.00
      Term of the Loan in Months ...............          3
      Compensating Balance (%) .................      20.00
      Is the loan discounted? (Y) or (N) .......          N

      Interest (Discount) .....................$     125.00

      Compensating Balance ....................$    1000.00

      Effective Rate (APR) (%) .................      13.10

[F1]=HELP   [F2]=REVIEW   [F3]=CALC   [F5]=REDO   [F9]=PRINT   [ESC]=MENU
```

quires the borrower to maintain a 20 percent compensating balance. Thus, on the \$5,000 loan, the compensating balance would be (\$5,000)(0.20) = \$1,000. This compensating balance is credited to the borrower's checking account, but the borrower does not have access to it. This, in turn, has the effect of raising the periodic rate because the funds actually available (\$5,000 - \$1,000 = \$4,000) are less than they were under the original set of circumstances. The following calculations show how the effective rate would be determined using Equations 16.1 and 16.2:

$$\text{Periodic Rate} = \frac{\$125}{\$4{,}000} = 0.03125$$

$$\text{Effective Rate} = (1.0 + 0.03125)^4 - 1.0$$

$$= .1310 = 13.10\%$$

Using PROFIT+ to Calculate the Effective Rate on a Loan Requiring a Compensating Balance Exhibit 16.4 shows how Choice 1 on the PROFIT+ Effective Rates on Short-Term Loans submenu can be used to calculate the effective rate on the simple interest loan with a compensating balance in the example that was just discussed. Here, again, principal is $5,000, the interest rate is 10 percent, the term of the loan is three months. The compensating balance percentage is 20 percent, and the loan is not discounted.

Add-on Interest Loans

An add-on interest loan is one in which interest is figured on the principal, then it is added to the principal to arrive at the loan's face value. The face value is then divided by the number of months over which the loan is to be repaid to obtain the loan payment. For an example, assume that $4,000 is borrowed for six months at 12 percent add-on interest. Interest is ($4,000)(0.12)(6/12) = $240; the face value is $4,000 + $240 = $4,240; and the monthly payment is $4,240/6 = $706.67. Expressed as a time line, the loan appears as follows:

	1	2	3	4	5	6
($4,000)	/	/	/	/	/	/
	$706.67	$706.67	$706.67	$706.67	$706.67	$706.67

From the time line, you should see immediately that a problem exists in determining the periodic rate using Equation 16.1. Namely, how much money does the borrower have available for the full term of the loan? Only at the beginning of the loan does it have the full $4,000 available, because after each payment is made, less and less of the principal is paid back. The way around this problem is a rather simple one. It uses the method that you studied in Chapter Four of this guide for determining yields and growth rates. Specifically, the periodic rate is obtained by solving for "i" in Equation 4.6:

$$PV = PMT\left(\frac{1}{i} - \frac{1}{i(1+i)^n}\right) \qquad \textbf{(4.6)}$$

where PV = the loan principal

PMT = the loan payment

n = the number of loan payments

i = the periodic rate.

In our example, the PV is $4,000, the PMT is $706.67, and n is six. Using this information in Equation 4.6 to solve for "i," we obtain 0.0169 as the periodic rate.

Once you have the periodic rate, you can "plug" it into Equation 16.2 to obtain the effective rate on the loan.

Exhibit 16.5

```
PROFIT+                                                    PROFIT+
        E F F E C T I V E   R A T E S   O F   S H O R T - T E R M   L O A N S

                             ADD-ON INTEREST

     Loan Principal ............................      4000

     Interest Rate (%) .........................     12.00

     Term of the Loan in Months ................         6

     Interest ................................$     240.00

     Loan Payment ............................$     706.67

     Effective Rate (APR) (%) ..................     22.28

 [F1]=HELP  [F2]=REVIEW  [F3]=CALC  [F5]=REDO  [F9]=PRINT  [ESC]=MENU
```

$$\text{Effective Rate} = (1.0 + 0.0169)^{12} - 1.0$$
$$= .2228 = 22.28\%$$

In the preceding calculation, the "m" used to calculate the effective rate was 12. When working with a loan with monthly payments, it is the payment period that is used to determine the value of "m." Thus, there are 12 monthly payments in one year.

Using PROFIT+ to Calculate the Effective Rate on an Add-on Interest Loan
Examine the PROFIT+ Effective Rates on Short-Term Loans submenu in Exhibit 16.1. Choice 2 on the menu allows you to determine the effective rate of interest on add-on interest loans. Exhibit 16.5 shows how this routine can be used to solve the add-on interest example that was worked above.

Trade Credit

Trade credit is credit between businesses. It appears on the seller's books as accounts receivable and on the buyer's books as accounts payable. In effect, the typical trade credit terms can be divided into two components: (1) free trade credit, and (2) costly trade credit. Take, for example, the trade credit terms 2/10, net 30. They imply that a 2 percent cash discount is offered if payment is made by the tenth day; otherwise, the net (full) amount of the invoice is due by the thirtieth day. Perhaps the easiest way to see that these terms have both a free and a costly component is to examine a hypothetical purchase under the terms.

Assume that Andrew Corporation purchases $1,000 of goods under the 2/10, net 30 terms. If the firm pays by the tenth day, it must remit $1,000 - (0.02)($1,000) = $980 to its supplier. For payment on the thirtieth day, the full $1,000 is due. Pictured as a time line, the situation appears as follows:

	10th	30th
	$980	$1,000

The free component in this situation is the first ten days of the credit period. If payment is made by the tenth, the trade credit is without cost to Andrew. The costly component is evident: if payment is made on the thirtieth day, Andrew must pay $20 more for the goods that it purchased. This means that Andrew's cost of goods sold will be $20 more, and its gross profit $20 less than it otherwise might have been. While $20 does not sound like much, multiplying that amount by the number of thousands of dollars of goods that the firm purchases during the year means many lost dollars of profit.

Our concern here is to translate this costly trade credit component into an effective annual rate of interest, so that it can be compared with other forms of borrowing. If, for example, its effective cost is greater than that of bank financing, the firm would be advised to borrow from the bank to take advantage of the cash discount.

The method for determining the effective cost of trade credit is similar to that used for the other forms of short-term financing discussed in this chapter. It involves calculating the periodic interest rate, and then using it to obtain the effective annual rate. While we could use dollar amounts in Equation 16.1 to calculate the periodic rate, it is simpler to use percentages. Thus, we can modify Equation 16.1 as follows to determine the periodic rate for trade credit:

$$\text{Periodic Rate} = \frac{\text{Cash discount percent}}{100 - \text{Cash discount percent}} \qquad \textbf{(16.3)}$$

For 2/10, net 30 terms, therefore, the periodic rate would be

$$\text{Periodic Rate} = \frac{2}{100 - 2} = 0.0204.$$

We can then use Equation 16.2 to determine the effective annual rate of the costly trade credit component. To do this, however, we must know the length of the lending period so that we can calculate the number of lending periods there are in one year. Looking back at the time line given in the example, you can see that the lending period is 20 days—the difference between the last day on which the cash discount can be taken and the end of the net period, and there are 360/20 = 18 of these periods in one year. The general way to determine the length of the lending period is to subtract the discount period from the net period. Continuing with the example, the effective rate of the costly component is calculated as follows:

$$\text{Effective rate} = (1.0 + 0.02041)^{18} - 1.0$$

$$= .4386 = 43.86\%$$

(Note: Many texts simply multiply the periodic rate of interest times the number of lending periods per year to obtain the approximate effective rate of interest. In our example, this would yield an approximate effective rate of (0.0204)(18) = 36.72%. This approximation obviously understates the true effective annual rate for costly trade credit.)

Using PROFIT+ to Calculate the Effective Rate of Costly Trade Credit Choice 3 on the Effective Rates on Short-Term Loans submenu gives you the ability to calculate the effective rate of interest on trade credit. Exhibit 16.6 shows how this routine is used to determine the effective rate for terms of 2/10, net 30. (In addition to providing the effective annual rate calculated using Equation 16.2, PROFIT+ also determines the approximate effective rate. This figure, while it understates the true cost of passing up discounts, is provided because it is calculated using the approximation method discussed in most beginning financial management textbooks.)

SUMMARY

This chapter provided a review of simple and discount interest loans, add-on interest loans, and trade credit; showed how the effective annual rate of each is calculated; and introduced you to the PROFIT+ routine for handling each effective rate calculation. The method used for determining the effective rate both in this chapter and by PROFIT+ employs the concept of compounding. Some introductory textbooks use methods for determining approximate effective rates that do not employ compound interest.

Exhibit 16.6

```
PROFIT+                                                    PROFIT+
      E F F E C T I V E   R A T E S   O F   S H O R T - T E R M   L O A N S

                              TRADE CREDIT

        Cash Discount (%) .........................        2

        Length of Discount Period in Days .........       10

        Net Period in Days ........................       30

        Approximate Effective Rate (%) ...........     36.73

        Effective Rate (APR) (%) .................     43.86

 [F1]=HELP  [F2]=REVIEW  [F3]=CALC  [F5]=REDO  [F9]=PRINT  [ESC]=MENU
```

END-OF-CHAPTER PROBLEMS

1. Calculate the effective annual rate of interest on the following simple interest loans using your PROFIT+ software:

	Principal	Interest Rate%	Term in Months
a.	$1,000	11	2
b.	$1,000	11	4
c.	$1,000	11	6
d.	$1,000	11	8
e.	$1,000	11	10
f.	$1,000	11	12

2. Calculate the effective annual rate of interest on the following simple interest loans using your PROFIT+ software:

	Principal	Interest Rate%	Term in Months
a.	$1,000	6	3
b.	$1,000	8	3

	Principal	Interest Rate%	Term in Months
c.	$1,000	10	3
d.	$1,000	12	3
e.	$1,000	14	3
f.	$1,000	16	3

3. Calculate the effective annual rate of interest on the following simple interest loans using your PROFIT+ software:

	Principal	Interest Rate%	Term in Months
a.	$2,000	11	3
b.	$4,000	11	3
c.	$6,000	11	3
d.	$8,000	11	3
e.	$10,000	11	3
f.	$12,000	11	3

4. Summarize, in words, what you learned from working problems 1, 2, and 3.

5. Work problems 1, 2, and 3 assuming that each loan is discounted.

6. Work problems 1, 2, and 3 assuming that each loan bears simple interest and a 15 percent compensating balance.

7. Work problems 1, 2, and 3 assuming that each loan is discounted and requires a 15 percent compensating balance.

8. Summarize, in words, what you learned from working problems 5, 6, and 7.

9. Smith, Brown, and Washington, Inc., is negotiating with First County Bank for an $80,000, six-month loan. First County has offered to make the loan at 10.5 percent simple interest. What is the effective rate of interest on the loan?

10. Aaron King, treasurer of Ginger Snap Products, recently approached several banks regarding the terms each would offer on a three-month, $150,000 loan. King obtained the following offers:

First National Bank—14 percent, simple interest, no compensating balance.

Second National Bank—13.5 percent, discount interest, no compensating balance.

Third National Bank—12 percent, simple interest, a 20 percent compensating balance.

Fourth National Bank—11.5 percent, discount interest, a 10 percent compensating balance.

Rank the alternatives from the one with the lowest effective rate to the one with the highest rate.

11. Sharon Gomez, vice-president of finance of Containerization, Inc., is negotiating with several banks regarding the terms each would offer on a nine-month, $1,650,000 loan. Gomez obtained the offers shown below. Rank the alternatives from the one with the lowest effective rate to the one with the highest rate.

First State Bank—13 percent, simple interest, a 15 percent compensating balance.

Second State Bank—12.7 percent, discount interest, no compensating balance.

Third State Bank—13.5 percent, simple interest, no compensating balance.

Fourth State Bank—12.0 percent, discount interest, a 20 percent compensating balance.

12. Calculate the effective rate of interest on each of the following add-on interest loans (assume monthly payments):

a. $7,500, 12 percent, 6 months

b. $5,400, 10 percent, 12 months

c. $8,700, 9 percent, 12 months

d. $1,150, 7 percent, 6 months

e. $7,600, 11 percent, 9 months

f. $9,990, 10.5 percent, 12 months

13. Johnson Energy Corporation's bank recently offered to lend the firm $225,000 at 9.5 percent add-on interest. What is the effective rate of interest on this loan if it is to be paid off in nine equal monthly payments?

14. Barbara Sutherlind, owner of Barb's Corner Craft Shops, Inc., is negotiating a $12,000, four-month loan with a local bank. The bank has offered Sutherlind the alternatives shown below. Rank the alternatives from the one with the lowest effective rate to the one with the highest rate.

Alternative 1: 11 percent, discount interest, no compensating balance.

Alternative 2: 10 percent, discount interest, no compensating balance.

Alternative 3: 9 percent, simple interest, 20 percent compensating balance.

Alternative 4: 6.5 percent, add-on interest, amortized in four equal monthly payments.

15. Calculate the effective rate of interest for the nonfree component of the following trade credit terms:

a. 1/10, net 30

b. 1/10, net 45

c. 1/10, net 60

d. 2/10, net 30

e. 2/10, net 45

f. 2/10, net 60

g. 3/10, net 30

16. Summarize, in words, what you learned from working problem 15.

17. Gherhardt Corporation projects an increase in sales for the coming month, but the company needs an additional $75,000 to finance the inventories needed for these sales. The funds can be raised from Greene County Bank at a 12 percent simple interest with a 15 percent compensating balance for one month. Alternatively, Gherhardt can finance the inventories by no longer taking cash discounts, thus increasing accounts payable. The company purchases under terms of 2/15, net 45.

a. Based strictly on an interest rate comparison, how should Gherhardt obtain the financing that it needs?

b. What additional qualitative factors should the company consider prior to making its final decision? (Consult the chapter on short-term financing in your financial management textbook if you need assistance with answering this question.)

Chapter Seventeen
Capital Budgeting Basics

Of all the decisions that financial managers must make, those involving the investment in fixed assets have some of the most long-lasting effects on the firm due to the life spans of these assets. The entire process of planning for the acquisition of fixed assets is called *capital budgeting*, and it is with one segment of this planning process--evaluating capital spending proposals--that this chapter deals.

THE CAPITAL BUDGETING PROCESS

Project Generation

Capital budgeting consists of many tasks. At the beginning of the process is the generation of ideas for potential capital projects. Since the phrase *investment in fixed assets* is such a general one, it should come as no surprise that there are many different types of capital projects, ranging from such necessary expenditures as repairing a leaky roof or repairing a damaged piece of machinery to replacing an older piece of equipment with a more modern and efficient one, purchasing a new typewriter, building an entire new production facility to produce a new line of products, or constructing a new home office building. As different types of projects are proposed, you should understand that the evaluation of each may require a different type of analysis and a different level of sophistication. For example, large, risky projects generally demand more detailed and sophisticated evaluation than do small, relatively riskless projects.

Project Evaluation

Estimating Cash Flows After ideas for projects have been generated, the next step in the capital budgeting process is to determine the economic feasibility of the proposed projects. For some types of projects, for example repairing a leaking roof that threatens to damage some expensive equipment, the expenditure may be an obvious economic necessity. For others, for example building a plant to manufacture a new product, very detailed cost/benefit analysis might be necessary. For projects demanding more detailed analysis, the first, the most important, and the most difficult step in the analytical process is the estimation of the cash outflows and inflows associated with the project. This step is vital to the evaluation process because any cost/benefit analysis must be based on these cash flow estimates. Regardless of the level of sophistication of the analytical techniques to be used, the ultimate results are only as good as the cash flows on which they are based. The estimation of cash flows is difficult because these flows, especially the inflows, frequently have to be projected for several years into the future.

Since a variety of factors influence the cash flows for various types of capital projects, it is beyond the scope of PROFIT+ to provide formats for calculating cash flows under all circumstances. Instead, PROFIT+ provides a spreadsheet for determining the cash inflows for a typical "new" (rather than for a "replacement") project.

The first thing that you need to understand about calculating a project's cash inflows is that cash flows, not accounting profits, must be used. Whereas accounting profits subtract a noncash charge against income (depreciation expense) cash flows do not. In general, the net cash inflow for a project is determined by first estimating the net income the project will produce in a particular year, and then adding the depreciation expense associated with the project to net income. In the last year of a project's life, any inflows from the recovery of net working capital and the after-tax salvage value of the project must also be included as cash inflows. Exhibit 17.1 shows the general format for calculating cash inflows for a new capital spending proposal. (For a more complete discussion of calculating cash inflows, refer to Chapter 10 of *Fundamentals of Financial Management,* 4th ed., by Eugene F. Brigham, or to Chapter 16 of *Essentials of Managerial Finance*, 8th ed., by J. Fred Weston and Eugene F. Brigham.)

The PROFIT+ routine for determining cash inflows will be presented later in this chapter after you have learned about methods for ranking and selecting capital spending proposals.

Exhibit 17.1

Format for Calculating Net Cash Inflows

Sales
- Costs (except depreciation)
- Depreciation Expense
Operating Income
- Taxes
Net Income
+ Depreciation Expense
Net Cash Inflow

Terminal year cash inflows: Recovery of net working capital
Salvage value (1 - tax rate)

Selection/Ranking Methods Once cash flows have been estimated, the next step in the analysis of a capital spending proposal is to evaluate the flows using an appropriate selection/ranking method. Selection/ranking methods are techniques designed to help you answer at least two questions about capital projects:

1. Is the project an "acceptable" one? That is, do the projected benefits outweigh the projected costs?

2. Where does an acceptable project rank when compared with other acceptable projects that are competing for the same investment dollars? (Note: Economic theory holds that all projects whose benefits outweigh their costs should be financed and undertaken. In practice, arbitrary limits are sometimes placed on the amount of capital spending a firm is willing to undertake during a particular period. This practice is termed *capital rationing*.) Ranking is also necessary for mutually exclusive projects--ones that are separate proposals for accomplishing the same basic task.

Although many selection/ranking methods have been used or proposed in the past, the most widely used methods are called *discounted cash flow*, or DCF, methods. These techniques take into consideration that money has time value and accordingly use present value calculations to adjust future cash flows for the effects of time. The interest, or discount, rate used with the DCF techniques is the firm's *cost of capital*. This rate is a measure of the overall percentage cost of the firm's long-term sources of financing. The idea here is that a project should earn at least as much as the funds invested in it are costing, or it should not be undertaken. (Chapter Twenty of this guide provides a more detailed discussion of cost of capital.) The two most popular DCF methods are the *net present value* (NPV) method and the *internal rate of return* (IRR) method.

Net Present Value A project's NPV is the difference between the present value of its projected net cash inflows and the initial cost of the project (with the present values calculated using the firm's cost of capital as the appropriate discount rate). A project is acceptable under the NPV technique if it has a positive NPV (i.e., the present value of the projected benefits exceed the present value of the costs). Projects with higher NPVs are ranked above those with lower NPVs. Expressed in equation form, the NPV method appears as follows:

$$NPV = PV(\text{Net cash inflows}) - \text{Initial cost}$$

$$NPV = \sum_{t=1}^{n} \frac{CF_t}{(1 + k)^t} - C \tag{17.1}$$

where CF_t = net cash inflow in time period t
k = the cost of capital
C = the initial cost of the project (initial cash outflow).

Internal Rate of Return A project's IRR is the discount rate that makes the present value of its net cash inflows equal to the initial cost of the project. In this sense, the IRR computed for a project is similar to the rate of return earned on any investment, for example, the yield to maturity on a bond. IRR answers the following question: "If a project has an initial cost of X dollars, and we project that it will return us Y dollars per year for n years, what percentage return on our investment does this stream of inflows represent?" When using IRR, a project is acceptable if the calculated IRR is greater than the firm's cost of capital. When IRR is greater than the cost of capital, you are projecting that the return on the invested funds (the IRR) will be greater than the cost of those invested funds (the cost of capital). Other things being equal (and an in-depth study of capital budgeting will teach you that they frequently are not), projects with higher IRRs rank above those with lower IRRs. Arithmetically IRR is calculated by solving for "r" in the following equation:

$$0 = \sum_{t=1}^{n} \frac{CF_t}{(1 + r)^t} - C \tag{17.2}$$

where r = the project's internal rate of return.

The preceding discussion provides only the basic rationale and methodology involved with using the NPV and IRR techniques. You should refer to your financial management textbook to learn more about how these methods are used and what limitations they possess.

THE PROFIT+ CAPITAL BUDGETING BASICS ROUTINE

As can be seen from Exhibit 17.2 (the Capital Budgeting Basics submenu), Option 17, Capital Budgeting Basics, on the Main Menu includes routines for computing NPV and IRR when the cash inflows and outflows for a project are already known and for determining the net cash inflows for a new capital spending proposal along with the project's NPV and IRR. (In general, these routines are best suited for normal capital spending proposals. "Normal" projects are those that have an initial cash outlay followed by a series of cash inflows.) PROFIT+ uses Equation 17.1 to calculate NPV and Equation 17.2 for computing IRR, and it follows the format in Exhibit 17.1 for determining net cash inflows. The Net Cash Inflow routine limits the length of a projcct to cight ycars.

Exhibit 17.3 shows how Choice 1 on the Capital Budgeting Basics submenu, "NPV and IRR given cash outflow, cash inflows, and cost of capital," can be used to solve the following sample problem:

Sample Problem: Millan Furniture Company, Incorporated, is considering purchasing a piece of equipment for use in manufacturing a proposed new line of dining room furniture. The initial cost of the equipment is estimated to be $120,000, and the projected net cash inflows for the project are as follows:

Year	*Inflow*	*Year*	*Inflow*
1	*$14,000*	*5*	*$42,000*
2	*16,000*	*6*	*30,000*
3	*24,000*	*7*	*20,000*
4	*42,000*	*8*	*10,000*

The firm's cost of capital is 14.5 percent. What are the project's NPV and IRR? Is the project acceptable?

Exhibit 17.2

```
PROFIT+                                                    PROFIT+
              C A P I T A L   B U D G E T I N G   B A S I C S

  There are two basic capital budgeting routines available:

  ▶ 1.  NPV and IRR given cash outflow, cash inflows and cost of capital. ◀

    2.  NPV and IRR with spreadsheet for calculating cash inflows.  Cash
        outflow and cost of capital are given.

               Use ↑↓ to make your selection and press [RETURN]
                                      or
                     type the number preceding your selection.

                    [F1]=HELP  [F2]=REVIEW  [ESC]=MENU
```

Exhibit 17.3

```
PROFIT+                                                    PROFIT+
                          N P V   A N D   I R R
Cash Outflow:  120000.00   Cost of Capital % :  14.50   # Yrs:    8.000

       INFLOW          INFLOW          INFLOW          INFLOW          INFLOW
  1:   14000.00   2:   16000.00   3:   24000.00   4:   42000.00   5:   42000.00
  6:   30000.00   7:   20000.00   8:   10000.00

  Net Present Value:     -9353.55      Internal Rate of Return:   12.26

  [F1]=HELP  [F2]=REVIEW  [F3]=CALC  [F5]=REDO  [F9]=PRINT  [ESC]=MENU
```

The solution to the sample problem in Exhibit 17.3 shows that the project's NPV is negative and that its IRR is less than the firm's cost of capital. This indicates that the project is unacceptable.

The next sample problem requires that cash inflows be determined prior to the calculation of NPV and IRR. Exhibit 17.4 shows how Choice 2 on the Capital Budgeting Basics submenu can be used with this problem. (Note: The problem is taken from *Essentials of Managerial Finance*, 8th ed., by J. Fred Weston and Eugene F. Brigham, pp. 516-518.)

Sample Problem: Houston Trucking Company is considering purchasing a new delivery van at a cost of $10,000. In addition to its purchase price, the van requires an investment in net working capital of $3,000, which will be recovered when the van is sold. The van has a five-year ACRS life (depreciation expense: yr. 1 = $2,000, yr. 2 = $3,200, yr. 3 = $2,000, yr. 4 = $1,400, and yr. 5 = $1,400); additional sales attributable to the new van will amount to $28,000 per year for five years; and Houston expects to be able to sell the van for $500 at the end of its five-year service life. Operating costs (fuel, labor, and so forth) will amount to $20,000 per year; Houston's marginal federal-plus-state income tax rate is 40 percent; and its cost of capital is 10 percent. What net cash inflows will the project produce in each year of its service life, and what are the project's NPV and IRR?

Exhibit 17.4

PROFIT+ PROFIT+

N P V & I R R W I T H C A S H I N F L O W C A L C U L A T I O N

Net Cash Outlay: 13000 Cost of Capital %: 10.0 Project Life: 5

	1	2	3	4	5
Sales........	28000	28000	28000	28000	28000
Costs (except deprec.)....	20000	20000	20000	20000	20000
Depreciation.	2000	3200	2000	1400	1400
Tax Rate (%).	40	40	40	40	40
Taxes........	2400	1920	2400	2640	2640
A-T Income...	3600	2880	3600	3960	3960
+ Deprec.	2000	3200	2000	1400	1400
Sal. Value...					500
A-T Sal. Val.					300
Net WC Rcry..					3000
Net Cash Inflow.......	5600	6080	5600	5360	8660

NPV: 10361.20 IRR: 36.25 %

[F1]=HELP [F2]=REVIEW [F3]=CALC [F5]=REDO [F9]=PRINT [ESC]=MENU

SUMMARY

This chapter briefly discussed some of the topics associated with capital budgeting and introduced you to the PROFIT+ routines that are related to these topics. As you will learn when reading your financial management textbook, capital budgeting is a very complex subject and deserves a great deal more attention and study than this guide can provide. Use PROFIT+'s Capital Budgeting Basics routine to help you learn about those aspects of the capital budgeting process for which it is designed, but be cautioned that the programs included here are designed to provide you with only an introduction to this very important area of corporate financial management.

END-OF-CHAPTER PROBLEMS

1. Calculate the NPV and the IRR for a $30,000 project that has the cash inflows given in the following table. Is the project acceptable? Why or why not? (Cost of captial = 14%.)

Year	Inflow
1	$ 3,500
2	5,500
3	7,500
4	10,000
5	10,000
6	5,000
7	6,000

2. Nealland Sellers, Inc., is considering the acquisition of a new, fully automated Bradley planer. The machine will cost $175,000. Nealland's planners estimate that the planer will produce the following net cash inflows over its nine-year life:

Year	Inflow
1	$10,250
2	22,000
3	38,500
4	56,850
5	56,850
6	50,000
7	40,000
8	30,000
9	10,000

a. If Nealland uses a cost of capital of 13 percent, should the firm purchase the planer? Why or why not?

b. If the company's cost of capital is 10.5 percent, is the project acceptable? Why or why not?

c. Nealland just received word that the planer's supplier will reduce its price by $8,000 if Nealland will make its purchase within the next ten days. Given this reduced price, answer parts a and b.

3. The net annual cash inflows for Projects A22 and B56 are shown in the table given below. Both projects have an initial cost of $26,000.

Year	Inflows for Project A22	Inflows for Project B56
1	$16,000	$8,600
2	7,800	8,600
3	7,800	9,500
4	2,100	9,500

a. If the firm uses a 14 percent cost of capital, what are the NPV and IRR of each project?

b. If the projects are independent (i.e., if they are not mutually exclusive), should each be accepted?

c. If the projects are mutually exclusive, which project should be accepted? (Note: You may have to consult your financial management textbook for help on this one!)

d. How would your answers to parts a, b, and c change if the company's cost of capital were 18 percent, rather than 14 percent?

4. The Cory Construction Company is considering purchasing a new crane that has an initial cost of $126,000. Estimates suggest that the new piece of equipment will produce the following net cash flow stream over the next eight years:

Year	Flow	Year	Flow
1	$32,000	5	$25,000
2	42,000	6	25,000
3	45,000	7	25,000
4	35,000	8	30,000

a. If the company's cost of capital is 14 percent, what are the NPV and the IRR for this project? Is the project acceptable?

b. If the cost of the project was $160,000, rather than $126,000, would your answers to part a change?

c. Assuming an initial cost of $126,000, how would your answers to part a change if the firm's cost of capital were 15 percent? If it were 16 percent?

5. Projects M and N both have an initial cost of $7,500, are being evaluated using a cost of capital of 14 percent, and are projected to generate the following net cash inflows over the next five years:

Year	Inflows for Project M	Inflows for Project N
1	$4,100	$1,000
2	3,000	1,500
3	2,000	2,000
4	1,500	3,000
5	1,000	4,100

a. What are the NPV and the IRR for each project?

b. If the two projects are independent, is each acceptable?

c. If the firm's cost of capital decreased to 9 percent, would your answers to parts a and b be affected?

d. If the firm's cost of capital were 17 percent, would your answers to parts a and b be affected?

e. Which project's NPV is more sensitive to changes in the assumed cost of capital? Why? (Note: To answer the "why" part of this problem, you may have to consult your financial management textbook.)

6. Brian Goodrich, manager of the Kansas City Division of Smithfield Manufacturing Corporation, is in the process of deciding between two new machines from separate suppliers. Since the machines perform identical tasks, Goodrich must choose only one of them (i.e., they are mutually exclusive projects). Machine A will cost more, but it will be less expensive to operate; it will cost $45,000, while Machine B will cost $35,000. The firm uses a 10 percent cost of capital to evaluate projects of this type. Goodrich estimates the life of both machines to be six years, during which time the net cash inflows for Machine A will be $13,250 per year and those for Machine B will be $10,600 per year. Calculate the NPV and IRR for both machines, then decide which one, if either, Goodrich should recommend.

7. Benton, Inc., is evaluating a project suggested by its research and development department. Use the following information to answer parts a through d of this question:

Net Cash Outflow	$13,200
Project Life	6 years
Cost of Capital	15%
Salvage Value in year 6	1,600

	Year 1	Year 2	Year 3	Year 4	Year 5	Year 6
Sales	$15,000	15,000	15,000	15,000	15,000	15,000
Costs (except deprec.)	$10,000	10,000	10,000	10,000	10,000	10,000
Depreciation	$ 3,200	5,120	3,200	2,240	2,240	0
Tax rate	40%	40%	40%	40%	40%	40%

a. What are the annual net cash inflows for this project?

b. What are this project's NPV and IRR?

c. Is the project acceptable?

d. How would your answers to parts b and c change if Benton's cost of capital were 12 percent, rather than 15 percent?

8. Jay Engleton of Ruston, Inc., is evaluating the purchase of a new sales vehicle for his firm. Use the following estimates to answer parts a through d of this question:

Net cash outflow	$21,440
Project life	6 years
Cost of capital	10%
Salvage value in year 6	2,000
Net working capital recovery in year 6	2,240

	Year 1	Year 2	Year 3	Year 4	Year 5	Year 6
Sales	$18,000	18,000	18,000	18,000	18,000	18,000
Costs (except deprec.)	$12,500	12,500	12,500	12,500	12,500	12,500
Depreciation	$ 3,840	6,144	3,840	2,688	2,688	0
Tax rate	40%	40%	40%	40%	40%	40%

a. What are the annual net cash inflows for this project?

b. What are this project's NPV and IRR?

c. Is the project acceptable?

d. How would your answers to parts b and c change if Ruston's cost of capital were 12 percent, rather than 10 percent?

9. Matthews Corporation is evaluating project K344. The project has an initial cost of $170,000. The project will also require an additional investment in net working capital of $24,000, which will be recovered at the end of the project's life. Over the project's five-year ACRS life, depreciation expenses will be: yr. 1 = $34,000, yr. 2 = $54,400, yr. 3 = $34,000, yr. 4 = $23,800, and yr. 5 = $23,800; projected new sales attributable to project K344 will amount to $420,000 per year for five years; and Matthews expects the project's salvage value to be $11,000 at the end of its five-year service life. Operating costs (exclusive of depreciation) are estimated to be $360,000 per year; the firm's marginal income tax rate is 38 percent; and its cost of capital is 11 percent. (Note: Remember to add the additional investment in net working capital to the project's initial cost to obtain the net cash outlay.)

a. What net cash inflows will the project produce in each year of its service life?

b. What are the project's NPV and IRR?

c. Is project K344 acceptable? Why or why not?

d. A recent letter from the project's design engineer suggests that its cost could be $179,000 rather than $170,000. This would change annual depreciation expenses to: yr. 1 = $35,800, yr. 2 = $57,280, yr. 3 = $35,800, yr. 4 = $25,060, and yr. 5 = $25,060. How would this cost increase affect the project's acceptability?

10. The Maine Lobster Company is evaluating the installation of a new processing line. In the table on the following page you will find the projections the firm has made regarding the costs and cash inflows for the line. Use this information to answer parts a through d of this question:

Net cash outflow	$111,040
Project life	5 years
Salvage value in year 5	2,000
Net working capital recovery in year 5	11,200

	Year 1	Year 2	Year 3	Year 4	Year 5
Sales............	$93,000	94,000	95,000	90,000	88,000
Costs (except deprec.)........	$62,500	63,500	62,000	50,000	47,000
Depreciation....	$19,968	31,949	19,968	13,978	13,977
Tax rate.........	40%	40%	40%	40%	40%

a. Is the project acceptable at a 14 percent cost of capital?

b. Is the project acceptable at a 12 percent cost of capital?

c. Is the project acceptable at a 10 percent cost of capital?

d. Would your answers to parts a through c change if the firm's marginal income tax rate were 34 percent?

Chapter Eighteen
Net Present Value Sensitivity Analysis

CAPITAL PROJECT EVALUATION AND RISK

In Chapter Seventeen, no mention was made of how risk affects the evaluation of capital projects. Yet some of the projects a company is contemplating will be more risky than others. For example, one project might involve purchasing equipment to expand production of an existing product, while another requires that the company invest in facilities to produce an entirely new product with which it has had very little experience. Obviously, the second of these two projects would be more risky than the first.

Where projects of different risk are being analyzed, should the same standards be used to evaluate each? Simple logic should lead you to answer no to this question. Higher-risk projects should be required to produce higher returns than those of average risk, just as projects with lower-than-average risk should be expected to produce returns that are below average. Probably the simplest method for recognizing that projects possess different levels of risk is to group projects into three categories: high risk, normal risk, and low risk. Then, when using the NPV and IRR methods for evaluating the projects, use a higher-than-normal cost of capital for high-risk projects, a lower-than-average cost of capital for low-risk projects, and an average cost of capital for projects of normal risk. There also exist various methods that are beyond the scope of this guide for handling the question of differential risk.

Measuring Project Risk: Sensitivity Analysis

Although providing subjective measures of project risk such as those mentioned above (i.e., high, normal, and low risk) is at least a step in the direction of realizing the problem of differential project risk, it is neither a very sophisticated nor an objective method. Given these deficiencies, other techniques have been developed to assist in measuring the relative riskiness of a project. One of these methods is NPV sensitivity analysis, which shows how much a project's NPV will change in response to a given change in a single input variable when other inputs are held constant. That is, sensitivity analysis (which is really just a form of the "what if?" analysis) helps the manager determine how sensitive NPV is to changes in the various factors that have been used in its calculation: changes in the determinants of net cash inflows, project cost, and cost of capital. Other things being equal, the more sensitive NPV is to changes in the input variables, the more risky will be the project under consideration.

Sensitivity analysis begins by examining the base, or most likely, case for a particular capital budgeting project. After the NPV for this base case has been calculated, sensitivity analysis requires that each key input variable be changed by some given percentage--both above and below the base value--while all other variables are held constant. As each individual change is made, the project's NPV is recalculated, the result is recorded, and the NPV is plotted (either graphically or algebraically) against the variable being altered. The slopes of the lines relating NPV to each key variable show how sensitive NPV is to changes in each. The steeper the slope of a particular relationship, the more sensitive NPV is to changes in that variable. Management's task then is to decide whether that variable's value could be different from the most-likely-case value used for the base case. If there is a great deal of uncertainty about the value of a variable with a steeply sloped sensitivity line, this would increase the project's risk more than would uncertainty regarding a variable whose sensitivity line was less steeply sloped. In general, where more than one project is being examined, those projects with the most steeply sloped sensitivity lines should be thought of as being the most risky. That is, small differences from the base case in their input variables lead to much larger changes in NPV.

The PROFIT+ NPV Sensitivity Analysis Routine

Your PROFIT+ software contains a structured routine (Option P, NPV Sensitivity Analysis, on the Main Menu) for conducting NPV sensitivity analysis on a capital project. The routine is referred to as being structured because it has been written to work with a particular type of capital project: one whose cash inflows are projected to be the same during each year of its life. Using your inputs for the base values of the following variables:

Unit sales per year
Sales price per unit
Variable costs per unit
Fixed costs except depreciation
Depreciation expense
Income tax rate
Project salvage value
Cost of capital
Expected project life
Initial project cost,

PROFIT+ first calculates the annual expected cash inflows for the project, then determines the project's NPV at the base value for each variable. (See Chapter Seventeen of this guide for a review of how the net cash inflows are calculated.) Next, PROFIT+ takes one variable at a time, changes it plus and minus 10 percent from the base value, recalculates cash inflows and the NPV given each of these changes, and then computes the slope of the sensitivity line relating NPV to each of the variables. The slope is calculated using the following formula:

$$\text{Slope} = \frac{\text{Percent change in NPV}}{\text{Percent change in X}} \tag{18.1}$$

where X = the particular input variable being changed.

PROFIT+ makes no judgments as to the relative riskiness of a particular project. It is up to you to make such judgments as it would be for the manager of a business.

Exhibits 18.1 and 18.2 show how the PROFIT+ NPV Sensitivity Analysis routine can be used to solve the following sample problem:

Sample Problem: The following estimates have been made concerning the cash flows and other relevant data for Project Y.

Unit Sales per Year	*3,000*
Sales Price per Unit	*$73.00*
Variable Costs per Unit	*$45.00*
Fixed Costs except Depreciation	*$50,000*
Depreciation Expense	*$17,000*

Exhibit 18.1

PROFIT+ PROFIT+

N P V S E N S I T I V I T Y A N A L Y S I S

I N P U T S

Unit Sales Per Year	3000
Sales Price Per Unit	73.00
Variable Costs Per Unit	45.00
Fixed Costs Except Depreciation	50000.00
Depreciation Expense	17000.00
Income Tax Rate (%)	40.00
Salvage Value	15000.00
Cost of Capital (%)	11.00
Expected Project Life in Years............	5
Project Cost at Time Period 0.............	100000.00

[F1]=HELP [F2]=REVIEW [F5]=REDO [F9]=PRINT [ESC]=MENU [PGDN]=ANALYSIS

Exhibit 18.2

PROFIT+ PROFIT+

N P V S E N S I T I V I T Y A N A L Y S I S

VARIABLE	NPV at Base Value of Variable - 10%	NPV AT BASE VALUE OF VARIABLE	NPV at Base Value of Variable + 10%	Slope of Sensitivity Line for Variable
Unit Sales	-12757.86	5869.46	24496.78	31.736
Sales Price	-42694.63	5869.46	54433.55	82.740
Var. Costs	35806.23	5869.46	-24067.31	-51.004
FC excl. Dep.	16957.15	5869.46	-5218.23	-18.890
Dep. Expense	3356.25	5869.46	8382.67	4.282
Tax Rate	8382.67	5869.46	3356.25	-4.282
Cost of Capital ..	8987.11	5869.46	2891.60	-5.073
Salvage Value	5335.35	5869.46	6403.57	0.910
Life	-1704.86	5869.46	13058.69	12.249
Cost	15869.46	5869.46	-4130.54	-17.037

[F1]=HELP [F2]=REVIEW [F5]=REDO [F9]=PRINT [ESC]=MENU [PGUP]=INPUTS

Income Tax Rate	*40%*
Project Salvage Value.	*$15,000*
Cost of Capital.	*11%*
Expected Project Life	*5 years*
Initial Project Cost	*$100,000*

Conduct NPV sensitivity analysis on this project using the given data as the base case.

SUMMARY

In the preceding problem had you been given another project with which you could have compared the slopes of Project Y's sensitivity lines, you could have commented on the relative riskiness of the two projects. The one with the greater slopes would have been the riskier of the two. In the absence of another project for comparison, sensitivity analysis can be used to help the analyst identify to which input variables the project is most sensitive. In the case of Project Y, for example, the slopes of the lines relating NPV to unit sales, sales price, and variable costs were the steepest. To carry this example a bit further, the slope of the line relating NPV to sales price was 51.50. This means that a one percentage point change in sales price from the base value produces a 51.50 percent change in NPV—a relationship about which the planner would definitely want to know! Being aware of this information shows you the input variables for which the accuracy of your estimates is most critical.

END-OF-CHAPTER PROBLEMS

1. Commerce Novelties Corporation is considering purchasing a new piece of equipment to manufacture its new platinum golf tee/calculator combination. The following projections have been gathered for the project:

Unit Sales per Year	8,500
Sales Price per Unit	$80.00
Variable Costs per Unit	$50.50
Fixed Costs except Depreciation	$125,000
Depreciation Expense	$42,500
Income Tax Rate	40%
Project Salvage Value	$30,500
Cost of Capital	12%
Expected Project Life	6 years
Initial Project Cost	$250,000

a. Conduct NPV sensitivity analysis on this project.

b. To which of the input variables does the project's NPV appear to be most sensitive? How can this information be of use to management?

c. On simply a subjective basis, without having any other projects for comparison, comment on the riskiness of this project.

2. Franko Robotics, the company that was considering Project Y, the project analyzed in Exhibits 18.1 and 18.2, is also considering another project, Project Z. Projections for Project Z are given in the following table:

Unit Sales per Year	3,000
Sales Price per Unit	$74.00
Variable Costs per Unit.	$46.00
Fixed Costs except Depreciation	$44,500
Depreciation Expense	$17,000
Income Tax Rate	40%
Project Salvage Value	$12,000
Cost of Capital	11%
Expected Project Life	5 years
Initial Project Cost	$100,000

a. Conduct NPV sensitivity analysis on Project Z.

b. To which of its input variables does Project Z's NPV appear to be most sensitive? Why?

c. Which of Franko's two projects, Y or Z, appears to be the riskier? Support your answer.

d. The base case cost of capital for both Projects Y and Z was 11 percent. Given your answer to part c, would you advise Franko's management to use the same cost of capital to evaluate both of these projects? Why or why not?

3. Florida Foundries, Inc., is evaluating a new project. The following information has been gathered:

Unit Sales per Year	12,000
Sales Price per Unit	$25.00
Variable Costs per Unit.	$19.54
Fixed Costs except Depreciation.	$32,000
Depreciation Expense	$20,000
Income Tax Rate	40%
Project Salvage Value	$10,000

Cost of Capital.	13%
Expected Project Life..................................	7 years
Initial Project Cost	$110,000

a. Conduct NPV sensitivity analysis on this project.

b. Does the project appear to be acceptable?

c. To which of its input variables does the project's NPV appear to be most sensitive? Why?

d. Would your answers to parts b and c change if the sales price per unit were $28.00, rather than $25.00? Why or why not?

e. Would your answers to parts b and c change if the sales price per unit were $23.00, rather than $25.00? Why or why not?

4. Juanita Merced, assistant manager for planning of West Coast Innovations, Inc., has been given the task of determining the riskiness of a new capital spending project. The project, whose cost is $200,000, is expected to produce 100,000 units per year that can be sold for $7.62 each. The best estimates that Merced can obtain suggest that variable costs per unit will be $5.92, fixed costs excluding depreciation will amount to $125,000, depreciation expense will be $40,000 per year over the project's ten-year life, and the project's salvage value will be $25,000. The firm's marginal income tax rate is 40 percent, and its cost of capital is 14 percent.

a. Conduct NPV sensitivity analysis on this project.

b. Does the project appear to be acceptable?

c. To which of its input variables does the project's NPV appear to be most sensitive? Why?

d. Would your answers to parts b and c change if the firm's cost of capital were 12, percent rather than 14 percent? Why or why not?

e. Would your answers to parts b and c change if the firm's cost of capital were 16 percent, rather than 14 percent? Why or why not?

5. Chuck Thomas is considering purchasing a computerized t-shirt imprinting system that he can operate in a local shopping mall. The initial cost of the system will be $25,000. Each year over the five-year life of the system, Thomas believes that he should be able to sell 7,500 t-shirts at an average price of $8.50 each. The system's supplier has told Thomas that variable cost will amount to $4.25 per shirt sold. Fixed costs (except depreciation expense), composed primarily of booth space rental, will amount to $12,000 per year, and depreciation expenses will be

$5,000. Due to wear and tear and expected technological advances over the next five years, Thomas does not anticipate that the system will have any significant salvage value. Thomas' income tax rate is 34 percent, and the appropriate cost of capital is 16 percent.

a. Conduct NPV sensitivity analysis on the t-shirt imprinting system.

b. Does it appear that Thomas should buy the system?

c. To which of its input variables does the system's NPV appear to be most sensitive? Why?

d. If you were Thomas, how would your answer to part c affect your decision-making process?

6. Hasenpfeffer Company has two capital spending proposals that it is evaluating this year. The following information has been accumulated for each project:

	Project 1	**Project 2**
Unit Sales per Year	9,700	7,800
Sales Price per Unit	$360.00	$250.00
Variable Costs per Unit	$290.00	$172.00
Fixed Costs except Depreciation	$120,000	$55,000
Depreciation Expense	$200,000	$200,000
Income Tax Rate	39%	39%
Project Salvage Value	$50,000	$50,000
Cost of Capital	15%	15%
Expected Project Life	10 years	10 years
Initial Project Cost	$2,000,000	$2,000,000

a. Undertake a NPV sensitivity analysis for each project.

b. Which project appears to be of greater risk? Support your answer.

c. Would your answer to part b influence how each project was evaluated? (Hint: Would it have any effect on the cost of capital used to evaluate each project?) Why or why not?

d. If the projects are independent, which, if either, should be accepted? Support your answer.

e. If the projects are mutually exclusive, which, if either, should be accepted? Support your answer.

Chapter Nineteen
Breakeven Analysis and Leverage

Two subjects that are of importance to both financial analysis and financial planning are breakeven analysis and leverage. In classes that are prerequisite to your financial management class you have learned that breakeven analysis is undertaken to determine at what level of sales or output a firm must operate for total revenues to cover total costs. Leverage is a term used to refer to the tendency of profits to change at a faster rate than sales due to the presence of fixed costs in a firm's cost structure. Since one important determinant of a company's breakeven point is the amount of fixed costs it carries, and since leverage is caused by fixed costs, the two subjects must somehow be related.

This chapter explains the concepts of breakeven analysis and leverage, shows how the two concepts are related, and demonstrates how your PROFIT+ software can be of assistance in performing some of the calculations associated with these two aspects of financial management.

BREAKEVEN ANALYSIS

The purpose of breakeven analysis is to determine the level of operations (i.e., sales) that is necessary for the firm's total revenues to cover total costs. Below this point the company will be incurring an operating loss, and above this point operating profits will be generated. Fundamentally, breakeven analysis involves the division of a firm's operating costs into two categories: those that are fixed over the relevant range of operations and those that vary with the level of operations.

Fixed costs include such items as executive and staff salaries, general office expenses, rental expenses, and depreciation on plant and equipment. Such items as the cost of raw materials, the wages of production workers, and sales commissions are examples of variable costs. Once these two types of costs have been identified, breakeven analysis proceeds by calculating, either graphically or algebraically, the level of sales where total revenues equal total costs--this level is the breakeven point.

While you might be more familiar with the determination of breakeven points using graphical solutions, software such as PROFIT+ relies on algebraic formulas when undertaking breakeven analysis. Consequently, the explanations that follow are presented in algebraic, rather than graphic, form. (For a more complete discussion of breakeven analysis, including both graphs and formulas, refer to your financial management textbook. Chapter 9 of *Essentials of Managerial Finance,* 8th ed., by J. Fred Weston and Eugene F. Brigham, contains such a discussion.) The following symbols will be used in our discussion:

P = Selling price per unit
Q = Quantity of units sold
S = Total sales revenue (= PQ)
v = Variable cost per unit
Qv = Total variable costs
F = Total fixed costs
TC = Qv + F = Total Costs
I = Interest expense

Using the preceding symbols, the breakeven point can be defined as the place where total revenues equal total costs, or

$$S = TC \tag{19.1}$$

To determine the breakeven point, the equation must be expanded as follows:

$$PQ = Qv + F \tag{19.2}$$

Then, the breakeven quantity (Q') can be defined algebraically by solving for Q'.

$$\begin{aligned} PQ' &= Q'v + F \\ PQ' - Q'v &= F \\ Q'(P - v) &= F \\ Q' &= \frac{F}{P - v} \end{aligned} \tag{19.3}$$

Exhibit 19.1

```
PROFIT+                                                         PROFIT+
          B R E A K E V E N   A N A L Y S I S   A N D   L E V E R A G E

   This routine has two options:

 ▶ 1.  Breakeven point calculation, given fixed costs, selling price, and
       variable costs per unit.

   2.  Breakeven point, degree of operating leverage, degree of financial
       leverage, and combined leverage effect, given complete income
       statement data.

            Use ↑↓ to make your selection and press [RETURN]
                                  or
                type the number preceding your selection.

                   [F1]=HELP  [F2]=REVIEW  [ESC]=MENU
```

The breakeven point in sales dollars can be determined by multiplying the breakeven quantity (Q') by the selling price per unit (P). In Equation 19.3, Q' is a function of two factors: F (total fixed costs) and P - v (which is frequently called the contribution margin). The *contribution margin* is the portion of each unit's selling price that is left to cover fixed costs and to produce profits.

The PROFIT+ Breakeven Analysis Routine

Option Q, Breakeven Analysis and Leverage, on the PROFIT+ Main Menu contains a program for solving for the breakeven point. As can be seen from Exhibit 19.1, selecting this option brings up the Breakeven Analysis and Leverage submenu. Choice 1 on this submenu calls up a routine that calculates the breakeven point, given fixed costs, the selling price, and variable costs per unit. The routine uses Equation 19.3 in its calculations. Exhibit 19.2 shows how Choice 1 on the Breakeven Analysis and Leverage submenu can be used to solve the following sample problem:

Sample Problem: The Knoxville Spring Company would like to determine its breakeven point for the coming year based on the following information: total fixed costs = \$20,000; variable costs per unit = \$1.00; and selling price per unit = \$2.50.

Exhibit 19.2

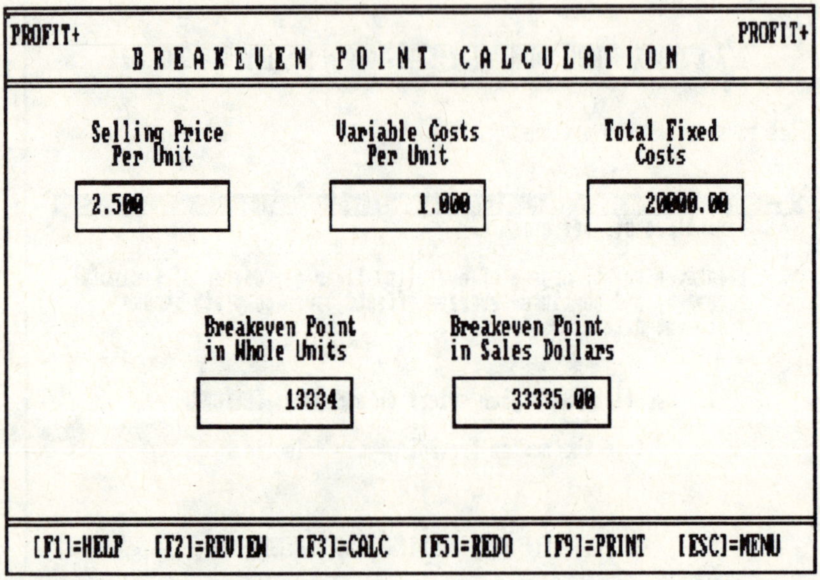

(Note: PROFIT+ follows the common practice of rounding the breakeven point to the next higher unit. In the example, the actual solution to Equation 19.3 gave a result of 13,333.333 units. This has been rounded to 13,334 units by PROFIT+.)

LEVERAGE

Leverage, or the tendency for profits to change at a faster rate than sales, is an important concept in financial management. Any discussion of leverage must begin by explaining that there are really two types of leverage that can be present in a business: operating leverage and financial leverage. Operating leverage is caused by the presence of fixed operating costs in the firm's operating cost structure, whereas financial leverage arises due to the existence of fixed-cost financing (primarily debt) in the firm's capital structure. Both of these types of leverage, when working together, can produce a significant "levering" effect on a company's profits.

If something is operating in your firm's cost structure that will cause, for example, profits to increase by 20 percent when sales have increased by only 8 percent (or a 20 percent decline when sales have dropped by 8 percent), naturally it is important to understand that it is there. In addition to this rather obvious significance, however, leverage is an important factor in the determination of the appropriate, or optimum, financial structure for a business. It is with this latter point in mind that we will begin a more detailed discussion of the concept of leverage.

Optimum Financial Structure

The determination of the optimum blend of debt and equity in a firm's capital structure involves a risk-return trade-off. Using greater proportions of debt financing increases the risk to which a business exposes itself and prompts stockholders to require a higher rate of return on their investment. Other things being equal, a higher required rate of return will cause the market price of the firm's common stock to decline. (Remember the constant growth dividend model? $P_0 = D_1/(k_s - g)$.) But other things frequently are not equal, because using higher proportions of debt financing can also lead to higher expected growth rates, and higher expected growth rates cause stock prices to rise. Thus, determining the optimum financial structure for a firm means that the financial manager must balance the risks associated with using increasing amounts of debt with the benefits that debt can produce for the firm.

Business Risk

One of the primary determinants of how much debt a firm can take on is the amount of business risk that firm has. Business risk can be defined as the uncertainty that is inherent in the projection of future levels of operating income (frequently called "Earnings Before Interest and Taxes," or EBIT). Examining the abbreviated income statement in Exhibit 19.3 should help explain why business risk has such an impact on the amount of debt a firm can use in its capital structure. As you can see from this income statement, it is out of operating income, or EBIT, that a firm must make the interest payments on its debt. Thus, the more uncertain the firm (and its creditors) are about future levels of EBIT, the more uncertain will be its ability to cover its interest payments, and the less able it will be to finance its operations with debt.

Although many factors have an impact on the amount of business risk a firm has (demand variability, sales price variability, labor and raw material price variability, for example), one of its main determinants is the importance of fixed costs in the firm's operating cost structure--the amount of operating leverage it possesses.

Exhibit 19.3

Sales
- Variable Costs
- Fixed Costs
Operating Income (EBIT)
- Interest Expense
Pretax Income
- Income Taxes
Net Income

Operating Leverage

Operating leverage is the tendency for operating income (EBIT) to change at a faster rate than sales due to the presence of fixed costs in a firm's operating cost structure. As fixed costs become more significant, EBIT becomes more sensitive to changes in sales. One of the simplest ways to understand why operating leverage works as it does is to think back to our discussion of breakeven analysis. In that discussion, fixed costs were defined as those that remain constant over the relevant range of operations. Remembering this, think about what happens to fixed costs per unit of sales as more (or fewer) units are produced and sold. As sales increase, fixed costs per unit decline, and as sales decrease, fixed costs per unit increase. That is, as more units are sold, each unit is responsible for covering a smaller amount of fixed costs, thus allowing a greater proportion of the sales price of each unit to go toward profit (and vice versa). So, it is how "thickly" or "thinly" fixed costs are spread on a per unit basis that gives rise to operating leverage. The more fixed costs a firm has relative to variable costs, the greater will be the impact of operating leverage.

The amount of operating leverage a firm has at any one time can be measured by calculating the *degree of operating leverage* (DOL). DOL can be defined as the ratio of the percentage change in EBIT that will result, other things being equal, from a change in sales to the percentage change in sales.

$$\text{DOL} = \frac{\text{Percentage change in EBIT}}{\text{Percentage change in sales}}$$

A degree of operating leverage of 2, for example, would tell the observer that, other things being equal, a 10 percent decrease in sales from the given level would produce a 20 percent decrease in EBIT. A DOL of 1.6 would imply that, other things held constant, a 16 percent increase in operating income would result from a

10 percent increase in sales. For any given level of sales, sales price, and cost structure, the degree of operating leverage present in a firm can be calculated using Equation 19.4.

$$DOL = \frac{Q(P - v)}{Q(P - v) - F} \tag{19.4}$$

Other things being equal, a high degree of operating leverage implies that a small percentage change in sales will produce a much greater change in operating income, leading to a higher amount of business risk. A high level of business risk generally means that a firm is less able to incur high levels of debt financing.

Financial Leverage

The other type of leverage that can be present in a firm is financial leverage--the tendency for profits (earnings per share and/or return on equity) to change at a faster rate than EBIT due to the presence of fixed-cost financing in a firm's capital structure. In other words, financial leverage is caused by the fixed interest expenses (and to a lesser extent the fixed preferred stock dividends) that are incurred when a firm uses debt financing (or preferred stock financing) in its capital structure. The fixed nature of interest expenses means that, as EBIT increases (decreases) proportionately lesser (greater) amounts of each EBIT dollar must be used to cover those expenses, thus leaving greater (lesser) amounts remaining as profits. The potential positive effect of financial leverage can be the attractive benefit of debt financing. On the other hand, its potential negative effect on profits causes debt financing to be more risky than equity financing.

The *degree of financial leverage* (DFL) measures how much financial leverage a firm has at any one time. It is defined as the ratio of the percentage change in before-tax profits that results, other things being equal, from a change in EBIT to the percentage change in EBIT.

$$DFL = \frac{\text{Percentage change in before-tax profits}}{\text{Percentage change in EBIT}}$$

A DFL of 1.5 implies that, other things being equal, a 20 percent change in EBIT will lead to a 30 percent change in before-tax profits (and a like change in after-tax profits, earnings per share, and return on equity). Equation 19.5 can be used to calculate the degree of financial leverage a firm has under a given set of circumstances.

$$DFL = \frac{EBIT}{EBIT - I}$$

(19.5)

The Combined Leverage Effect

If you will examine the income statement given in Exhibit 19.3 in light of the discussions of operating and financial leverage, you will see that operating leverage comes into play between sales and operating income, and that financial leverage has its effect between operating income and before-tax profits. Since both of these types of leverage can be present in the same firm, they can work together to produce a combined, or total, leverage effect between the top of the income statement and its bottom-line profit figure. This total effect is called the *combined leverage effect* (CLE) and can be defined as the ratio of percentage change in before-tax profits that results, other things being equal, from a change in sales to the percentage change in sales.

$$CLE = \frac{\text{Percentage change in before-tax profits}}{\text{Percentage change in sales}}$$

If, for example, a firm has a CLE of 3, this implies that, other things being equal, a 15 percent change in sales from the given level will produce a 45 percent change in before-tax profits.

CLE can be calculated in two ways. The first recognizes that the CLE is the product of the firm's DOL and DFL, and determines it accordingly.

$$CLE = DOL \times DFL$$

(19.6)

The second method for calculating CLE uses income statement data from the base. This method is represented in Equation 19.7.

$$CLE = \frac{Q(P - v)}{Q(P - v) - F - I}$$

(19.7)

The PROFIT+ Degrees of Leverage Routine

In addition to containing the breakeven routine discussed earlier in this chapter, the Breakeven Analysis and Leverage submenu shown in Exhibit 19.1 also contains a

Exhibit 19.4

```
PROFIT+                                                         PROFIT+
   B R E A K E V E N   P O I N T  &  D E G R E E S   O F   L E V E R A G E

 Selling Price / Unit ...      2.000 | Interest Expense .......    10000.00
 Units Sold ............      150000 | Income Tax Rate (%) ....          40
 Variable Costs / Unit ..      1.000 | # of Shares of Common
 Fixed Operating Costs ..   60000.00 |   Stock Outstanding.....       10000

          INCOME STATEMENT             Degree of
                                       Operating Leverage .....        1.67
  Sales ................   300000.00
  - Variable Costs .....   150000.00   Degree of
  - Fixed Costs ........    60000.00   Financial Leverage .....        1.13
  Op. Income (EBIT) ....    90000.00
  - Interest Expense ...    10000.00   Combined
  Income Before Tax ....    80000.00   Leverage Effect ........        1.88
  - Income Tax .........    32000.00
  After-tax income .....    48000.00   Breakeven Point:
  Earnings per Share ...        4.80    in Units ..............       60000
                                        in Dollars ............   120000.00

 [F1]=HELP   [F2]=REVIEW   [F3]=CALC   [F5]=REDO   [F9]=PRINT   [ESC]=MENU
```

routine for determining the DOL, DFL, and CLE for a firm, given base-case income statement information. (This routine also includes the firm's breakeven point in its output.) It uses Equations 19.3 through 19.6, respectively, to calculate the breakeven point, the DOL, the DFL, and the CLE. In addition, the routine also prints out an income statement similar to the one shown in Exhibit 19.3 along with the earnings per share figure for the firm.

Exhibit 19.4 shows how Choice 2 on the Breakeven Analysis and Leverage submenu can be used to solve the following sample problem:

Sample Problem: Using the income statement information in the table below, compute the breakeven point, the degrees of operating and financial leverage, and the combined leverage effect for Billbright Incorporated. What does each of the figures you have calculated mean?

Billbright Incorporated:
Income Statement Data

Selling Price	*$2.00*
Unit Sales	*150,000*
Variable Cost per Unit	*$1.00*
Fixed Operating Costs	*$60,000*
Interest Expense	*$10,000*

Income Tax Rate	*40%*
Number of Shares of Common Stock Outstanding	*10,000*

The results from the preceding sample problem can be interpreted as follows:

1. A breakeven point of 60,000 units implies that Billbright Incorporated must produce and sell approximately 60,000 units for its sales revenues to just cover its total costs. (Total sales = Total costs at BE point = 60,000 units x $2 selling price per unit = $120,000.)

2. A DOL of 1.67 implies that, other things being equal, a 1 percent change in sales from the given level (150,000 units) will produce a 1.67 percent change in EBIT.

3. A DFL of 1.13 means that, other things being equal, there will be a 1.13 percent change in before-tax profits, after-tax profits, earnings per share, and return on equity for each percentage point change in EBIT from the given level ($90,000).

4. Other things being equal, a CLE of 1.88 implies that each 1 percentage point change in sales from the given level should produce a 1.88 percent change in before-tax profits, after-tax profits, earnings per share, and return on equity.

SUMMARY

As with many other topics covered in this guide, you have been introduced to just the highlights of breakeven analysis and leverage. To get a more complete view of the importance of these topics to financial management, you should refer to the chapters in your financial management textbook that deal with these topics. Chapter 9 of Essentials of Managerial Finance, 8th ed., by J. Fred Weston and Eugene F. Brigham, or Chapter 15 of *Fundamentals of Financial Management,* 4th ed., by Eugene F. Brigham, are excellent reference chapters for this purpose.

END-OF-CHAPTER PROBLEMS

1. Determine the breakeven point for Blue Jeans Corporation, given the following information:

Total Fixed Costs	$35,000.00
Variable Costs per Unit	$45.35
Selling Price per Unit	$95.75

a. Other things being equal, if the Blue Jeans Corporation could increase its selling price to $115 per unit, what would be its breakeven point?

b. Other things being equal, if Blue Jeans could decrease its variable costs per unit to $44.55, what would be its breakeven point?

2. The Well-known Walter Cookie Company operates two of its "Just Like Home" cookie counters in St. Louis. Cookies sell for $0.60 each, variable costs per cookie amount to $0.07, and the firm's fixed costs for the two outlets combined are $68,000.

a. What is Well-known Walter's breakeven point in cookies? In dollars?

b. The firm is anticipating that, because of a recent increase in the prices of chocolate and sugar, its variable costs per cookie will soon rise to $0.078. Other things held constant, how would this increase affect the firm's breakeven point?

c. If, in response to the increase in its variable costs, the firm increased its price per cookie to $0.65, how would its breakeven point be affected?

3. The Blacklock Company is considering a move to automate its production facility. Presently, total fixed costs are $75,000 and variable costs per unit are $12.85. If it were to proceed with the automation project, the firm estimates that variable costs per unit would decline to $6 and fixed costs would increase to $147,000. If Blacklock's selling price per unit is $42, how would the proposed automation affect its breakeven point?

4. The Universal Knowledge Corporation's current selling price and cost structure are as follows:

Total Fixed Costs	$23,000.00
Variable Costs per Unit	$11.50
Selling Price per Unit	$24.96

a. What is the firm's breakeven point?

b. The firm is presently negotiating a new labor agreement that it believes will raise the wages of production workers and increase the variable costs of manufacturing to $12.76 per unit. If total fixed costs and selling price do not change, what effect will the anticipated wage increase have on the company's breakeven point?

5. The following table contains income statement information for the Illinois Lamp Company.

Selling Price	$121.00
Unit Sales	17,000
Variable Cost per Unit	$46.22
Fixed Operating Costs	$565,000
Interest Expense	$64,000
Income Tax Rate	40%
Number of Shares of Common Stock Outstanding	140,000

a. What is Illinois Lamp's breakeven point?

b. What are the degrees of operating and financial leverage and the combined leverage effect for the company?

c. What does each of your answers to part b imply?

d. By what percentage could Illinois Lamp's sales decline before earnings per share are eliminated?

6. Ralph Dean, the financial manager for Williams Corporation, is examining his firm's cost structure in light of some changes that might take place in the future. Initially, Williams would like to calculate the effect these changes will have on the company's breakeven point, on its degrees of operating and financial leverage, and on its combined leverage effect. Williams has gathered the following information regarding the firm's current operations:

Selling Price	$12.00
Unit Sales	66,500
Variable Cost per Unit	$6.88
Fixed Operating Costs	$149,000
Interest Expense	$29,000
Income Tax Rate	38%
Number of Shares of Common Stock Outstanding	60,000

a. What are Williams' current breakeven point, degrees of operating and financial leverage, and combined leverage effect?

b. If all other inputs remained the same but selling price was decreased to $10.75, how would each of the values calculated in part a change?

c. If, in addition to the decreased selling price, interest expenses increased to $44,000, how would each of the values calculated in parts a and b change?

d. What would be the additional impact on the values calculated above if, in addition to the changes already considered in parts b and c, Williams' fixed costs increased to $175,000?

e. Interpret and discuss the results of your calculations in parts a through d. Why is it important that Dean know the effects that the anticipated changes will have on the firm's breakeven point, degrees of operating and financial leverage, and combined leverage effect?

f. Assuming that the changes suggested in parts b, c, and d do occur, by what percentage could Williams' sales decline before earnings per share would be eliminated?

7. The Household Gadget Corporation is examining its cost structure because management believes that the structure will undergo some changes in the near future. The firm's initial concern is to calculate the effect these changes will have on the company's BE point, DOL, DFL, and CLE. Use the following information about Household's present operations to answer the questions asked below:

Selling Price	$21.50
Unit Sales	125,500
Variable Cost per Unit	$15.88
Fixed Operating Costs	$353,000
Interest Expense	$200,500
Income Tax Rate	39%
Number of Shares of Common Stock Outstanding	250,000

a. What are Household Gadget's current breakeven point, degrees of operating and financial leverage and combined leverage effect?

b. If all other inputs remained the same but selling price increased to $24.00 how would each of the values calculated in part a change?

c. If, in addition to the increased selling price, interest expenses decreased to $150,000, how would each of the values calculated in parts a and b change?

d. What would be the additional impact on the values calculated above if, besides the changes already made, the firm's fixed costs decreased to $275,000?

e. Discuss the results of your calculations in parts a through d. Why is it important to know the effects that the anticipated changes will have on the firm's BE point, DOL, DFL, and CLE?

f. Assuming that the changes suggested in parts b, c, and d do occur, by what percentage would Household Gadget's sales have to decline to eliminate earnings per share?

Chapter Twenty
Marginal Cost of Capital Basics

THE COST OF CAPITAL

A business must have assets to operate. To acquire these assets, management has to seek out ways to finance them. Evidence of this financing shows up on the claims side of the firm's balance sheet as various types of debt, preferred stock, and common stockholders' equity. These sources of financing, frequently called capital, are not obtained without cost, because those who provide the business with funds require a return on their investments. Management should be aware of the cost of these funds, since the vitality and growth of the firm depend on management's ability to take the funds, invest them in the business, and earn rates of return that are greater than the cost of the invested dollars. (If a firm earns exactly as much as its invested funds are costing, it can survive, but will not grow.)

The *cost of capital* is the phrase ordinarily used to refer to the cost of the funds invested in the business. It is an average measure of the cost of each of the components of a firm's capital structure: debt, preferred stock, and common stockholders' equity. Because growth requires that a firm earn more on its investments than the cost of the funds used for those investments, and long-term survival demands rates of return that are at least equal to the cost of funds, the cost of capital is a very important topic in financial management. It is used as a discount, or hurdle, rate in capital budgeting; it is employed as a measure to help determine the optimum capital structure; and it is also important in making decisions regarding working capital policy, leasing, and bond refunding.

Although cost of capital is such an important topic (or possibly more accurately, *because* it is such an important topic), it is one that cannot be fully addressed in a guide such as this. Instead, the basics required for use of PROFIT+'s cost of capital software will be discussed. You should refer to your financial management textbook for a more thorough discussion of the topic. (Chapter 17 of *Essentials of Managerial Finance*, 8th ed., by J. Fred Weston and Eugene F. Brigham, and Chapter 14 of *Fundamentals of Financial Management,* 4th ed., by Eugene F. Brigham, provide detailed discussions of the cost of capital.)

CAPITAL COMPONENTS AND THEIR COSTS

The first step in computing a firm's weighted average cost of capital is to identify the components of the firm's capital structure, and then determine the costs of each of these components. For simplicity, the firm with which you are working here has only three capital components: debt, preferred stock, and common stockholders' equity. As you read the following paragraphs dealing with the costs of each of these components, you should realize that each cost is based on the current market cost, rather than the historic cost, of the component. This is because the cost of capital is an *opportunity cost* concept, and the financial manager is concerned with what returns investors are expecting today on their investments, not the returns that investors were demanding in the past.

Component Cost of Debt

The component cost of debt is most frequently defined as the after-tax interest rate on the firm's new debt. Because the cost of capital averages the cost of debt along with the costs of preferred and common stock, all three of these costs must be stated in the same terms with respect to taxes. Since returns to preferred and common stockholders come from after-tax dollars, whereas interest to creditors is paid from before-tax income, the interest rate on debt must be adjusted to reflect the tax-deductible nature of interest. This adjustment is accomplished by taking the before-tax interest rate on new debt times one minus the firm's marginal tax rate as follows:

$$\text{Component Cost of Debt} = k_d(1 - t) \tag{20.1}$$

where k_d = interest rate on the firm's new debt

t = the firm's marginal tax rate.

Component Cost of Preferred Stock

The component cost of preferred stock is defined as the preferred dividend divided by the price per share that the firm would receive when issuing new preferred stock. (The price per share received by the firm is equal to the selling price, less any flotation costs.) This calculation is represented as follows:

$$k_p = \frac{D_p}{P_n} \tag{20.2}$$

where k_p = component cost of preferred stock

D_p = preferred dividend

P_n = net issuing price of new preferred stock.

Component Cost of Common Stockholders' Equity

Whereas debt and preferred stock both have a cost to the firm that is evident to most students, the cost of common stockholders' equity is sometimes more difficult to see. If, however, you will realize that the costs of both debt and preferred stock are the returns investors require from those components, and then remember that common stockholders also require a return on their investments, you should be able to understand why common stockholders' equity has a cost to the firm. If the firm does not provide the required return to suppliers of common equity--either in the form of dividends or capital growth--those investors will withdraw their financial support. That is, they will sell their stock and invest elsewhere where they *can* earn the required return.

Given that common equity does have a cost (the return required by common stockholders), at least two basic factors complicate the determination of what that cost is for a firm at a particular point in time. The first of these, and definitely the more perplexing, is that the cost of common equity is not an objective, contractually set cost such as those of bonds and preferred stocks. Therefore, it must be estimated using one of several techniques, rather than simply observed. The second complicating factor arises because common equity can take two forms: retained earnings and/or newly issued common stock. As you shall see later in this chapter, there exists an important reason for these two forms of equity to have different costs. In the paragraphs that follow, alternative methods for computing the component cost of retained earnings will be discussed. Then a discussion of the component cost of new common stock will be presented.

Component Cost of Retained Earnings At least three methods have been suggested for determining the component cost of retained earnings. The first of these, the Capital Asset Pricing Model (CAPM) approach, uses modern capital market theory to estimate the return required by a firm's equity holders. It does this by estimating each of the values included in the equation for the security market line (SML), shown as follows:

$$k_s = k_{rf} + b(k_m - k_{rf}) \tag{20.3}$$

where k_s = required rate of return on the firm's common stock

k_{rf} = risk-free rate of interest (usually estimated as either the rate on U.S. Treasury bonds or that on 30-day U.S. Treasury bills)

b = the "beta coefficient" for the firm's stock (measures the riskiness of the stock)

k_m = the rate of return for the "market" (frequently called the return on a stock of "average" risk).

This method requires several estimates as its inputs: the analyst must decide which interest rate to use as the "risk-free" rate, the beta must be estimated, and the "market" return must be estimated. Thus, the CAPM approach for determining the required rate of return on common equity is not as objective, or straightforward, as it might first appear. (For a complete discussion of the CAPM, see Chapter 6 of either *Fundamentals of Financial Management,* 4th ed. by Eugene F. Brigham, or *Essentials of Managerial Finance*, 8th ed. by J. Fred Weston and Eugene F. Brigham.)

A second method sometimes used for determining the required rate of return on a firm's common stock is based on the logic that a company's stock is riskier than its bonds, and therefore should yield a return that is greater than that of its bonds. Thus, the cost of common equity is determined by adding a *risk premium* of two to four percentage points to the interest rate on the company's long-term debt. Here, again, the calculated return is not a precise one, since the analyst must estimate the proper risk premium to add to the interest rate on the firm's long-term debt.

The final alternative discussed here for estimating the return required by a firm's common stockholders is the *dividend yield plus growth rate approach*, which assumes that the return stockholders are seeking is made up of two components: a dividend yield and a capital gain, or growth, component. This approach, also called the *discounted cash flow* (DCF) method, can be represented as follows:

$$k_s = \frac{D_1}{P_0} + g$$

(20.4)

where k_s = expected rate of return on common equity

D_1 = next expected common dividend

P_0 = current market price of the firm's stock

g = expected growth, or capital gain, rate (often, this is interpreted as the growth rate projected by security analysts).

Once more, the estimated return obtained by this method is just that—an estimate. It is based on the next *expected* dividend and the *expected* growth rate for the stock. Thus, the required rate of return on common equity, as estimated by all three of the above methods, is not an exact measure. In practice, it is usually most convenient to obtain reliable estimates for the DCF method. Because of this, PROFIT+ uses the DCF approach in calculating the cost of retained earnings.

Component Cost of New Common Stock If, over and above retained earnings, a firm is issuing new common stock to finance its operations, it must use the cost of this new stock as the estimate of its cost of common equity when determining the weighted average cost of capital. This being the case, why is the cost of new common stock different from that of retained earnings? The answer is that the flotation costs of selling new stock tend to increase the rate of return the firm must provide to its stockholders. Flotation costs increase the cost of new common equity because they decrease the proceeds that the firm receives when selling the new stock. As can be seen from Equation 20.5, this has the effect of raising the effective dividend yield the company must pay, which, in turn, raises the required rate of return on the stock.

$$k_e = \frac{D_1}{P_0(1 - F)}$$

(20.5)

where k_e = component cost of new common stock

F = the percentage flotation cost of selling new shares of common stock

$P_0(1 - F)$ = the net price per share realized by the firm when it sells new common stock.

WEIGHTED AVERAGE COST OF CAPITAL

A widely accepted method for determining a firm's cost of capital is to calculate a weighted average of the component costs of the firm's capital structure. The term *weighted* simply means that the relative importance (i.e., weight) of a particular component cost used in calculating the average is based on the percentage of the company's capital structure represented by that component.

Optimum, or Target, Capital Structure

A firm that is attempting to maximize its value will strive to determine its optimum capital structure. That is, its management will seek that blend of debt, preferred stock, and common equity financing that maximizes the price of the firm's common stock. Once this optimum, or target, capital structure has been established, the firm will attempt to raise new funds in a manner that will maintain the optimum blend. For example, if a firm has determined that its optimum capital structure consists of 40 percent debt, 20 percent preferred stock, and 40 percent common stockholders' equity, and it must raise \$1000 during the coming year, it would attempt to raise that amount according to the following schedule: \$400 debt, \$200 preferred stock, \$400 common stockholders' equity (either retained earnings or the sale of new common stock). (For discussions of how firms determine their target capital structures, see Chapter 18 of *Essentials of Managerial Finance*, 8th ed., by J. Fred Weston and Eugene F. Brigham, and/or Chapter 15 of *Fundamentals of Financial Management*, 4th ed., by Eugene F. Brigham.)

Calculating the Weighted Average Cost of Capital

Once the component costs and the weights of their respective components have been determined, the computation of the weighted average cost of capital requires the following calculations:

$$k_a = W_d k_d(1 - T) + W_p k_p + W_s k_s \quad \textbf{(20.6)}$$

where W_d = percentage of debt in the firm's capital structure

W_p = percentage of preferred stock in the firm's capital structure

W_s = percentage of common stockholders' equity in the firm's capital structure.

(Note: If new common stock has been used to raise equity capital, then k_e should be used in the above equation, rather than k_s.)

The Marginal Cost of Capital

Within a given period of time, as a firm seeks to obtain more and more dollars of financing, at some point those funds will probably be available only at higher and higher costs. This being the case, there will come a point when the firm's cost of capital begins to rise. To estimate where this point lies and what the firm's cost of capital will be beyond this point, you can construct a *marginal cost of capital (MCC) schedule* for the business. This schedule shows the cost of obtaining an additional dollar of capital (i.e., the marginal cost) as more and more funds are sought. Since economic theory tells us that value is maximized where marginal costs equal marginal revenues, it is the marginal cost of capital that should be used when making various decisions within the firm, for example, when evaluating capital spending proposals.

The marginal cost of capital is simply the weighted average cost of obtaining an additional dollar of financing and can be calculated using the approach discussed earlier in this chapter, which is summarized in Equation 20.6.

Breaks in the MCC Schedule Whenever the cost of a capital component increases and causes the firm's MCC to rise, a "break" is said to have occurred in the MCC schedule. Being able to identify these break points helps the financial manager be better able to determine the firm's marginal cost of capital. A *break point* is defined as the dollar value of new capital that can be raised before an increase in the firm's weighted average cost of capital occurs.

While break points can result from an increase in the cost of any capital structure component, the most common first break point to be encountered is the retained earnings break point--the point at which the firm must switch from using retained earnings (internal equity) to selling new common stock (external equity) to raise its equity funds. When this switch occurs, the higher cost of external equity causes the firm's MCC to increase.

For any given situation, the retained earnings break point can be calculated using the following equation:

$$BP_{re} = \frac{\text{Available retained earnings}}{W_s} \tag{20.7}$$

One of the PROFIT+ routines described in the following section computes the retained earnings break point using Equation 20.7.

Exhibit 20.1

```
PROFIT+                                                        PROFIT+
     M A R G I N A L   C O S T   O F   C A P I T A L   B A S I C S

This routine gives you three options:

 ▶1. MCC calculation given the costs of the capital structure components.

  2. MCC calculation along with the calculation of the costs of the cap-
     ital structure components.

  3. MCC calculation along with the calculation of the costs of the cap-
     ital structure components and the retained earnings break point.

              Use ↑↓ to make you selection and press return
                                  or
               press the number that precedes your choice.

              [F1]=HELP   [F2]=REVIEW   [ESC]=MENU
```

THE PROFIT+ COST OF CAPITAL ROUTINE

Option R, Cost of Capital Basics, on the PROFIT+ Main Menu calls up the Marginal Cost of Capital Basics submenu shown in Exhibit 20.1. As can be seen in this exhibit, the submenu offers you three choices for calculating cost of capital. Each of these choices is discussed, and a sample problem using each is presented, in the following paragraphs.

MCC Calculations Given the Costs of the Capital Structure Components

Choice 1 on the Marginal Cost of Capital Basics submenu calculates MCC when provided with the dollar values of each of the three components of a firm's optimal capital structure: the after-tax costs of debt, preferred stock, and common stockholders' equity. The routine also calculates the weight of each component from your inputs. Exhibit 20.2 shows how Choice 1 can be used to help answer the following sample problem:

Exhibit 20.2

PROFIT+ PROFIT+

MCC GIVEN COMPONENT COSTS

Component	Amount of this Component in the Target Capital Structure	Weight %	After-Tax Component Cost %
Long-term Debt	6000.00	41.38	7.00
Preferred Stock	1000.00	6.90	15.00
Common Equity	7500.00	51.72	16.00

Marginal Cost of Capital (%): 12.21

[F1]=HELP [F2]=REVIEW [F3]=CALC [F5]=REDO [F9]=PRINT [ESC]=MENU

Sample Problem: Sharpe, Incorporated, has the following capital structure, which it believes is optimal:

Debt	*$6,000*
Preferred Stock	*$1,000*
Common Stockholders' Equity	*$7,500*

If the after-tax cost of its debt is 7 percent, the component cost of its preferred stock is 15 percent, and the component cost of stockholders' equity is 16 percent, what is the firm's weighted average marginal cost of capital?

MCC Calculation along with the Calculation of the Costs of the Capital Structure Components

Choice 2 on the Marginal Cost of Capital Basics submenu determines MCC and the costs of the capital structure components when you supply the appropriate inputs. You must inform the routine whether external equity is being used, whereupon PROFIT+ will identify with an asterisk the cost of equity (internal or external) that was used in the MCC calculation. PROFIT+ also calculates and displays the weight of each component.

Exhibit 20.3

```
PROFIT+                                                          PROFIT+
   M C C   W I T H   C O M P O N E N T   C O S T   C A L C U L A T I O N

Interest Rate on New L-T Debt (%) ............... 14.000    Component Costs
Tax Rate (%) .................................... 34.000
Dividend on New Preferred Stock ................. 10.000    Debt....  9.240
Net Price of New Preferred Stock ................ 92.000    Pfd.
Common Dividend Expected for Year 1 .............  2.000    Stock... 10.869
Projected Capital Gain (Growth Rate)                        Int.
  for Common Stock in Year 1 (%) ................  8.000    Equity.. 12.000
Current Market Price of Common Stock ............ 50.000   *Ext.
Percentage Flotation Cost for                               Equity.. 12.705
  Selling New Common Stock (%) .................. 15.000
                                                              Weight
Amount of L-T Debt in Capital Structure ......... 6000000.00  33.33 %
Amount of Pref. Stock in Capital Structure ...... 2000000.00  11.11 %
Amount of Com. Equity in Capital Structure ...... 10000000.00 55.56 %
Is external equity being used?  <Y>es or <N>o ... Y

  MARGINAL COST OF CAPITAL (%) ..............................  11.347

[F1]=HELP  [F2]=REVIEW  [F3]=CALC  [F5]=REDO  [F9]=PRINT  [ESC]=MENU
```

Exhibit 20.3 shows how Choice 2 can be used to solve the following sample problem:

Sample Problem: The Weinstein Company's financial manager is calculating the firm's marginal cost of capital for the year. He has accumulated the information in the following table. Use this information to calculate the cost of each capital structure component, the weight of each component, and Weinstein's MCC.

Interest Rate on L-T Debt	*14%*
Income Tax Rate	*34%*
Dividend on New Preferred Stock...............	*$10*
Net Price of New Preferred Stock	*$ 92*
Expected Common Div. for Year 1	*$ 2*
Projected Com. Stock Growth Rate	*8%*
Market Price of Common Stock..................	*$ 50*
Flotation Cost of New Com. Stock..............	*15%*
Capital Structure:	
Long-term Debt	*$ 6,000,000*
Preferred Stock....................................	*$ 2,000,000*
Common Equity....................................	*$10,000,000*

External equity will be used during the year.

Exhibit 20.4

```
PROFIT+                                                              PROFIT+
M C C   W / C O M P O N E N T   C O S T   &   R - E   B R E A K   P O I N T

Interest Rate on New L-T Debt (%) ............... 13.000    Component Costs
Tax Rate (%) .................................... 39.000
Dividend on New Preferred Stock ................. 12.000    Debt....  7.930
Net Price of New Preferred Stock ................ 90.000    Pfd.
Common Dividend Expected for Year 1 ............. 3.000     Stock... 13.333
Projected Capital Gain (Growth Rate)                        Int.
  for Common Stock in Year 1 (%) ................ 6.000     Equity.. 10.615
Current Market Price of Common Stock ............ 65.000   *Ext.
Percentage Flotation Cost for                               Equity.. 11.244
  Selling New Common Stock (%) .................. 12.000
Retained Earnings Estimated for the Year ........ 500000.00
Size of the Capital Budget for the Year ......... 2400000.00
                                                                   Weight
Amount of L-T Debt in Capital Structure ......... 5000000.00       27.78  %
Amount of Pref. Stock in Capital Structure ...... 4000000.00       22.22  %
Amount of Com. Equity in Capital Structure ...... 9000000.00       50.00  %
  RETAINED EARNINGS BREAK POINT ............................ 1000000.00
  MARGINAL COST OF CAPITAL (%) ............................. 10.788

[F1]=HELP  [F2]=REVIEW  [F3]=CALC  [F5]=REDO  [F9]=PRINT  [ESC]=MENU
```

MCC Calculation along with the Calculation of the Costs of the Capital Structure Components and the Retained Earnings Break Point

Choice 3 on the Marginal Cost of Capital Basics submenu performs all the calculations included in Choice 2. In addition, when provided with estimates of the amount of available retained earnings and the size of the capital budget for the year, the routine also determines the retained earnings break point and indicates with an asterisk which equity component was used to calculate MCC.

Exhibit 20.4 shows how Choice 3 can be used to solve the following sample problem:

Sample Problem: Compute the weight and cost of each capital structure component, the retained earnings break point, and the MCC for Master Sound Corporation using the following information:

Interest Rate on L-T Debt	*13%*
Income Tax Rate	*39%*
Dividend on New Preferred Stock....................	*$12*
Net Price of New Preferred Stock	*$90*
Expected Common Div. for Year 1	*$3*
Projected Com. Stock Growth Rate	*6%*

Market Price of Common Stock	*$65*
Flotation Cost of New Com. Stock	*12%*
Capital Structure:	
Long-term Debt	*$5,000,000*
Preferred Stock	*$4,000,000*
Common Equity	*$9,000,000*
Projected Retained Earnings	*$ 500,000*
Size of Capital Budget	*$2,400,000*

SUMMARY

This chapter outlined the basics of computing the costs of the components of a firm's capital structure, the weighted average marginal cost of capital for a firm, and the retained earnings break point in a firm's marginal cost of capital schedule. Although the numerical calculations presented here might appear to be rather simple, remember that the capital structures of most firms are much more complicated than the simple three-component structure presented here. (Most large firms, for example, have several different bond issues outstanding.) In addition, you should realize that the "real work" associated with determining a firm's cost of capital is not the arithmetic that PROFIT+ is performing for you, but the effort that must be expended in the estimation of the component costs--especially the cost of equity--and the prediction of how these costs will be affected as the firm attempts to attract additional funds.

END-OF-CHAPTER PROBLEMS

1. The financial manager of In-Line Systems, Inc., is determining the firm's marginal cost of capital for the coming year. She has estimated that In-Line's capital components will have the following costs:

After-tax Interest Rate on L-T Debt	8.5%
Cost of Preferred Stock	14.0%
Cost of New Common Equity	17.0%

The firm has the following capital structure, which is considered optimum:

Long-term Debt	$250,000
Preferred Stock	$100,000
Common Stockholders' Equity	$650,000

a. What is the weight of each of the components of the firm's capital structure?
b. What is the marginal cost of capital for In-Line Systems, Inc.?

2. Use the following information regarding Smithfield Books Company to answer parts a through d of this question:

After-tax Interest Rate on L-T Debt....................	9.2%
Cost of Preferred Stock..................................	12.0%
Cost of New Common Equity..........................	15.0%

Smithfield has the following capital structure, which the firm's management considers optimum:

Long-term Debt	$6,500,000
Preferred Stock...	$2,500,000
Common Stockholders' Equity	$9,750,000

a. What is the weight of each component of Smithfield's capital structure?

b. What is Smithfield's MCC?

c. How would the firm's MCC be affected if the after-tax cost of debt were 10 percent, rather than 9.2 percent?

d. Assuming all other inputs were back to their base values, how would Smithfield's cost of capital be affected if the cost of preferred stock were 14 percent, rather than 12 percent?

3. AI Computers is attempting to determine which of three capital structures will have the lowest cost. Information on each of the alternatives is shown in the table below. Which capital structure will produce the lowest cost of capital?

ALTERNATIVE A:

Capital Component	Amount of this Component	Component Cost
L-T Debt	$100,000	7.5%
Preferred Stock	0	---
Common Equity	$700,000	17%

ALTERNATIVE B:

Capital Component	Amount of this Component	Component Cost
L-T Debt	$200,000	8.6%
Preferred Stock	0	---
Common Equity	$600,000	17%

ALTERNATIVE C:

Capital Component	Amount of this Component	Component Cost
L-T Debt	$500,000	10%
Preferred Stock	0	---
Common Equity	$300,000	19%

4. Use the following information dealing with the capital structure of Artichoke Corporation to answer parts a through c of this question.

Capital Component	Amount of this Component	Component Cost
Debt	$300,000	6.8%
Preferred Stock	$100,000	13.0%
Common Equity	$550,000	15.5%

a. What is Artichoke's present cost of capital?

b. How would the firm's cost of capital change if the cost of common equity increased to 16.5 percent?

c. If, in addition to the increased cost of equity, the company's costs of debt and preferred stock increase to 8 and 14 percent, respectively, how will the firm's cost of capital be affected?

5. Given the information in the following table, determine the weight and cost of each capital component and the MCC for Masters and Son Company:

Interest Rate on L-T Debt	13%
Income Tax Rate	39%
Dividend on New Preferred Stock	$4
Net Price of New Preferred Stock	$48
Expected Common Div. for Year 1	$4
Projected Com. Stock Growth Rate	7%
Market Price of Common Stock	$82
Flotation Cost of New Com. Stock	12%

Capital Structure:	
Long-term Debt	$26,000,000
Preferred Stock	$14,000,000
Common Equity	$60,000,000

External equity will be used during the year.

6. Joel Johnson, financial vice-president for Johnson, Smith and Wheyland Corporation (JSW), is determining the firm's marginal cost of capital for the year. He has determined that JSW would have to pay 13.5 percent interest on new long-term debt, and that new preferred stock with a dividend of $12 could be sold to net the firm $90. The expected dividend on the firm's common stock is $1.22, and analysts project that the common stock growth rate will be 10 percent. If JSW were to sell new stock, flotation costs would amount to 15 percent of the present market price, which is $46 per share. The firm's present capital structure, which Johnson believes is optimal, is composed of $36 million in long-term debt, $12 million in preferred stock, and $52 million in common stockholders' equity. JSW's marginal income tax rate is 39 percent.

a. What is the weight and cost of each of the components of JSW's capital structure?

b. If JSW uses no external equity during the coming year, what will be its MCC?

c. If the firm makes use of external equity, what will be its MCC for the coming year?

7. Given the information in the following table regarding the capital structure of Anchor Scales Corporation, provide answers to parts a through d of this question:

Interest Rate on L-T Debt	12.5%
Income Tax Rate	40%
Dividend on New Preferred Stock	$9
Net Price of New Preferred Stock	$85
Expected Common Div. for Year 1	$3
Projected Com. Stock Growth Rate	6%
Market Price of Common Stock	$60
Flotation Cost of New Com. Stock	14%
Capital Structure:	
Long-term Debt	$16,000,000
Preferred Stock	$ 4,000,000
Common Equity	$40,000,000

a. What is the weight and the cost of each component of Anchor Scales' capital structure?

b. If the firm uses no external equity, what is its MCC?

c. If the firm sells new common stock during the year, what is its MCC?

d. How would your answers to parts a though c change if the expectations for Anchor Scales' common stock dividend and growth rate increased to $3.50 and 8 percent, respectively?

8. Compute the weight and cost of each capital structure component, the retained earnings break point, and the MCC for Building Blox Corporation using the following information:

Interest Rate on L-T Debt	15%
Income Tax Rate	34%
Dividend on New Preferred Stock	$10
Net Price of New Preferred Stock	$92
Expected Common Div. for Year 1	$1
Projected Com. Stock Growth Rate	5%
Market Price of Common Stock	$28
Flotation Cost of New Com. Stock	15%
Capital Structure:	
Long-term Debt	$3,000,000
Preferred Stock	$1,000,000
Common Equity	$8,000,000
Projected Retained Earnings	$ 200,000
Size of Capital Budget	$ 800,000

9. Use the information in the following table regarding Telephone Cable, Inc., to answer parts a through d of this question:

Interest Rate on L-T Debt	13.8%
Income Tax Rate	40%
Dividend on New Preferred Stock	$ 8
Net Price of New Preferred Stock	$72
Expected Common Div. for Year 1	$1.80
Projected Com. Stock Growth Rate	7%
Market Price of Common Stock	$36
Flotation Cost of New Com. Stock	13%
Capital Structure:	
Long-term Debt	$40,000,000

Preferred Stock..................................	$10,000,000
Common Equity..................................	$100,000,000
Projected Retained Earnings.....................	$ 8,000,000

a. What is the weight and the cost of each component of Telephone Cable's capital structure?

b. If the firm were planning a $10 million capital budget for the coming year, what would be its MCC?

c. If Telephone Cable were planning a $14 million capital budget for the coming year, what would be its MCC?

d. If you worked the problem correctly, you should have obtained different answers for parts b and c. What made these answers differ?

10. Susan Taylor, assistant to the financial vice-president for Bethany Products Corporation, is determining the firm's marginal cost of capital for the year. She has determined that Bethany would have to pay 14 percent interest on new long-term debt, and that new preferred stock would require a dividend of $7.50 and could be sold to net the firm $45.50. The expected dividend on the company's common stock is $2.50, and analysts project that the capital gains rate will be 6 percent on the firm's stock for the coming year. If Bethany were to sell new stock, flotation costs would amount to 12 percent of the present market price, which is $62.50 per share. The firm's present capital structure, which Taylor feels is optimal and should be maintained, is composed of $126 million in long-term debt, $28 million in preferred stock, and $268 million in common stockholders' equity. Bethany's marginal income tax rate is 40 percent, and the size of its capital budget for the coming year is $20 million.

a. What is the weight and cost of each of the components of Bethany's capital structure?

b. If Bethany can retain $8 million, what will be its MCC?

c. If the firm can retain $13 million, what will be its MCC for the coming year?

d. If you worked parts b and c correctly, they should have had different answers. Why did their answers differ?

Chapter Twenty-One
PROFIT+ Calc

WHY PROFIT+ CALC?

The primary characteristic of PROFIT+ that makes it both practical and attractive for use in the beginning financial management class is that it is not based on a commercially available electronic spreadsheet program. As a consequence, you do not have to learn how to use a spreadsheet (and your instructor does not have to take away from valuable lecture time to teach about using a spreadsheet) prior to "getting into" PROFIT+. As you have seen, all you must know to use PROFIT+ is the basic structure of the type of problem you wish to work. PROFIT+ provides prompts in simple English for all of your inputs. What is sacrificed by using this approach, however, is the ability to adapt the software to particular, or unusual, situations. The spreadsheets that make up PROFIT+ are designed to work problems that are stated in certain formats, and while you have a certain amount of flexibility in their use, PROFIT+ does not give you the ability to alter these standard formats. Learning how to program an electronic spreadsheet would give you the ability to overcome this limitation. This chapter, and PROFIT+ Calc, give you this ability.

WHAT IS PROFIT+ CALC?

In response to the desire by some users of PROFIT+ to go beyond the standard spreadsheets that make up the bulk of its routines, a basic introductory spreadsheet program, PROFIT+ Calc, has been included as Option S on the Main Menu. PROFIT+ Calc is laid out similarly to classic spreadsheet programs. While it is not intended to completely replace these programs, it will allow you to learn what a spreadsheet is all about.

Spreadsheets, of which PROFIT+ Calc is one, were born out of the observation that many problems are commonly solved using a pencil, paper, and a calculator. Calculating sales projections, departmental budgets, engineering estimates, and the like, are all done in this manner.

PROFIT+ Calc combines the familiarity and convenience of a pocket calculator with the powerful memory and electronic screen capabilities of the personal computer. With PROFIT+ Calc, the screen becomes a window that shows part of the larger worksheet. You can access different parts of the sheet at will, displaying any 22 by 8 section of the 50 by 26 sheet.

The screen is divided into a 22 by 8 grid of rows and columns. The intersection of these rows and columns is called a *cell.* At each cell you can enter a number, a label, or an equation. Because of this capability, you can design routines for dealing with the particular characteristics of the problem that you wish to solve.

Formatting commands allow you to customize the appearance of the data in the worksheet, both on a global and local level. Global formatting applies to all of the cells, while local formatting applies only to individual cells. (Local formatting takes precedence over global formatting.) In this manner, you can make your spreadsheet look like a balance sheet or income statement, a cash budget, a capital project cash inflow spreadsheet, or an income tax form.

The real power of PROFIT+ Calc lies in its ability to *remember* the equations and numbers used as you define your problem. If you need to change a number on the worksheet, you need merely change that number and PROFIT+ Calc will recalculate all the numbers that relate to it. Recalculation makes PROFIT+ Calc a powerful tool. This allows you to easily correct mistakes, as well as ask "what if?" questions (just as you have done with the other PROFIT+ routines).

To set up these models, you must decide what items you want to show and where you want them on the spreadsheet. After you have decided on a layout, you can enter titles, labels, and other textual information to show where the data is to go. Next you enter the raw data, such as prices, rates of interest, or any other numbers, into the cells you have designated for them. Finally, you enter the equations that will be used to calculate intermediate values and the final numbers in which you are interested.

Once you establish the format for a particular application, you can change the numbers at will. PROFIT+ Calc will take care of calculating new answers for the equations based on the new values you just entered, as well as handling the formatting of those cells so that they are displayed in a pleasing and useful manner. You can save the entire worksheet to a file and recall it later, print the worksheet on the printer to obtain a hard copy, or print a copy to a disk file, which you may enter into a word processor as a table.

In an hour or two, you can learn enough of the elementary features of PROFIT+ Calc to enable you to solve simple problems. As you use PROFIT+ Calc and become more familiar with it, you will learn the more advanced commands and techniques, such as how to have PROFIT+ Calc total and average the results located in other cells.

This chapter serves both as an introduction to spreadsheets in general and as an introduction, tutorial, and user's manual for PROFIT+ Calc. The remainder of the chapter is organized into three main sections. The first of these is an overall discussion of the features and design of PROFIT+ Calc. The second is an instructional section, containing lessons that have been structured to foresee some of the problems and questions that will arise as you learn PROFIT+ Calc. These lessons will lead you from initiating a PROFIT+ Calc session through various exercises that illustrate how PROFIT+ Calc can assist in solving problems. The exercises should be read and studied while you are sitting at your computer, since they are designed to lead you through the features of PROFIT+ Calc. The third section of the chapter summarizes the PROFIT+ Calc commands. It contains a description of each of the commands available to you. As you use the advanced features of PROFIT+ Calc and become more familiar with them, you will find yourself spending more time in this section.

The best way to learn PROFIT+ Calc is to use it. Do not be afraid of making mistakes and experimenting. No matter what you type at the keyboard, you cannot hurt the computer or the PROFIT+ Calc routine. By becoming familiar with PROFIT+ Calc as a supplement to the other PROFIT+ routines, you will have acquired the use of a powerful software package that will be of use not only in your financial management classes, but also in other classes in the business curriculum and in your personal life.

AN OVERVIEW OF PROFIT+ CALC

In the preceding paragraphs, you were given a general idea of what an electronic spreadsheet is and what general features are contained in PROFIT+ Calc. In the paragraphs that comprise this section, you will gain a more thorough understanding of the spreadsheet and how it functions.

Running PROFIT+ Calc

To run PROFIT+ Calc, select Option S from the Main Menu. When you do this, you will be presented with an introductory screen that contains a variety of descriptive information regarding the program. Pressing [RETURN] while on the introductory screen will take you to the main PROFIT+ Calc routine.

Exhibit 21.1

Spreadsheet Format

The PROFIT+ Calc spreadsheet is a matrix made up of 1,300 cells divided into 50 rows and 26 columns. Each cell is displayed as a maximum of 8 positions. As a result, only 22 rows and 8 columns are displayed on the screen at any one time. As can be seen in Exhibit 21.1, the rows are labeled numerically and the columns are labeled alphabetically, starting at the upper-left corner of the matrix. Thus the first cell in the upper-left corner would be A1. When the program starts up (refer to Exhibit 21.1), it will show cells A1 through H22 on the screen. (The Goto command, discussed later in this chapter, allows you to display the remainder of the matrix.)

Cursor and Status Line

The current cell is indicated by an inverse video cursor. When PROFIT+ Calc is first run, the current cell will be A1, as is shown in Exhibit 21.1. The top line of the screen is the status line. This line is used to give more information about the current cell and to prompt you for more information when executing a Special Command. Values will be shown unformatted in full precision (with as many decimal places as are possible) on the status line, although they will have either a global or local format applied to them when displayed in the cell of the matrix on the screen. The global and local formats control how the value is displayed and printed. How values are formatted will be discussed later in the chapter.

Cursor Manipulation

The cursor can be moved to any cell on the screen through the use of the cursor (arrow) keys on your keyboard. Each time one of the cursor arrow keys is pressed, the current cell changes appropriately, as indicated by the inverse video cursor. In Exhibit 21.2, for example, the cursor has been moved to cell D10. By using these keys, you can move the cursor anywhere on the screen. The status line at the top of the screen will change to indicate the new cell position and the contents of the new cell.

The Goto command can be used to move the cursor directly to any cell in the matrix. This command takes a few more keystrokes than the cursor movement keys, but will save keystrokes when moving to a location more than a few cells away. Also, the Goto command allows you to move to a cell that is off the screen. If the cell is off the screen, and the Goto command is used to access it, then the cell will be put at the upper-left corner of the screen. You will learn how to use the Goto command in the tutorial included in this chapter.

Exhibit 21.2

Exhibit 21.3

You may also move the screen window by a full page (screen). The [PG UP] and [PG DN] keys move the screen 22 lines, while holding down the [CTRL] key and simultaneously pressing the left or right arrow key will move the screen 8 columns left or right, respectively.

Entering Data

You can enter three types of data into the current cell. The first type of data is a numerical value. To tell PROFIT+ Calc that a value is to be entered into the current cell, press the = key. PROFIT+ Calc will respond by clearing the status line and prompting you for the value to be entered, as is shown in Exhibit 21.3. You enter a value and press [RETURN] when done. The status line will be cleared, and PROFIT+ Calc will display the new contents of the current cell.

The second type of data that can be entered is a label. This is useful for labeling columns or rows of data. To tell PROFIT+ Calc that a label is to be entered into the current cell, press the ' key. PROFIT+ Calc will respond by clearing the status line and prompting you for a label. At this point, you enter a label and press [RETURN]. PROFIT+ Calc will enter the label and display the contents of the current cell. Labels can have up to eight characters per cell. If a longer label is desired, more characters can be entered and the label will be automatically continued into the next cell. (By taking advantage of this feature of PROFIT+ Calc, you can fill up the entire width of the screen with a label, or heading, for your spreadsheet. You can even use PROFIT+ Calc as a crude word processor by making use of its ability to allow labels longer than the cell width.)

The third type of data that can be entered into the current cell is an equation. How equations are entered will be explained during the PROFIT+ Calc tutorial. For now, suffice it to say that with an equation you perform a variety of arithmetical operations on the contents of individual cells, or on a variety of different cells.

Clearing the Screen

Occasionally the screen may become cluttered with unwanted material. Or you may wish to clear any highlighted cells back to normal brightness. Pressing the [HOME] key causes PROFIT+ Calc to redraw the display. It does not alter the information in any of the cells.

Cancel

There will be times when you want to stop PROFIT+ Calc from updating the screen (which can be slow). For instance, PROFIT+ Calc is drawing the screen and you realize that you have another change to make, and then will need to update the screen again. You may press the [END] key, and PROFIT+ Calc will immediately return control to you. After you make your change, you can press the [HOME] key and PROFIT+ Calc will redraw the entire display.

THE PROFIT+ CALC TUTORIAL

The following tutorial teaches you how to build a basic spreadsheet and use the primary features of PROFIT+ Calc. For the sake of convenience, the tutorial is divided into a series of lessons. Go through these lessons while sitting in front of your computer with PROFIT+ running.

Lesson 1

To run PROFIT+ Calc, choose Option S from the PROFIT+ Main menu. When you have PROFIT+ Calc running, you should first see the PROFIT+ Calc introductory screen. After reading the screen, press [RETURN] and you will see the PROFIT+ Calc outline on the screen with rows 1 through 22 displayed on the left and columns A through H displayed across the top of the screen (see Exhibit 21.1). At the intersection of a row and column is a cell. As was explained in the preceding section, in each cell you can enter a label (text), a value (constant), or an equation (formula).

The top line of the screen is the status line, which gives the contents of the current cell. The current cell is indicated on the screen by an inverse video cursor. When the program is first run, the cursor will be in cell A1, and the status line will show "A01 = (blank)," which indicates that nothing has been entered into cell A1. This status line is used to display the cell contents and receive user interaction. When PROFIT+ Calc is waiting for the user to issue a command, this line will show the contents of the current cell.

Movement of the cursor is done through the cursor control (arrow) keys. To move to cell A2, you would press the down arrow key. To access a cell that is off the screen, use the Goto command. The Goto command is entered by pressing /G. PROFIT+ Calc will respond by clearing the status line and asking which cell to go to. This can be a cell on or off the screen. If it is off the screen, PROFIT+ Calc will clear the screen and display a new section of the matrix with the requested cell in the upper-left corner of the screen. Even for movement on the screen, the Goto command can be easier than the cursor keys if the user has to move more than a few cells. In addressing cells, you may specify either A01 or A1 as you please. Take a minute or two at this point to practice moving the cursor around the screen using the arrow keys, and around the spreadsheet using the Goto command. When you are through practicing, use the Goto command to return the cursor to cell A1.

Moving the cursor and window around are fairly straightforward, as you have seen, but so far the worksheet should be empty. Writing on the worksheet is just as easy. Before going further, press the [HOME] key to clear the screen and rebuild the window on the screen. Make certain that you are on cell A1, and press the ' key. Enter "SALES" (without the quotation marks) and press [RETURN]. Upon pressing the quote key ('), PROFIT+ Calc responds by clearing the status line and prompting you for the label to go into cell A1. As you enter "SALES," PROFIT+ Calc displays it on the status line. The [BACKSPACE] key can be used to correct any errors before you press [RETURN], which tells PROFIT+ Calc to enter the label in the current cell (A1). (Should you discover that you have made an error after you have pressed [RETURN], simply press the ' key and reenter the label. The same applies for errors made when entering values or equations.)

Each cell can normally hold up to eight characters. If the label you desire to enter is longer than eight characters, PROFIT+ Calc will allow you to enter nine characters in the cell and automatically continue the label in the next cell. (The ninth character goes into the space between the cells.) In this way, you can have long titles and labels in the PROFIT+ Calc matrix. At this point, the status line should read A01=SALES.

Now move the cursor to B1 by pressing the right arrow key. When the status line reads B01=(blank), press the = key. (This key may be used with or without the shift key being pressed.) PROFIT+ Calc will prompt you for a value to go in B1. You can then enter a number up to eight digits long. When you have the number, press [RETURN] to tell PROFIT+ Calc to enter the number in the matrix. Spend several minutes practicing entering labels and values into your spreadsheet. When you are through, press /N to return to the Calc Introduction screen and obtain a new spreadsheet. (PROFIT+ Calc will ask you to confirm that you really want a new sheet. Type Y in response to its question.)

To prepare your spreadsheet for the next part of this lesson, enter the following values into the indicated cells:

A1: 1000
B1: 1000

To enter an equation, you must go to the Equation command by pressing the / key. PROFIT+ Calc will respond by displaying all the commands available to you. To execute the Equation command, press the E key. PROFIT+ Calc will then prompt for the Equation to go in the current cell. Equations can have cell references, numbers, the five math operators (+, -, *, /, ^), and ten levels of parentheses. From cell C1, enter the equation A1 + B1 and press [RETURN]. The status line will show the equation you have just entered and its current value. Thc ccll will display this value (2000).

If you changed the value in cell B1, you would have to ask PROFIT+ Calc to recompute the value of the equation in C1. To do this, you enter /C, which tells PROFIT+ Calc to go through the matrix and calculate all of the equations, placing the new values in the cells. In this fashion, you can make several changes and, when finished with the changes, tell PROFIT+ Calc to compute the new values. Since this may take the longest of any of the commands, you should make as many changes as possible before recomputing. At this point, change the value of B1 to 2000 and press /C. PROFIT+ Calc will respond by recalculating the value of C1 and displaying the new value (3000) highlighted so that you can see what happened. The cursor disappears while PROFIT+ Calc is busy executing your command. Its reappearance is the signal that you may enter your next command.

PROFIT+ Calc can calculate your spreadsheets either by row or by column; that is, one row at a time, or one column at a time. The default setting is by row. Some spreadsheets you develop--cash budgets, for example--may require column-by-column calculation. (This is because some values in lower-numbered rows are based on values in higher-numbered rows.) To change to calculation by column, type /Z, and respond by typing C when you are asked if you wish to calculate by row or by column. (Simply press [RETURN] in answer to the other questions that PROFIT+ Calc asks you at this point. We will learn about the significance of these questions later on in this chapter.) Practice by entering the following equations into the cells that are indicated:

D1: C1 + 1000
E1: (D1 + B1) / 6
F1: E1 - 900
G1: F1 ^ 2
H1: G1 ^ .5

When you have entered these equations, type /C. PROFIT+ Calc will recalculate the matrix and display the appropriate values in cells D1 through H1. If you have entered your equations correctly, your spreadsheet should look like the one shown in Exhibit 21.4.

After entering values, labels, and equations into the matrix and computing the results, you can save the PROFIT+ Calc matrix as a file so that it can be recalled later. The command to do this is the SAVE command, /S. PROFIT+ Calc will respond by prompting for a filespec, or name, to give to the matrix you are saving.

Exhibit 21.4

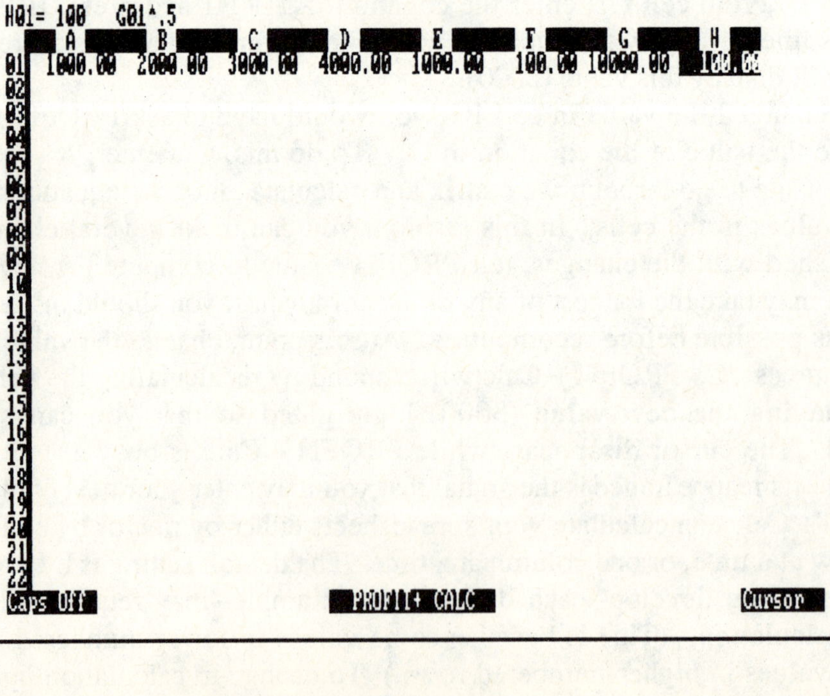

(You are also shown the default file name, which will be used if you press [RETURN]. It is suggested that you format a blank floppy disk, label it "PROFIT+ Calc Files," and then make a habit of always using it to save the files that you create while using PROFIT+ Calc. Alternatively, you can use your PROFIT+ Storage Disk for this purpose.) Appropriate file names must begin with a letter and can have no more than eight characters. So that PROFIT+ Calc will know in which drive to save a file, you should preface each file name with the letter of the drive (A: or B:). File names such as the following are all legal:

A: PROB1.CAL
B: PR-1.CAL
A: PROBLEM.CAL
B: PROBLEM

If you do not provide an extension (the three letters that follow the period in the file names), PROFIT+ Calc will use the file-type .CAL to indicate that this is a PROFIT+ Calc spreadsheet file. After entering the filespec, PROFIT+ Calc will ask you to insert the correct disk for the file, giving you a chance to swap disks. Place your PROFIT+ Calc Files disk in the drive you have specified and press [RETURN]. Your file will be saved.

ALWAYS REMEMBER TO REPLACE YOUR PROFIT+ CALC FILES DISK WITH THE PROFIT+ DISK THAT YOU REMOVED PRIOR TO SAVING (OR LOADING) A FILE!

Otherwise, you could cause PROFIT+ to terminate prematurely. At this point, type /S, and save the sample file on which you have been working. Name the file "A:TUTOR1.CAL." (Remember to replace your PROFIT+ Calc Files disk with the PROFIT+ disk after you have saved the file.)

After you have saved the matrix to a file, you can use the LOAD command, /L, to load the file back into the PROFIT+ Calc matrix. First, type /N to obtain a new spreadsheet, so you will know that the load command has worked. PROFIT+ Calc will respond by restarting from the beginning, with a new, empty matrix. Now execute the LOAD command by typing /L. PROFIT+ Calc will ask you for the name of the file to be loaded, just as with the SAVE command. Make certain to type the appropriate drive name and a colon in front of the name of the PROFIT+ Calc file you want to retrieve. Place your PROFIT+ Calc Files disk in the appropriate drive, and type the file's name--in this case, "TUTOR1.CAL." PROFIT+ Calc will display the spreadsheet when it is loaded into your computer's memory. If you give PROFIT+ Calc the name of a nonexistent file, an error message will appear on the status line. Press [RETURN] to recover. The name you give becomes the new default file name. (Remember to replace your PROFIT+ Calc Files disk with the PROFIT+ disk after you have loaded the file.)

The one last command that will be covered in lesson one is the QUIT command, which terminates the PROFIT+ Calc program. PROFIT+ Calc does NOT automatically save the data in the matrix when you quit. It is up to you to save any matrix that you believe is worth keeping. To exit the PROFIT+ Calc program, type /Q , which will return you to the PROFIT+ Main Menu after asking you if you really want to quit.

Lesson 2

In this lesson, you will learn more about the power of PROFIT+ Calc, building on the basic principles introduced so far. You will set up an example and build from there.

Exhibit 21.5 shows the spreadsheet that will be used in this lesson. In column A is a series of labels for the corresponding rows of information. In row 1 is a series of values that label the corresponding columns. First, enter the labels in column A. If you do not have a clear screen, press /N to get a new matrix. Move the cursor to A2 and press the quote key to enter a label. Now enter "A/L RATE" and press [RETURN]. Do the same thing for cells A3 through A7, so that they look like the cells in Exhibit 21.5. Now use the = key to enter the corresponding values for cells B1 through G1 and cells B2 through G2.

At this point, all the values in the first two rows are being displayed with two decimal places, even though you entered the top row as simple integers. To get your matrix to look like the one in Exhibit 21.5, you will have to use the Format command. The Format command has two options--global and local. The global format applies to all cells that have not yet been assigned a specific local format. When you assign a cell a local format, that takes precedence over the global format. When PROFIT+ Calc first starts up, the global format is two decimal places.

In Exhibit 21.5, row 1 is formatted locally to integer. To set the local format for row 1, press /F to execute the Format command, then press L to set a local format. PROFIT+ Calc will now ask if you want the cells displayed as integer, or 0-7 decimal places. Enter I for integer. Now tell PROFIT+ Calc that you want this format to apply to the top row of cells by entering B1, pressing [RETURN], then entering G1, and pressing [RETURN]. At this point, your spreadsheet should look like rows 1 and 2 of Exhibit 21.5, as well as column A. If not, trace back through the first part of the lesson to pick up anything you might have missed.

Exhibit 21.5

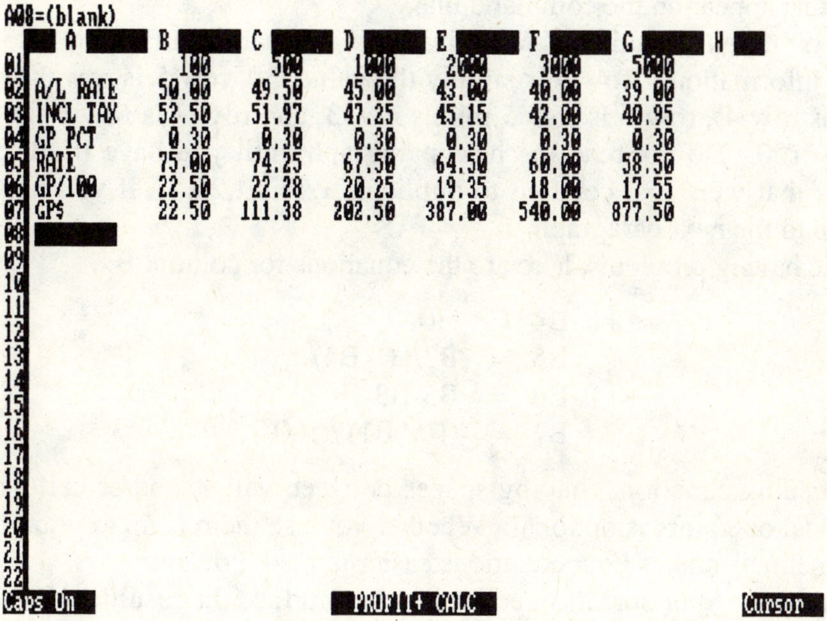

A08=(blank)

	A	B	C	D	E	F	G	H
01		100	500	1000	2000	3000	5000	
02	A/L RATE	50.00	49.50	45.00	43.00	40.00	39.00	
03	INCL TAX	52.50	51.97	47.25	45.15	42.00	40.95	
04	GP PCT	0.30	0.30	0.30	0.30	0.30	0.30	
05	RATE	75.00	74.25	67.50	64.50	60.00	58.50	
06	GP/100	22.50	22.28	20.25	19.35	18.00	17.55	
07	GP$	22.50	111.38	202.50	387.00	540.00	877.50	
08								
09								
10								
11								
12								
13								
14								
15								
16								
17								
18								
19								
20								
21								
22								

Caps On PROFIT+ CALC Cursor

Row 3 of Exhibit 21.5 is 105 percent of row 2 (row 2 plus a 5 percent tax). For this, you will need to enter an equation in B3. Move the cursor to cell B3 and enter /E to enter the equation. Now enter B2*1.05 and press [RETURN]. B3 now has the correct formula in it, but there are five more cells to fill. Rather than enter the same equation five times, you will learn to use the Replicate command.

The Replicate command is used in PROFIT+ Calc to copy formulas, values, and labels into a series of cells. In the case of formulas, you have the option of copying the formula exactly, or relative to where it is placed. To execute the Replicate command, enter /R. PROFIT+ Calc will then ask you for the source cell. In this case, enter B3 and press [RETURN]. If your cursor is at B3 you may simply press [RETURN] and PROFIT+ Calc will enter the value of the current cell. PROFIT+ Calc will next ask if there is to be a multiple number of cells in the source. Press N for no. If you were going to copy part of a whole row or column, you would enter Y for yes. PROFIT+ Calc now asks if the replicate is absolute or relative. If you choose A for absolute, all of the cells would have the equation B2*1.05 in them, which is not what you want to occur; thus you want to replicate relative to the location of the equation. Press R for relative. Next PROFIT+ Calc wants to know where to replicate the equation. You will be prompted for the first and last cells in the target range. Enter C3, [RETURN], G3, and [RETURN]. PROFIT+ Calc will now replicate the equation into the cells that we want, and the new equations will reference the cell directly above them, not to B2. To confirm this, use the arrow keys to move through cells C3 to G3. As you move, look at the equations that appear on the command line.

At this point, you should be able to finish off the matrix in Exhibit 21.5 with the following information. Row 4 is simply the value .30, row 5 is row 3 divided by (one minus row 4), row 6 is row 5 minus row 3, and row 7 is row 6 times row 1 divided by 100. Do not read the next paragraph until you have tried to use the commands that were just covered to duplicate Exhibit 21.5. If you need a little help, go on to the next paragraph.

If you are having problems, here are the equations for column B:

```
B4 = .30
B5 = B3/(1 - B4)
B6 = B5-B3
B7 = (B6*B1) / 100
```

In the preceding equations, having spaces between values and/or cell names and mathematical operators is optional. Whether you use them is up to you. Including spaces sometimes makes your equations easier to read, however.

When you have your spreadsheet working to produce the results in Exhibit 21.5, save it with the name "TUTOR2.CAL."

Lesson 3

In this lesson, you will learn some of the more advanced features that make entering data into the matrix a bit easier. Load the "TUTOR2.CAL" file from lesson 2 back into the PROFIT+ Calc spreadsheet. First, we will blank a series of locations with the Blank command. Enter /B and PROFIT+ Calc will ask for the series of cells to be blanked. Enter B2, press [RETURN], enter G2, and press [RETURN]. PROFIT+ Calc will erase the contents of locations B2 through G2. Now move the cursor to B2. Before reentering the values, tell PROFIT+ Calc to automatically jump across the row. To do this, enter /J and select R for row. Now whenever a label or value is entered in a cell, PROFIT+ Calc will automatically jump to the cell to the right of the current cell. To skip a cell in the row, you may simply press [RETURN]. Try it out by reentering the values that were in row 2.

Now you will learn how to use the Print command, /P. When printing, only 8 columns of information will fit on an 80-character wide printer, or 14 columns of information on a 132-character wide printer. PROFIT+ Calc will prompt you for the column where you wish to start printing. If your spreadsheet is too wide to print at one time you will have to print it in two or more parts. To print the spreadsheet from lesson 2, turn on your printer and make certain that it is on line, execute the Print command by entering /P, and tell PROFIT+ Calc to start with column A. PROFIT+ Calc will then print the first 8 or 14 columns, depending on your printer width.

To change the printer width, use the /Z command, which changes a number of the PROFIT+ Calc default values. These are the order of calculation (by row or by column) as you learned earlier; your printer width; print output file or device; and the Bold flag. In each case, PROFIT+ Calc shows you the current default and prompts you for a new value. To leave a value as defined, you may simply press [RETURN].

If you have an 80-column printer, you should enter 80 when prompted for printer width. This will prevent PROFIT+ Calc from trying to print past the end of your paper. When PROFIT+ Calc asks for the name of the print output file or device, press [RETURN] to keep the default device LST (your printer). (You could enter a file name and PROFIT+ Calc would store the print output for you to print later or to enter into a word processor.)

If you elect to leave the Bold feature on, values in the matrix that PROFIT+ Calc has just computed will be highlighted on the screen. For the Total and Average commands, the cells just totaled will be highlighted. Any command that rewrites the screen (e.g., HOME) will erase the highlighting, as will running the cursor over the cells. If you do not find this feature helpful, use /Z to turn Bold off.

The next command to be reviewed is the Modify Value command, /M. This command will allow you to perform a calculation on a series of values (not equations), and leave the new value in the cells. It has no effect on equations or labels. For an example, we will increase the values in row 2 by 11 percent using the Modify Value command. To do this, enter /M, to which PROFIT+ Calc will respond "Finish equation :". PROFIT+ Calc assumes the value in the cell to be modified to be the first term of the modify equation, so just enter *1.11 and press [RETURN]. PROFIT+ Calc will then ask for the range of cells to be modified. Tell PROFIT+ Calc to use cells B2 through G2. PROFIT+ Calc will then modify these values for you. To see the entire results on the whole matrix, enter /C and PROFIT+ Calc will use the new values as input to the equations that reference those cells. The Modify Value command can use all of the facilities available in the regular equation mode: cell references, numbers, the five math operators, and ten levels of parentheses.

There are two PROFIT+ Calc commands that write equations for you. These are the Total and Average commands. To use these commands, move the cursor to the cell where you wish the resulting equation to be placed, then execute the appropriate command, /T for Total or /A for Average. PROFIT+ Calc then prompts for the source range for the cells to be totaled or averaged, and places both the equation and the value of the total or average in the current cell. If the Bold feature is on, the source range for the total or average will be highlighted.

Two of the most powerful commands at your disposal are the Insert and Delete commands. These commands allow you to make room in the matrix for new data by inserting a blank row or column or to delete a row or column without leaving a blank space. When these commands are executed, PROFIT+ Calc automatically modifies all equations in the matrix so that they reference the same data, even though it has been moved to a new location.

For example, suppose you wanted to add a column labeled 200 between columns B and C of the spreadsheet on which you have been working. To do so, move to column C and execute the Insert command by typing /I and selecting C for column insert. PROFIT+ Calc will move all of the columns from C through Z one column to the right, losing the data in column Z, and creating a new, blank column C. Finally all equations will be altered, such that any reference to (for instance) C5, will now reference D5.

The Delete command performs just the opposite of the Insert command. To delete column C, move the cursor to any cell in the column, enter /D, and select C to delete a column. This will cause columns D through Z to be moved one column to the left, placing a blank column in column Z and deleting column C. Finally all equations that referenced any cell that was moved will be updated to reference the same data in its new location.

WORDS OF CAUTION
Be careful when deleting or inserting columns and rows!
PROFIT+ Calc can easily wipe out a series of values in an instant.

The Window command allows the user to display either row 1 or column A on the screen at all times. For example, go to cell A50 and execute the Window command, /W, and select the row option by entering R. You will now see row 1 where the top row is. This allows you to place labels for data in row 1 or column A and see them from anywhere in the matrix.

The [END] key can be used to save time using PROFIT+ Calc by canceling unwanted screen rewrites. Any time PROFIT+ Calc is redrawing the entire screen (for example, after a Goto to a cell off the screen, at the end of the /Z command, or after you press [HOME]), you may press the [END] key and PROFIT+ Calc will immediately stop drawing the screen and be ready to accept a new command. You may also cancel a Print (/P) or a Compute (/C) command. In the latter case, any cells that were not redrawn will still retain their old values.

Finally, a word about series. A number of PROFIT+ Calc commands (/B, /F, /T, etc.) ask you to enter the first and last cells of a series. Normally these cells will be in a straight line on a row or column. However, you may, if you like, enter a block series. For instance, you could use /B to blank out the block of cells C2-C5, D2-D5, and E2-E5 by entering the series C2-E5. PROFIT+ Calc considers a block series to be all cells from the starting column to the ending column on each row from the start to the end of the series. In effect, you are entering the upper-left and lower-right corners of a rectangle.

Lesson 4

This final lesson will cover a single feature--plotting bar graphs. PROFIT+ Calc can offer such a feature only with limitations. For one, you can only draw horizontal bar graphs. Second, you must scale the graph yourself (i.e., PROFIT+ Calc will not automatically scale the graph to fit within a window). Third, if you wish to make the graph smaller, you must manually erase the bars with the Blank command (/B). Fourth, you cannot graph negative numbers. And fifth, the resolution is limited to one-half character width. Despite these limitations, the bar graphs you can draw provide a pleasing visual presentation of your results.

To draw a bar graph, arrange the results to be plotted in a column. In the example shown in Exhibit 21.6, labels have been placed in column A and results in column B. Next, put a single scale factor in column C next to each result to be plotted. This is most easily done by entering the scale factor in the top cell of the column and replicating it through the rest of the column. (The scale factor is the number by which each value to be graphed is multiplied to obtain the number of characters to be used in the graph.) The value of this scale factor will depend on the magnitude of the data and the desired size of the graph. You cannot see the scale factor in Exhibit 21.6 because the bar graph is displayed in its place, but the value used is 15. (The status line does indicate that the value in C4 is 15, however.) Whereas solid bars appear in Exhibit 21.6, what character you see when you print a bar graph will depend on what printer you use and how it interprets the code it is sent. The bars may be printed using the letter "X" or some other character.

After you have entered the labels shown in Exhibit 21.6, the values in column B, and the scale factor 15 in column C, draw the graph by formatting the scale factors as bars. To do this, enter /F for format, L for local, B for bar graph, and then the first and last cell addresses of the column of scale factors (C4 and C20). PROFIT+ Calc will redraw the entire screen, showing the bar graph.

PROFIT+ Calc draws the graph by multiplying the scale factor in the cell formatted as a bar graph by the value in the cell immediately to the left, and then creating a label consisting of that many half-characters wide bars. This label is extended into the cells to the right, as far as the screen permits. The scale factor is retained in the first cell of the bar graph but is not displayed. (You can, however, see it on the status line.) If the last character in the bar is only a half character, it will be brighter than the rest of the bar. If the graph is not as wide as you wish, you can modify the scale factor in the entire column with the /M command,

Exhibit 21.6

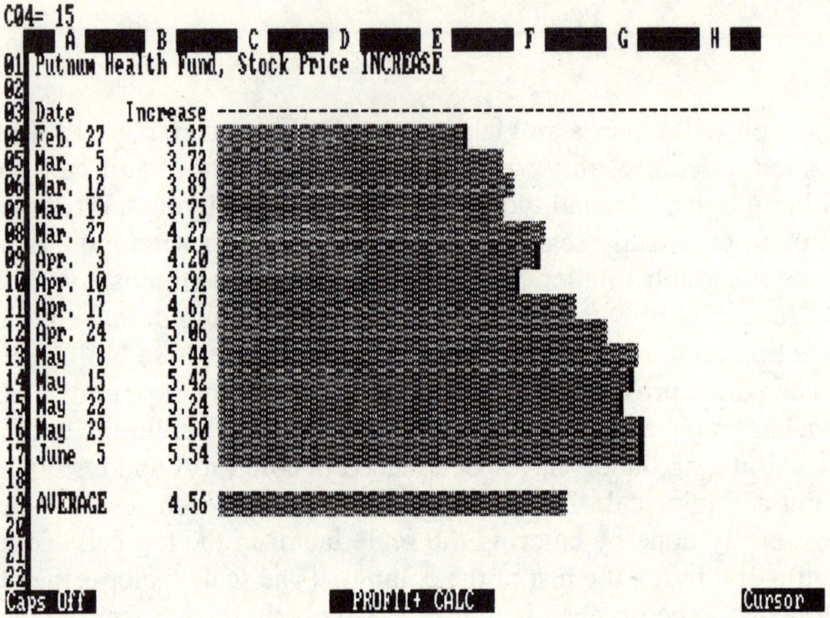

followed by [HOME] to redraw the screen. If the graph is too wide, first erase the labels extending beyond the scale factors with the /B command, and then proceed to modify the scale factors (otherwise parts of the first bar graph will remain in the cells).

SPECIAL COMMANDS OVERVIEW

In the tutorial, you used the PROFIT+ Special Commands to perform such tasks as entering equations, saving and loading spreadsheets, formatting cells, going to a particular cell, replicating a series of values, and so on. The Special Commands allow you to manipulate the contents of the PROFIT+ Calc spreadsheet. These commands are accessed by pressing the / key and then selecting the appropriate command. Any commands that use cell references for source ranges or target ranges apply to cells off the screen as well as on the screen. So you can, for example, replicate to locations off the screen. The PROFIT+ Calc Special Commands are listed alphabetically and described in this section so that you can have a reference source as you use the spreadsheet.

/A Average

This command allows you to average a series of cells and put the result in the current cell, as indicated by the inverse video cursor. Thus you should position the cursor to the cell where you want the average to appear and type /A. PROFIT+ Calc will prompt for the first and last cells you want included in the equation. You should enter each cell when asked and press [RETURN]. PROFIT+ Calc will then write the equation for the average of that series of cells and its value in the current cell. If the Bold option is on, the cells of the series being averaged will be highlighted. The Average command first displays the total of the range, then changes it to the average.

/B Blank

This command is used to blank out (erase) a series of cells, either in a row or column. To erase a series of cells, press /B and give PROFIT+ Calc the starting and ending cells of the series. PROFIT+ Calc will erase everything from the cells in the series (values, labels, equations, and local formatting). In this, as in all other commands, when PROFIT+ Calc prompts you for a cell, pressing [RETURN] defaults to the current cell. Thus to blank the current cell, you could type /B [RETURN] [RETURN].

/C Compute

Depending on the order in which you wish the program to proceed, PROFIT+ Calc will go through the matrix either row by row or column by column, computing and displaying the current values of all equations in the matrix. The default order is by row, but you can use the /Z command to change to calculation by column. If the Bold option is on, each computed value will be highlighted. You may cancel the Compute command by pressing the [END] key.

/D Delete

This command deletes either an entire row or an entire column of a PROFIT+ Calc spreadsheet. When a column or row is deleted, the following columns or rows are all moved up one location and the new last column or row is left blank. PROFIT+ Calc then alters the equations in the matrix to reference the new locations of the cells. To use the Delete command, move the cursor to the column or row to be deleted and press /D, then tell PROFIT+ Calc whether you want to delete a column or a row. *Be careful with this command as you cannot recover the deleted results unless you have previously saved the matrix.*

/E Equation

This command allows you to enter an equation into the current cell. You may use numbers with decimals or fractions, cell references, the five main math operators (+, -, *, /, ^), and ten levels of parentheses. To enter an equation, type /E, the desired equation for that cell, and press [RETURN]. There are no priorities among the operators. Each is evaluated as it is encountered reading left to right. Thus 3-1*2 equals 4, not 1. Because there are no priorities among the operators, you should make heavy use of parentheses to group calculations. If, for example, you want the result of the preceding equation to be 1, write it as follows: 3-(1*2). Whenever you are in doubt regarding whether to use parentheses, you should use them to avoid erroneous results.

/F Format

This command allows you to format the displayed and printed values of the cells. There are two main options to this command--global formats and local formats. The global format applies to all cells not locally formatted. A local format overrides the global format for that cell. Each cell may be formatted as an integer, or a decimal number with 0 to 7 decimal places displayed. To use the Format command, type /F and either G for global or L for local. Next enter any of the following: I for integer or 0 through 7 for that many decimal places. If you chose local formatting, PROFIT+ Calc will prompt for a series of cells to be formatted. As usual, you may press [RETURN] to indicate the current cell.

There are several special formatting commands that may be used but which are not mentioned in the Format prompt. If you enter G, PROFIT+ Calc will change a locally formatted cell back to the global format. If you enter D, PROFIT+ Calc will display the current system date. If you enter @, PROFIT+ Calc will display the current system time. The date and time will always be current up to the last time the cell was displayed. Thus when you reload the matrix tomorrow, you will get tomorrow's date and time. If you enter !, PROFIT+ Calc will change the value of that cell into a label (i.e., it will no longer be a number or an equation and will not change with /C). This may be used to "freeze" the date and time.

A format of type B will cause a bar graph to be drawn by multiplying those cells by the values in the cells to the left, and drawing a solid bar of that many half-characters in the current cell and extending to the right.

/G Goto

This command allows you to move the cursor to any cell in the matrix, whether on the screen or off. If the target cell is off the screen, the screen will be cleared and the target cell will be placed in the top left corner, if appropriate.

/H Help

This command displays a page of one-line instructions covering each of the Special Commands. When you are done reading Help, press any key to return to your place in the matrix.

/I Insert

This command is the complement of the Delete command. It allows you to insert either an entire row or an entire column. To execute this command, move the cursor to a cell before which you want a new column or row. Press /I and select either Row or Column. PROFIT+ Calc will insert a blank row or column, moving all subsequent rows or columns down one, with the last one dropping off the matrix. Finally, all equations are updated such that all references to cells that were moved are altered to point to the same data.

/J Jump

This command sets the Jump mode flag such that whenever you enter a value with the = key, a label with the ' key, or simply press the [RETURN] key, the cursor is moved one cell along the row or column. To use this option, type /J, then enter either R to move along the row, C to move down the column, or a space to turn off the Jump option.

/L Load

This command is used to load PROFIT+ Calc files saved on disk with the Save command. PROFIT+ Calc will prompt for a file name. You may enter the entire filespec. Always include the letter of the drive and a colon before your file name, always begin your file name with a letter, never make your file name more than 8 characters long, and always store your PROFIT+ Calc files on your PROFIT+ Calc Files disk (or on your PROFIT+ Storage Disk). If you omit the file type (the three letters follow the period after the file name), PROFIT+ Calc will append .CAL to the file name. Simply pressing [RETURN] will load the default file name shown on the status line, which is the last file you loaded or saved. *When you are through with your PROFIT+ Calc Files disk, remember to replace it with the PROFIT+ disk that you initially removed.*

/M Modify

This command allows you to modify the values of a series of cells. In doing this, PROFIT+ Calc will ask you to finish the equation used to modify the values, assuming the value of the cells to be modified as the first term of the equation. Thus to increase a series of cells by 50 percent and then subtract 10 from them, finish the equation with "*1.50-10." If the Bold option is on, the modified series will be highlighted.

/N New

This command reruns PROFIT+ Calc from the start, clearing all cells and resetting all default values.

/P Print

This command prints a section of the matrix on the printer. PROFIT+ Calc will print as many columns as will fit in the width of your printer (that you set with the /Z command). An 80-character wide printer will hold columns A-H, a 132-character wide printer will print columns A-N. PROFIT+ Calc will prompt for the column with which to start printing. As usual, pressing [RETURN] defaults to the current cursor position. You may also print a copy of your matrix to a disk file, which may then be used as input to a word processor. For this, you must change the default file/device name with the /Z command. The /P command will then write an ASCII file (i.e., a standard word processing file), which you can display on the screen, copy to your printer, or use as input to another program. You may cancel the Print command by pressing the [END] key.

/Q Quit

You use this command to exit PROFIT+ Calc. Make sure that all data has been saved before quitting. When you quit, PROFIT+ Calc returns you to the PROFIT+ Main Menu.

/R Replicate

This command allows you to replicate information from one part of the matrix to another. For values or formulas, this is a regular copy function; but for equations, PROFIT+ Calc can replicate the equation relative to its position so that it will reference the correct cells from the row or column of its new position. To use this command, type /R. PROFIT+ Calc will prompt for the cell to be replicated. You may press [RETURN] to indicate the current cell. PROFIT+ Calc will then ask if there is to be more than one cell used as the source. If you respond with a Y, PROFIT+ Calc will increment the source cell replicated from as it steps through the target range. Otherwise PROFIT+ Calc will copy only the one cell to all of the cells in the target range.

Next PROFIT+ Calc will ask if the replication is to be absolute or relative. Use absolute for labels, values, and equations that you want to be copied exactly as they are. Use relative replication for equations that must reference cells in the same position relative to their new location. Finally PROFIT+ Calc will prompt for the target range of the replication.

/S Save

This is the complement of the Load command. This command saves the PROFIT+ Calc matrix as a binary disk file. You are prompted for a filespec, which must include the drive name and can include a file extension. If you do not specify a file extension, PROFIT+ Calc will append .CAL to the file name. Pressing [RETURN] will save the default file name shown on the status line, which is the last file saved or loaded. All files should be saved on your PROFIT+ Calc Files (or PROFIT+ Storage) disk. *When you are through with your PROFIT+ Calc Files (or PROFIT+ Storage) disk, remember to replace it with the PROFIT+ disk that you initially removed.*

/T Total

This command generates the equation for the total of a series of cells and places both the equation and the resulting value in the current cell. The command works in a manner similar to that of the Average command. If the Bold feature is on, then the series totaled will be highlighted.

/W Window

This sets an internal flag that causes PROFIT+ Calc to display row 1 or column A on the screen at all times. This is used if you have labels in the first row or column that you wish to see even if you are displaying a part of the matrix beyond what originally fits on the screen. After typing /W, enter R for row, C for column, or a space to turn off the Window option. This option adds some extra time to all commands that change any cell being displayed.

/Z Change Default Settings

This command allows you to change certain default values used by the spreadsheet. PROFIT+ Calc will prompt you to enter the order of calculation--by row or by column--you wish to use. Next PROFIT+ Calc will prompt for the width of your printer. Enter the number of characters your printer can print across the page. PROFIT+ Calc will then ask for the name of a file for printed output. For this to go to your printer, leave the default value, LST, by pressing [RETURN]. To print to a disk file, enter any valid file name, such as "B:BUDGET.TXT." Finally, PROFIT+ Calc will ask if you want the Bold feature on or off. When Bold is on, PROFIT+ Calc will highlight the results of its calculations to distinguish them from constants. In the Total and Average commands, PROFIT+ Calc highlights the range that was just totaled or averaged. This can help avoid mistakes. Clearing the screen returns all cells to normal brightness, as does any other command that rewrites the screen. For all of the above prompts, pressing [RETURN] will retain the present setting.

SUMMARY

PROFIT+ Calc is a basic electronic spreadsheet package that provides you with an introduction to basic spreadsheet functions. In addition, the software is powerful enough that it should prove useful to you in business classes other than financial management and in your own personal life. In combination with the other PROFIT+ routines, PROFIT+ Calc is a component of a very utilitarian software package.

PROFIT+ Calc and portions of this chapter were adapted with permission from a public domain spreadsheet program entitled PC-Calc. The authors of PC-Calc, John L. Vandegrift and Guy C. Gordon, deserve both thanks for their generosity and credit for their efforts.

END-OF-CHAPTER PROBLEMS

1. With a new, blank PROFIT+ Calc spreadsheet on the screen, enter the following information into the indicated cells:

A1:	Spreadsheet Designers, Incorporated
A2:	1988 Pro Forma Income Statement
A3:	--
A4:	Sales
A5:	Less: Operating costs
A6:	Operating income
A7:	Less: Interest expense
A8:	Earnings before tax
A9:	Less: Income taxes
A10:	Net after-tax income
D4:	10000.00
D5:	D4 * .80
D6:	D4 - D5
D7:	400.00
D8:	D6 - D7
D9:	D8 * .40
D10:	D8 - D9

a. If you correctly designed your spreadsheet, net after-tax income should be 960.00. Now change sales to 12000.00 and recalculate. What after-tax income do you have now?

b. Each number in the spreadsheet is shown with two zeros displayed to the right of the decimal point. Use the format command to display all numbers as integers (i.e., with no decimal places).

c. Change sales back to 10000 and recalculate. Your after-tax income should now be 960 once again.

d. Place your PROFIT+ Calc Files (or PROFIT+ Storage) disk in drive A and save the pro forma income statement you developed. Give it the following name: A:EOC1.CAL.

e. Press /N to obtain a new spreadsheet. Now load the EOC1.CAL file that you just saved.

f. Beginning with row 15, add both labels and equations to your spreadsheet to calculate the following ratios:

Operating profit margin = operating income/sales
TIE = operating income/interest expense
Net profit margin = net after-tax income/sales

g. Change sales to 15000 and recalculate. What are the new values for net after-tax income and for each of the three ratios?

2. Use the following information for Intermediate Adventures Company to answer parts a through f of this question:

Cash	$ 50
Receivables	85
Inventories	100
Gross Fixed Assets	200
Accumulated Depreciation	50
Accounts Payable	50
Accrued Wages and Taxes	25
Mortgage Bonds	70
Common Stock and Paid-in Capital	100
Retained Earnings	140

a. Using PROFIT+ Calc, develop a pro forma balance sheet for Intermediate Adventures Company. Assume that the data are for the year ended December 31, 1988. (Make certain to use equations for all calculated values, and to show all intermediate totals, such as total current assets, net fixed assets, total current liabilities, etc.)

b. Below the spreadsheet space in which you have placed the balance sheet, calculate the following ratios for Intermediate Adventures (assume that the firm's projected sales for 1988 are $1000):

Current ratio = current assets/current liab.
Inventory t/o = sales/inventories
Average collection period = accounts receivable/(sales/360)
Total asset turnover = sales/total assets
Debt ratio = total debt/total assets

c. The company has been considering using cash to pay off $40 of its mortgage bonds. If it took this action, how would its pro forma balance sheet and the ratios calculated in part b be affected?

d. In addition to paying off $40 of its mortgage bonds, Intermediate Adventures is considering expanding its sales force. This initially would involve increasing both inventories and accounts payable to $150 and $100, respectively. What effect would this move have on the firm's balance sheet and the five ratios that you have calculated?

3. Use the information in the following table to develop a cash budget for the first three months of 1988 for the Turpin Corporation using PROFIT+ Calc. Assume that purchases are paid for the month following that in which they are made. Use one line to show both projected borrowing needs and surplus cash. Borrowing needs should show up as negative numbers, while surplus cash will appear positive. Use the PROFIT+ Calc /Z command to change the order of calculation to column by column. (This change is necessary because your cash budget will assume that the beginning cash balances for February and March are equal to the preceding month's cumulative cash balance. Since cumulative cash balance is one row farther down the spreadsheet than beginning cash balance, the correct figure would not be calculated if row by row calculation were used. Refer to Chapter Fifteen of this guide, or to your financial management textbook, for a review of cash budgeting.)

Sales for November 1987	$50,000
Sales for December 1987	$60,000
Cash Discount Percentage	2%
Collection Estimates:	
Percentage Collected during the Month of Sale	10%
Percentage Collected 1 Month Following Sale.....	70%
Percentage Collected 2 Months Following Sale....	20%
Purchases as a Percentage of Next Month's Sales....	70%

	January	**February**	**March**
Sales Forecasts:	$70,000	$60,000	$50,000
Payment Forecasts:			
Wages and Salaries	9,000	9,000	9,000
Rent	9,500	9,500	8,000
Miscellaneous	2,000	2,000	2,000
Taxes			8,500
Other	6,700		
Beginning Cash Balance	3,600		
Target Cash Balance	3,000	3,000	3,000

4. Use the formulas listed on the following page to develop a PROFIT+ Calc spreadsheet that will calculate future value, present value, present value of an annuity, and future value of an annuity. Be certain to make liberal use of parentheses when developing your formulas. Also be certain to allow for separate entry of each input into individual cells of your spreadsheet. For example, when

calculating future value, enter the present value in a separate cell, the nominal rate in a separate cell, and the number of years in a separate cell. (Hint: Before you enter the equations for calculating the final results, enter the formulas for calculating i and n in separate cells. This will make the development of the formulas much easier. Remember that the number of open parentheses in your equations must equal the number of closed parentheses.)

$$FV = PV(1 + i)^n$$

$$PV = FV/(1 + i)^n$$

$$FV_{annuity} = PMT \times \frac{(1 + i)^n - 1}{i}$$

$$PV_{annuity} = PMT \times \left(\frac{1}{i} - \frac{1}{i\,(1 + i)^n}\right)$$

Use the spreadsheet that you have developed to answer the following questions:

a. What is the future value of $100 deposited at 10 percent compounded annually for two years?

b. What is the future value of $1,000 deposited at 12 percent compounded quarterly for five years?

c. What is the present value of $100 to be received in two years if the discount rate is 10 percent compounded annually?

d. What is the present value of $1,000 to be received at the end of five years if the discount rate is 12 percent compounded monthly?

e. What is the future value of a $100, five-year ordinary annuity if the interest rate is 10 percent compounded annually?

f. What is the future value of an ordinary annuity of $100 per month for two years if the interest rate is 12 percent compounded monthly?

g. What is the present value of a $100, five-year ordinary annuity if the discount rate is 10 percent compounded annually?

h. What is the present value of an ordinary annuity of $100 per month for two years if the discount rate is 12 percent compounded monthly?

i. How could you modify your spreadsheet so that the future values and present values of both an ordinary annuity and an annuity due were reported?

5. Use the following information to develop a PROFIT+ Calc spreadsheet for determining Orlando Corporation's marginal cost of capital. Refer to Chapter Twenty of this guide for a review of how MCC is calculated, if necessary.

Orlando Corporation:
Capital Structure Information

Interest Rate on New Debt	14%
Marginal Tax Rate	40%
Dividend on New Pref. Stock	$10
Net Price of New Pref. Stock	$91
Expected Common Stock Dividend	$4
Projected Com. Stk. Growth Rate	8%
Current Mkt. Price of Com. Stock	$80
Present Capital Structure:	
Long-Term Debt	$400,000
Preferred Stock	$200,000
Common Stockholders' Equity	$400,000

a. What is Orlando Corporation's MCC?

b. How would Orlando's MCC be affected if the interest rate on new debt were 12 percent, rather than 14 percent?

c. Assuming an interest rate on new debt of 14 percent, how would the firm's MCC be affected if the present market price of its common stock were $60, rather than $80?

d. Assuming the base values, how would Orlando's MCC be affected if the growth rate projected for its common stock were 6 percent, rather than 8 percent?

6. Refer to Chapter Thirteen of this guide and develop a PROFIT+ Calc spreadsheet that will calculate the following values when given the appropriate inputs: economic order quantity (EOQ), average inventory in units and in dollars, and reorder point in units. Use your spreadsheet to calculate the preceding values, given the following sets of information:

a. Annual sales = 300,000 units; carrying costs as a percentage of purchase price = 20 percent; purchase price per unit = $5; fixed costs per order = $30; safety stock = 10,000 units; order lead time = 14 days

b. Annual sales = 150,000 units; carrying costs as a percentage of purchase price = 25 percent; purchase price per unit = \$8.55; fixed costs per order = \$50; safety stock = 5,000 units; order lead time = 10 days

c. Annual sales = 1,500,000 units; carrying costs as a percentage of purchase price = 30 percent; purchase price per unit = \$0.80; fixed costs per order = \$20; safety stock = 50,000 units; order lead time = 21 days

Chapter Twenty-Two
PROFIT+ Write

WHY PROFIT+ WRITE?

When PROFIT, the predecessor to PROFIT+, was first published, one of the first suggestions for an addition to the program involved the need for a routine that would allow students to print their name, class number, and/or other types of identification at the top of their PROFIT printouts. In response to this suggestion, the author wrote a "Print Your Name" routine that accomplished the desired task, and it was included in the second and later printings of PROFIT. Later, when PROFIT was reviewed prior to the development of PROFIT+, several reviewers indicated that it would be convenient for students to have a means by which they could include answers to the discussion questions that accompany problems in their printouts. The combination of these two suggestions--the need to print identification and to print discussion question answers--prompted the development of PROFIT+ Write.

WHAT IS PROFIT+ WRITE?

PROFIT+ Write is a simple text editor that allows you to include various types of verbal matter within your PROFIT+ printouts. You can use PROFIT+ Write to place a header, including your name and other identification, at the top of the first, or every, page of your PROFIT+ printouts. You can use PROFIT+ Write to intersperse discussions within your PROFIT+ printouts, as well. In fact, you can even use PROFIT+ Write as a very simple, but effective, stand-alone word processor.

Exhibit 22.1

Like the bulk of the PROFIT+ routines, PROFIT+ Write takes very little time to learn. In fact, you should be an accomplished PROFIT+ Write user within the five or ten minutes that it takes to read this chapter and run the routine for the first time.

The remainder of this chapter is spent explaining how to use PROFIT+ Write. You will find this explanation summarized on the PROFIT+ Write review screen that you call up from within the program with the [F2] key.

USING PROFIT+ WRITE

Option T on the PROFIT+ Main Menu calls up the PROFIT+ Write routine. When this option is selected, you are presented with the PROFIT+ Write screen shown in Exhibit 22.1. As you can see from this exhibit, the screen is composed of the usual PROFIT+ banner heading, a blank "note pad" delimited at both the left and the right margins by solid vertical lines, the active function key line, and the prompt line that reads, "Enter text (74 characters per line maximum). Press [RETURN]." The blinking cursor is located at the upper-left corner of the note pad and indicates the first position of the first line of text.

All that you must do at this point to begin using PROFIT+ Write is to start typing! As the prompt line indicates, you may enter a maximum of 74 characters per line. Any character on your computer's keyboard can be included in your text. At the end of every line of text, you must press [RETURN] to enter your text and to proceed to the next line of text. In this respect, PROFIT+ Write is like a typewriter because it does not support word wrap. (Word wrap is a characteristic of full-feature work processors. If you reach the right margin, the program will automatically "wrap" around to the next line of text and, if you are in the middle of a word, will bring the partially completed word to the first of the next line.) Also, [RETURN] must be pressed to enter the text.

Until you have pressed [RETURN], PROFIT+ Write does not recognize that text has been entered. While this generally is not a problem within the body of your text because you must remember to press [RETURN] to move from one line to the next, you must remember to press [RETURN] after you have entered your last line of text and after you have made changes in any text that you have already entered.

A single PROFIT+ Write document may be no more than 17 lines long. For headings to your printouts and answers to most discussion questions, this length should be sufficient. You can, however, compose discussions of greater length by typing and printing more than one 17-line document in sequence. Simply print a document, clear the PROFIT+ Write note pad, and continue with your discussion, stopping to print after each 17 lines.

Editing a PROFIT+ Write Document

You may use any of your computer's regular editing keys to edit a PROFIT+ Write document once it has initially been typed. Use the [TAB] key to move to the beginning of the line of text that you wish to edit. Once there, you can use the left and right arrow keys to position your cursor for editing. Pressing either of these arrow keys once will move the cursor one space in the direction of the arrow. Holding the [CTRL] key down and pressing the left or right arrow key will move the cursor five spaces to the left or right. Pressing the [END] key will move the cursor to the end of the line of text, while pressing the [HOME] key will reposition the cursor at the first character of the line.

In its default setting, the cursor is in the typeover mode. This means that, once you have positioned the cursor, any character that is typed will replace the character directly under the cursor. You may toggle the cursor to the insert mode by pressing the [INSERT] key. While in the insert mode, the character that you type is inserted at the point of the cursor. To indicate that the insert mode is active, the cursor becomes taller. Remember that the total length of a line, *including any new characters that you insert,* can be no more than 74 characters. Additional characters will be "pushed" off the right side of the note pad (into oblivion) if you inadvertently attempt to exceed the 74-character limit. Press [INSERT] a second time to toggle back to the typeover mode. You may use the [DELETE] key to erase the character directly under the cursor. Pressing the [BACKSPACE] key will erase the character to the cursor's immediate left.

REMINDER
Remember to press [RETURN] after you have edited a line of text!

Printing a PROFIT+ Write Document

PROFIT+ Write documents are printed to printer or disk in the same manner that all PROFIT+ work is printed. Simply press the [F9] key to initiate the printing process. If you do not want each line of your printout to begin flush with the left edge of your paper, you may insert several spaces at the beginning of each line of text. Remember, however, that each space occupies one of the 74 characters of line length that are allowed.

SUMMARY

PROFIT+ Write is an easy-to-use text processor designed to be used in conjunction with the other PROFIT+ routines. While the program is in no way intended to replace a full-feature word processor, you will find it to be very useful for its intended tasks: placing headers on and including discussions within PROFIT+ printouts. In addition, you may find it to be a simple word processor that is of use for other basic writing tasks.

APPENDIX

ANSWERS TO SELECTED END-OF-CHAPTER PROBLEMS

Chapter 3:

5. a. $30,050
   b. $34,730
   c. $30,986

Chapter 4:

5.	FV = $179,793.55	Interest = $55,793.55
8.	PV = $114,966.21	Interest = $35,483.79
11.	a. 13.20 years	
17.	FV = $60,803.34	Interest = $6,803.34
19.	a. $1,406.71	
26.	$108,885.72	

Chapter 5:

4. a. $859.491

Chapter 6:

8. a. 11.50%

Chapter 7:

4. a. $29.98
7. $30.70

Chapter 8:

2. E(Value) = 19.75% Var. = 8.837%
   Std. dev. = 29.727% Coef. var. = 1.505

5. Arith. mean = 13.33% Geom. mean = 11.419%
Var. = 5.473% Std. dev. = 23.393%
Coef. var. = 1.755

Chapter 9:

8. Beta = 1.33 k_s = 18.146% Value = $31.73

Chapter 10:

3. Current ratio = 2.0X Acid test ratio = 1.3X
Inv. T/O = 6.7X ACP = 75.4 days
Fxd. Asset T/O = 5.5X Tot. Asset T/O = 1.7X
Debt ratio = 61.7% Debt/Equity = 161.4%
T.I.E. = 2.3X
Profit margin = 1.2% Basic E.P. = 6.1%
ROA = 2.1% ROE = 5.4%

Chapter 11:

1.

	Source	**Use**
Cash	6.00	
Marketable Securities	30.00	
Accounts Receivable		42.00
Inventories		102.00
Gross Plt. and Equip.		396.00
Acc'd. Dep.	120.00	
Accounts Payable	36.00	
Notes Payable	48.00	
Accrued Wages		
Accrued Taxes	12.00	
Mortgage Bonds		24.00
Debentures	288.00	
Common Stock		
Paid-in Capital		
Retained Earnings	24.00	
Totals	564.00	564.00

Chapter 12:

1. a. Additional funds needed = $4.32 million
5. a. Receivables = -2.426 + 0.103(Sales)
   Inventories = 1.357 + 0.141(Sales)

Chapter 13:

1. a. EOQ = 5,774 units
   b. Average inventory = 6,887 units
   c. Average investment = $16,528.80
   d. Orders per year = 42
   e. An order should be placed every 9 days.
   f. Reorder point = 7,334 units

Chapter 14:

1. Under the assumptions given, the proposed change in credit policy would increase net income by $2.6 million. Make the change.

Chapter 15:

1.	January	February	March
Tot. Loans Outstd.	1400		
Surplus Cash		940	9000

Chapter 16:

10. Fourth National Bank — 13.87%
    Second National Bank — 14.72%
    First National Bank — 14.75%
    Third National Bank — 15.87%

12. a. 22.28%

15. a. Approximate effective rate = 18.18%
    Effective rate (APR) = 19.83%

Chapter 17:

1. The project is not acceptable. The internal rate of return (12.12%) is less than the cost of capital (14.00%), and the net present value (-$1,845.22) is less than zero.

6. a. Net annual cash inflows: Year 1 = 4280; Year 2 = 5000; Year 3 = 4280; Year 4 = 3896; Year 5 = 3896; Year 6 = 3960.

b. NPV = $2,993.20 IRR = 23.38%

c. The project is acceptable because NPV > 0 and IRR > cost of capital.

Chapter 18:

1. a. Slopes of Sensitivity Lines for Variables:

Variable	**Slope**
Unit Sales	4.44
Sales Price	12.04
Variable Costs	-7.60
FC excl. Depreciation	-2.21
Depreciation Expense	0.50
Tax Rate	-0.98
Cost of Capital	-0.94
Salvage Value	0.07
Life	1.80
Cost	-1.79

Chapter 19:

1. Initial breakeven point = 695 units

a. Breakeven point = 503 units

5. a. Breakeven point = 7,556 units

b. DOL = 1.80 DFL = 1.10 CLE = 1.98

Chapter 20:

1. a. Long-term Debt = 25%
   Pref. Stock = 10%
   Common Stock = 65%

   b. Marginal cost of capital = 14.57%

5.

	Weight	Cost
Long-term Debt	26.000%	7.930%
Pref. Stock	14.000%	8.333%
Common Stock	60.000%	

Int. eq. = 11.878%
Ext. eq. = 12.543%
Marginal cost of capital = 10.754%
(External equity used in the calculation of MCC.)

8.

	Weight	Cost
Long-term Debt	25.000%	9.900%
Pref. Stock	8.333%	10.870%
Common Stock	66.667%	

Int. eq. = 8.571%
Ext. eq. = 9.202%
Marginal cost of capital = 9.515%
(External equity used in the calculation of MCC.)
Retained earnings break point = $300,000